Plants from the Edge of the World

PLANTS
from the Edge of the World

New Explorations in the Far East

MARK FLANAGAN
and TONY KIRKHAM

TIMBER PRESS
Portland - Cambridge

Published in 2005 by
Timber Press, Inc.
The Haseltine Building
133 S.W. Second Avenue, Suite 450
Portland, Oregon 97204-3527, U.S.A.

Timber Press
2 Station Road
Swavesey
Cambridge CB4 5QJ, U.K.

www.timberpress.com

Printed in China

Library of Congress Cataloging-in-Publication Data

Flanagan, Mark.
  Plants from the edge of the world : new explorations in the Far East /
Mark Flanagan and Tony Kirkham.
      p. cm.
  Includes bibliographical references and index.
  ISBN 0-88192-676-0 (hardcover)
  1. Botany--East Asia. 2. Plant collecting--East Asia. 3. Flanagan,
Mark--Travel--East Asia. 4. Kirkham, Tony--Travel--East Asia. 5.
Botanists--Travel--East Asia. 6. Plant collectors--Travel--East Asia.
I. Kirkham, Tony. II. Title.
  QK379.5.E38F59 2005
  581.95--dc22

                                        2004012684

A Catalogue record for this book is also available from the British Library.

To Sally, Lesley, Callum, Jennifer,
Sophie and Robert

Thank you, with all our love, Tony and Mark

CONTENTS

'THE MOST IMPORTANT THING to look after is your stomach—treat it gently and sensibly and you won't go far wrong. Equally important are your feet; wear sensible boots and break them in before you go'.

This is some of the best advice I ever received, given by well-known plant explorer Frank Ludlow, who, with his friend and fellow explorer Major George Sherriff, is remembered today as half of the most successful plant hunting partnership in the history of Himalayan exploration. Between 1933 and 1949 they made seven expeditions to the mountains of the eastern Himalaya, including Bhutan and southeast Tibet, collecting specimens and introducing to cultivation seeds of a great many plants, especially rhododendrons, gentians, lilies, primulas and *Meconopsis*.

With my friend the late Len Beer, I benefited enormously from several meetings with Ludlow, visiting him at The British Museum (Natural History) in London in the spring of 1971. All this was in preparation for the University of North Wales, Bangor Expedition to East Nepal, of which Beer was leader and I a member. To sit in Ludlow's cubbyhole in the Botany Department listening to the great man telling us stories of his exploits was an experience I am never likely to forget. Ludlow's reminders of the practical aspects of an expedition certainly paid off, and there were several occasions subsequently when we had special cause to thank him. Sadly, he died the following year at the ripe old age of eighty-six.

Preparing for a plant hunting expedition, especially your first one, is naturally cause for great excitement and a certain apprehension. It is, after all, a prelude to adventure, and adventure is the lifeblood of any endeavour involving travel to pastures new. As a boy in a northern town in the 1940s, I would regularly set out, accompanied by my pals, into the Pennine moorlands north of my home, each time venturing further and further afield. We called it travelling to the land of the lost, and occasionally, it was we who became lost only to find our way home again, relieved and a little wiser. To us it was an adventure, passing from the known to the unknown, and later, as my interests and horizons spread to other counties then other countries, I began to think of myself as an explorer and more than that, an explorer with a special mission to see and study plants.

The Nepal Expedition of September–December 1971 was my first real taste of adventure in the high places and my first opportunity to travel in the footsteps of the great plant explorers of old. It mattered not to me that others had been there before. What really counted was that *I* had not, and my experience therefore would be very personal and very special. In the event, it proved to be a turning point in my life let alone my career, and things have never been the same since. It is the spirit of adventure that underpins Mark Flanagan's and Tony Kirkham's approach to the travels described in this book, and their writing strongly reflects their own sense of pioneering and achievement. Indeed, reading their varied accounts, which are written in the first person present, allows us the illusion of being fellow travellers, sharing at first hand their successes and disappointments, their highs and lows.

When Flanagan relates their experience of being lost in the mist-shrouded mountains of Taiwan with night fast approaching, their frustration and concern are ours too as we slip and slide across dangerous streams, forcing our way through dense thickets, hungry, exhausted and soaked to the skin. Likewise, the authors' encounters with mosquitoes in the woods by Vladivostok sound all too familiar, and their words persuade us that we too can hear their incessant humming and feel their myriad bites. But mosquitoes, mist, rain, cold, hunger, fatigue and worse are the stuff of adventure, without which the challenge is no challenge at all.

Given their Kew training, the authors not surprisingly have a very focussed and modern approach to their plant hunting. 'Temperate loop', 'target species', 'key locus' and other terms are freely used in the text, and we are constantly reminded of the task they have set themselves and the need to respect the Convention on Biological Diversity agreed at the Rio Earth Summit in 1992. We are introduced also to the people they travel with or encounter along the way, and a varied and richly charactered selection they are too. Their anecdotes are laced with a humour, often dry, that had me chuckling on several occasions, and they are not reticent in revealing the other's foibles and minor misfortunes, which demonstrates the strength of their friendship.

And then there is the entertainment. All who have travelled in the world's wild places will nod and smile on reading of the authors' efforts to bolster their own and their hosts' spirits with their singing and joking. It reminded me of the many occasions Len Beer and I sang our hearts out in the mountains of Nepal to help us cope with fatigue or atrocious weather as well as to keep our end up at campfire parties with our sherpas and porters. It was the same years later on the Sino-British Expedition to the Cangshan in the mountains of China, with yet more singing plus the pranks and jokes of our leader, an incorrigible and fun-loving Chinese professor. It all helps to make the world go round and, at the very least, is a way of relaxing at the end of a long or difficult day.

But what of the plants that form the heart and soul of this book? Northeast Asia is the source of a great many of our garden ornamentals, and during their travels through South Korea, Taiwan, Ussuriland and Hokkaido the authors encounter a goodly number of them. On Taiwan they find *Deutzia pulchra* and collect its seed. Twelve years later and I enjoy the privilege of growing one of the resultant seedlings, now a thumping shrub of 3 m (10 ft) with bold foliage and generous racemes of white blooms in spring whilst the conspicuous exfoliating, pinky-grey, cinnamon-bellied bark is a welcome bonus in winter. This is just one of the many ornamental plants introduced by the authors as seed to British cultivation.

Another is the pale peely-barked *Betula davurica* from South Korea, which I also have admired in the woods of the Changbai Shan on China's border with North Korea. Indeed, I remember climbing a tall specimen of this uncommon birch on a bright sunny morning in June 1983, collecting a handful of seed before enjoying the view from my high perch. Tony Kirkham's tree-climbing skills are called upon many times in securing precious seeds, and I can well imagine, therefore, his amazement when he comes one day in Hokkaido upon a mighty monarch birch, *Betula maximowicziana*, encased in scaffolding to facilitate seed gathering by a young forestry student.

Of special interest to plantsmen and gardeners are the seed collections made in the Ussuri region in the far-east corner of the Russian Federation, near Vladivostok and on the island of Sakhalin. Few modern British botanists or horticulturists have visited these locations, and the authors' account of the plants seen there is all the more interesting as a result. On Sakhalin, for instance, they collect seed of *Euonymus sachalinensis*, the true species, rather than the related and almost identical *E. planipes*, which commonly masquerades as this species in Western cultivation.

In Ussuriland, they encounter an immense tree of *Populus maximowiczii* towering at an estimated 40 m (130 ft), which reminds me of trees of similar size seen in Hokkaido in Japan and in China's Jilin Province. One of the most exciting accounts for me, however, details their visit to a site in the Vladivostok region to see *Microbiota decussata*, a dwarf spreading cypress- or juniper-like conifer first introduced to European cultivation around 1957 and eventually reaching Britain some sixteen years later. I remember first seeing this plant in a Dutch collection in the 1960s, and it was one of the first conifers I planted in my own garden in Winchester in 1977. Three years later, this same plant was filmed for the popular television show *Gardeners' World*. I will never forget presenter Geoffrey Smith's retort on being told that it had originated from somewhere to the east of Vladivostok: 'Goodness me, any further east and it would fall off the edge of the world'.

The instigation for the authors' travels we are told were the infamous gales of October 1987 that devastated woodlands, plantation and specimen trees over much of southeast England. Both the Royal Botanic Gardens, Kew, and its satellite garden at Wakehurst in Sussex suffered significant losses that resulted in a rethink of future planting practises and policies. From out of the destruction grew a desire and a determination to collect anew, in the wild, seeds of specific trees and shrubs to help replant and reorder the collections. All this is described by the authors (both of whom experienced firsthand the gales' destructive power) in chapter 1, and it is appropriate that, in their final chapter, following their collecting missions, we find them assessing early results on a tour of the new plantings. It is a cause for satisfaction and rejoicing, for many of their introductions are already thriving, and their dreams of a new renaissance are now a reality.

ROY LANCASTER

THE NARRATIVE THAT FOLLOWS IS TRUE. It is drawn from journals and field notes written at the time, in a factual and dispassionate way. Certain events may seem fantastic, even fanciful. Others are, perhaps, disquieting. But in writing this story we have been determined to reflect what really happened on our various travels without, to use a cliché, fear or favour. This approach did lead to certain concerns in that real people formed the basis of our overseas experiences, real people who gave a great deal of their time and energy to help us achieve our objectives. We have been careful not to misrepresent these people, nor to cast aspersions on their characters or personalities. Nevertheless, our interactions with them were personal, and an element of personal judgement inevitably enters our account. Fortunately, our relationship with collaborators was, without exception, a harmonious one and we can therefore write in an honest and positive way.

We also decided that we would write the main narrative, the events that happened to us whilst in the field, in the first person present; we felt this would allow the reader to experience events in a more immediate way. All other elements—the events that led up to the first trip, our work prior to each trip and the consideration of what we achieved—are written in the past tense. Such an approach does lead to a slightly awkward shift of tenses in the middle chapters, but we hope readers will forgive us our grammatical inadequacies for the sake of, what we hope is, a rip-roaring storyline.

Plants form a significant part of our book, and this inevitably brings the vexed question of taxonomy (plant naming) to the fore. This is a constantly changing area; new discoveries, detailed research and reinterpretation all can bring about a renaming of plants. At times it is difficult to know what the most accurate name for a particular plant is. The botanical names in this book are drawn from three sources. National and regional floras were used whilst working in the field. In some cases these are not fully up-to-date; several were also in the local language and we, therefore, relied upon the guidance of our collaborators. With well-known groups, we have had recourse to recently published monographs, maples being a good example. Finally, as our plants have grown and matured in cultivation they have been sent to botanists, in the herbarium at Kew or other institutions, who have provided us with an accurate identification. Almost inevitably, with so many plants covered, there may be an out-of-date name or a misidentification; for this we offer apologies in advance and hope that any reader who has sufficient knowledge will pass their observations on to us.

A word about E. H. Wilson: very quickly readers will come to realise the prominent role the great plant hunter Ernest Henry Wilson has played in our travels. Not as a living companion—his death in 1930 was greatly lamented at the time—but as an inspiration and exemplar. A great deal of historical information exists about Wilson's life, including at least two biographies; therefore, it is not the intention here to detail his career. Suffice to say that on many occasions we were aware that we were treading in the footsteps of a greater man, one who blazed a trail across the temperate parts of Asia at a time when air travel, four-wheel-drive vehicles and computers didn't exist. It has been a privilege to stand where Wilson stood and to see the landscape through his eyes. From Mark and Tony—Thank you, E. H. Wilson.

We hope readers will enjoy the story of our journeys and agree with us that nothing broadens the mind like travel.

MARK FLANAGAN
TONY KIRKHAM

ACKNOWLEDGEMENTS

O LUCKY MEN! By anybody's reckoning we have been two fortunate individuals. Fate dealt us a winning hand, not once but on four separate occasions. To be able to travel as we have, to experience what we did, to meet the wonderful people we came to know, to see with our own eyes what we saw, is good fortune indeed.

It would be remiss of us, however, to suggest that all this was just kismet. The kinds of journeys we undertook have a long gestation period, require lots of support and encouragement and rely on a great deal of hard work and goodwill, mainly on the part of collaborators overseas, who, at the beginning, were complete strangers. Not surprisingly we have a great many people to acknowledge and thank. We begin by recording our gratitude to Choi Myoung-Sub and Park Kwang-Woo for the forbearance and support they gave to two rookie collectors in South Korea in 1989. To Fuh-Jiunn Pan, who opened our eyes to the floral wealth, natural beauty and cultural heritage of Taiwan in 1992. To Peter Gorovoy and Sergei Lobanov, who supported us unstintingly during the demanding visit to the Russian Far East and Sakhalin Island in 1994. To Hideki Takahashi, who helped us complete the temperate loop during the visit to Hokkaido in 1997, thus realising a vision that began nearly ten years before.

As readers will discover, we also owe a great debt to the many people in England who provided the encouragement, support and opportunity for us to become professional plant collectors in the first place. To John Simmons,

EASTERN ASIA
The Temperate Loop

formerly Curator of Kew Gardens, and his Deputy Curator Ian Beyer, thanks are given for their farsightedness in giving horticulturists such as ourselves the opportunity to travel to faraway places. To Charles Erskine and Hans Fliegner, also of the Royal Botanic Gardens, Kew, for much practical advice, and to Tony Schilling, as Deputy Curator of Wakehurst Place and pioneer plant hunter in the Himalaya, for providing a role model to aspiring young travellers. Dr Nigel Taylor, the present Curator of Kew, continues to support overseas expeditions and was instrumental in setting up the trip to Hokkaido.

Thanks also to all the staff, in the gardens and nurseries at both Kew and Wakehurst Place, who have grown, planted and nurtured the many plants that we have reintroduced into the collections from these trips. The various taxonomists in the herbarium at Kew, but in particular to Susyn Andrews, who have determined and verified the identifications of the collections and herbarium specimens we brought back. To Jeanette Fryer, not just for her verifications of our collections of *Cotoneaster* but for her help with that genus in this book. Also to Yuji Kurashige, for information on the performance of our Taiwanese rhododendrons growing in Japan.

To Dr Peter Wyse-Jackson of the Botanic Gardens Conservation International, for introducing us to Igor Smirnov, who opened the doors to the far east of Russia for us. To Karen Bird of Portman Travel, who organised all our trips, ensuring that we caught the right flights to the right places at the right time.

To Anna Mumford, our editor, for her foresight, help, encouragement and patience, and Franni Bertolino Farrell, also of Timber Press, for painstakingly editing the manuscript and keeping our morale high during the difficult times at the PC with her entertaining e-mails of comments and corrections.

To Ros Johnson, the Plant Conservation Officer of the National Council for the Conservation of Plants and Gardens, who gave up her precious time to read and critique our first manuscript and, better still, for telling us it was pretty good! To Allen Coombes, Botanist at the Sir Harold Hillier Gardens, for a very thorough proof and name-check of our final draft, and Alan Fones for helpful comments and observations. To Jo Hall, for kindly painting the wonderful watercolour maps. Thanks to the archives of the Arnold

John Simmons
(photograph courtesy The Library & Archives,
Royal Botanic Gardens, Kew)

Charles Erskine
(photograph courtesy The Library & Archives,
Royal Botanic Gardens, Kew)

Arboretum, Harvard, for allowing us to use the photographs by Ernest Wilson. To Marilyn Ward of Kew's library, for help with references, pictures and manuscripts.

Sincere thanks go to Roy Lancaster, a fellow Lancastrian, plant hunter, boundless enthusiast and admirer of E. H. Wilson, for his inspiring foreword.

Our appreciation goes to everyone else, all the people too numerous to mention, who feature in the book and who helped make the expeditions successful and a pleasure to be part of.

Finally, we cannot give enough thanks to our two families, whom we adore. They have watched their husbands and fathers shoulder their packs and disappear for weeks on end. Their tolerant acceptance of our obsession with plant hunting can never be adequately repaid. They also provided the encouragement for us to put pen to paper and produce this account of our trips away, probably to find out what really happened. Sally, Lesley, Callum, Jennifer, Sophie and Robert, thank you.

CHAPTER 1

An Ill Wind

ON 13 OCTOBER 1987 the waters of the Bay of Biscay, the vast stretch of ocean on France's western seaboard, were calm and warm, unusually warm for the lateness of the season. Indeed these fickle waters were as warm as at any time during the past year. On the other side of the Atlantic, Hurricane Floyd, having vented its fury on the Sunshine State of Florida, was circling menacingly off the southeastern coast of the United States. West of the British Isles a huge volume of cold air drifted slowly south. These seemingly unconnected meteorological phenomena were about to unleash the most violent and destructive storm to be seen in England for over 250 years. A storm so malevolent that its effects, both physical and psychological, are still felt. A storm that would, incidentally, launch the plant hunting careers of Mark Flanagan and Tony Kirkham.

By 15 October a plume of warm, tropical Caribbean air had spun off from Hurricane Floyd and was pumped into the jet stream high above the Atlantic Ocean; it gained speed as it rose and was forced northeastwards. Meanwhile a depression, an area of low barometric pressure, developed near to northwestern Spain and began to move north, drawing energy from the warm waters of the Bay of Biscay. This depression began to deepen appre-

A satellite image of the Great Storm taken at 4.40 a.m. on 16 October 1987

(copyright University of Dundee, NERC Satellite Station)

ciably and pick up speed. As it met the cold air moving south, still more energy was gathered; priming was complete as the high-speed column of air from Hurricane Floyd plunged down from the jet stream. Early that evening, weather forecaster Michael Fish told viewers about a woman who had rung the BBC, saying she'd heard 'there was a hurricane on the way'. His infamous comment: 'Well, if you're watching, don't worry—there isn't'.

The climatological bomb exploded over northwestern France and the southeast of England with savage fury during the small hours of 16 October. Winds of up to 100 knots were recorded as the storm made land-fall on the Sussex coast at 2.00 a.m. It swept over the South Downs, lifting the roofs off picturesque cottages with knapped-flint walls in the quaint villages nestling at the foot of these gentle chalk hills. It sped on through the forested darkness of the Weald, destroying a hundred years of planting in the world-famous gardens of Nymans, Borde Hill and the satellite garden of the Royal Botanic Gardens, Kew, at Wakehurst Place. It felled every tree, bar a tenacious giant redwood by the house at Emmetts on top of the North Downs. Sometime before three o'clock in the morning it hit the outer suburbs of London. Kew Gardens lay unsuspecting and unprepared for its advent.

In bed in my flat in Hampton Hill, southwest London, I vaguely remember hearing a noise as a dustbin blew over and hit against a wall. I grunted and turned over. Nine kilometres (6 miles) to the east, Tony Kirkham was jolted awake by the crash of a tree uprooted by the first onslaught of the wind. For the next three hours he and his wife, Sally, watched in fascinated horror the maelstrom of activity unfolding before their eyes. Meanwhile, Lesley and I slept on in blissful ignorance.

The area where we lived was a new development, previously the site of a market garden and, hence, with a distinct lack of trees. Driving to work that morning I travelled a considerable distance before I realised that something terrible had happened. It was about 7.30 a.m. and the storm had all but blown itself out; however, evidence of its passing became clearer with each few hundred metres of my drive. Branches were strewn everywhere, the result of an unequal struggle. The occasional tree lay prone over a parked, and now flattened, car or rested at a frightening angle against a building. I managed to maintain my journey until just beyond the southern edge of Kew

Fallen tree blocking Kew Road on the morning of 16 October 1987

Gardens. A wonderful black walnut, which I had long admired, lay across Kew Road, and I could drive no further.

I climbed out of my car, and a familiar figure emerged from behind the tree's upturned root plate. Tony looked at me with a mixture of awe and disbelief. 'Wait until you get inside the Gardens', he said. 'It's a catastrophe'. Almost perversely the sun began to rise above the attractive detached Victorian houses that line Kew Road, heralding a beautiful autumn day. The sky was a cloudless blue and the air was warm, refreshed by the passage of the recently departed tempest.

Tony was right—it was a catastrophe! I walked around with Charles Erskine, head of the arboretum. Charlie, a sensitive man despite an opaque exterior with lashings of no-nonsense Scottish pragmatism, was clearly moved by what he saw. Having been in charge of the arboretum for ten years he had got to know many of the trees intimately. I can recall him standing by a fallen specimen of *Quercus bicolor*, the swamp white oak from the forests of the eastern and central United States. 'A favourite', he muttered forlornly under his breath. I still carry this mental picture—Charlie head bowed, body tense, a small figure next to the great bole of the oak, almost like a child contemplating the lifeless body of a beached whale and silently wondering at how something so powerful could be rendered impotent. Sadly the tragedy didn't end just there; this particular oak wasn't just a favourite but a UK champion tree, the biggest of its kind in the country. And so it went, tree after tree—champion trees, scientifically unique trees, historically important trees. Amongst the carnage was another tale, a tale of a lost heritage nurtured by previous generations of horticulturists, enjoyed by millions of visitors, valued by all who loved trees.

The second storm broke over us, almost as unexpectedly as the first, when the magnitude of what had happened overnight hit the world's press agencies. This was a very big news story, and as with every big news story an unseemly media scrum developed; every television company, every radio station, every newspaper wanted information and wanted it fast. Christine Brandt, Kew's lone public relations officer, was overwhelmed. How many trees had been lost? Were any irreplaceable? When would the gardens reopen? Were any historic buildings damaged? How would Kew ever recover? Like ravenous wolves the press corps swarmed over the battered and recumbent form of the Royal Botanic Gardens, Kew. As part of the media liaison team (among other duties) in the Living Collections Department, I was sucked into the vortex and spent a frantic day trying to assist Christine in meeting the requests of insatiable journalists.

Away to the south, almost forgotten in the frenetic first few hours of the morning, Wakehurst Place, Kew's country garden, was recovering from its own Armageddon. Sitting high up on the Sussex Weald the estate had taken the full impact of the storm within a few minutes of its landfall. Whereas Kew's tree losses would be numbered in hundreds, those at Wakehurst Place reached into five figures. The surrounding villages—Ardingly, Turners Hill, West Hoathly—were cut off and isolated, without electricity or telephones. Staff couldn't even reach the estate let alone set about the task of dealing with the situation. One of those who had more pressing concerns than the conditions at Wakehurst Place was Tony Schilling, its deputy curator. The

Post-storm clearance work commences at Kew

(photograph courtesy The Library & Archives, Royal Botanic Gardens, Kew)

impact of the storm had all but removed the roof of his cottage in the pretty Downland hamlet of Westmeston. Without the means to contact anyone at Wakehurst Place, Tony had to sit on his hands and await the emergency team of builders who had been contacted to make his house safe. The wait was to prove agonising.

Back at Kew an emergency meeting of the curatorial team, John Simmons, his deputy Ian Beyer and Charlie Erskine, had set out the bones of an initial response strategy. Once concluded Charlie cycled from John Simmons's office in Aiton House across the Somme-like landscape to the Stable Yard, where Tony and his arboretum colleagues, Mark Pitman and Mark Bridger, waited. Tony still recalls the tense atmosphere and the feeling of numb disbelief as Charlie walked into his office. He quickly outlined the plan—roads first, dangerous trees isolated or made safe, buildings inspected for damage and secured if hazardous, efforts to concentrate on the north-eastern corner of the gardens from the Main Gate to Victoria Gate—ironically the original Georgian kernel from which modern-day Kew had developed. All three supervisors left with a sense of purpose and determination; the long way back from catastrophe had started.

What then was the final head count? Had the storm been as devastating as was first thought? Perhaps more importantly, what was the response of garden staff to this huge psychological blow?

Kew's losses, accurately counted, amounted to eight hundred mature trees, which number included survivors that had to be felled after detailed inspection revealed them to be unsafe. At Wakehurst Place losses were estimated at fifteen thousand—no more accurate figure was possible: the difficult terrain, with steep-sided valleys, and the densely wooded nature of the site made precise counting impossible. It should also be realised that many of these trees were native species within the Loder Valley Nature Reserve and plantation exotics rather than specimen trees. Depressing as these figures might be, on an individual basis the losses were perhaps more profound still. Many trees from original introductions, with inestimable scientific and cultural value, were lost. Kew lost one of its original eighteenth-century Caucasian elms (*Zelkova carpinifolia*); a group of roble beeches (*Nothofagus obliqua*) from their first introduction in 1903 by the famous dendrologist H. J. Elwes were smashed to pieces.

Ulmus villosa, the endangered marn elm from the Himalaya, having survived two decades of Dutch elm disease was unceremoniously torn out of the saturated ground. Most of the celebrated hickory collection had either fallen in the night or had to be felled by a heartbroken Tony Kirkham, to make the area safe. The avenue of tulip trees (*Liriodendron tulipifera*) along the Broad Walk, having taken the full force of the winds, stood shattered or recumbent. Some locations around Capability Brown's Rhododendron Dell and the Bamboo Garden were impenetrable, even on foot, due to the crisscross of tree trunks and branch debris from the canopies of specimens more fortunate than their fallen neighbours. Other losses, such as *Malus trilobata*, *Maclura pomifera* and *Ehretia thyrsiflora*, stripped rarities from the arboretum, removing its stellar components like a football team shorn of its star players and now made to look ordinary.

A similar story unfolded at Wakehurst Place. The beautiful specimen of *Stewartia sinensis* from E. H. Wilson's 1901 introduction was destroyed; an original Wilson handkerchief tree (*Davidia involucrata*) was smashed back to

The lost *Zelkova carpinifolia* in front of the herbarium at Kew
(photograph courtesy The Library & Archives, Royal Botanic Gardens, Kew)

its primary scaffold branches. The unique specimen of the tender Mexican pine, *Pinus patula*, was no more, nor the elegant silver pendent lime (*Tilia tomentosa* 'Petiolaris') in the Carriage Ring: that this 25-m (80-ft) tree did not damage the Georgian stable block when it fell was nothing short of a miracle.

Despite some sanguine comments to the contrary, the informed view was that, yes, the storm had been as damaging as was first thought and, of course, not just at Kew and Wakehurst Place. Mercifully, given the severity of the storm, only eighteen people were killed in England, no doubt the result of the fact that by dawn the storm had all but cleared land and moved out to sea. The damage to property and infrastructure was immense. Despite all this however, popular angst kept returning to the loss of trees. Many people were deeply affected, in most cases for the first time, by the demise of well-known trees. Psychologists suggested that trees represent continuity in the human mind; they help to define peoples' environment whether it be a distant tree-clad ridge, the oak tree on the village green or the ancient churchyard yew. People felt a great sense of loss because the very thing they regarded as immutable and indestructible was revealed to be as mortal as humankind itself.

This conundrum of the psyche was also played out at Kew and Wakehurst Place as staff began the long and arduous recovery process. Remarkably, however, it began to drive the process almost as if it were turned on its head. The logic ran something like this. If trees have a finite life and we have just lived through a storm that exposed their mortality for all to see, isn't it even more important to ensure the continuity of tree collections so that future generations can enjoy what our forebears bequeathed to us? This powerful incentive was the driving force behind the amazing, Phoenix-like recovery that took place over the following weeks and months, and in the case of Wakehurst Place, years. Kew opened its gates to visitors within twelve days, though access was confined to a small area around the Princess of Wales Conservatory. Wakehurst Place likewise opened a limited area from 11 December 1987. Signs of hopefulness were everywhere. I watched with a mixture of emotion and admiration as Tony Schilling helped the aged Lady Price, the wife of the last private owner of Wakehurst Place, as she stood amongst the debris to plant a young handkerchief tree below the front lawns of the Mansion—a very public gesture of renewal. Tony Kirkham gained satisfaction from walking the nursery rows at Kew with Charlie Erskine in December 1987, selecting young saplings for that winter's planting programme.

Interestingly, several unexpected initiatives were also born out of the tragedy of the Great Storm of 1987. Never before had so many tree root systems, from so diverse a range of species, been exposed to view. For Dr David Cutler, of Kew's Jodrell Laboratory, this was too good an opportunity to miss. David and his colleagues already possessed a large volume of data about the anatomy of wood and the structure of tree root systems; such data, seemingly esoteric, has very practical applications. Cutler and his collaborators have done much to understand the complex interaction between tree roots and soil moisture; for example, the wrong tree growing on certain soils can result in shrinkage, which can disastrously undermine building foundations and bring about a collapse. One myth the scientists were able to conclusively explode was that tree roots ramify to great depths. In fact, on a very wide range of soil types, even very large trees have relatively shallow root systems, often only 1 m (3 ft 3 in) or so in depth. Tree roots are very much opportunistic and grow where the essential elements they need—moisture, oxygen and nutrients—are to be abundantly found. The shallowness of the root plates, witnessed at both sites, also caused a rethink of tree planting techniques. There appeared to be no need for the conventional deep tree pits; shallow, wider pits would ensure future tree planting was even more successful. Such an approach became a critical factor in the establishment of all the new collections Tony and I made.

Kew and Wakehurst Place also supplied timber from several species to aid researchers at the Forestry Commission's Alice Holt Lodge with their long-standing project looking at the ability of trees to isolate decay within their trunks. Other beneficiaries included a whole host of woodcarvers, who couldn't believe their luck when they gained access to previously unheard-of species of trees. I imagined a scene in my mind, a dinner party at which the host casually 'replies' to an admiring glance a guest has for a carved figure on the nearby mantel. 'Oh yes, that—I carved it from *Ehretia thyrsiflora* from Kew Gardens'. Amazed expressions all around. Perhaps the most striking wood carving that resulted from timber supplied by Kew is the marvellous work of art created by Robert Games, at that time a sixteen-year-old schoolboy from King's School in Gloucester; 'Kew Threatened by the Wind', made up of a thousand individual pieces of timber from thirty-three different species, now adorns a wall in the Victoria Gate Visitor Centre at Kew.

Another gratifying effect of the storm was the support received from botanical and horticultural institutions across the globe. In some cases this support was both immediate and tangible. For example, a team of arboricultural students from Askham Bryan College in Yorkshire, coordinated by lecturer Peter Hemsley, were at Wakehurst Place within a fortnight, assisting the in-house arborists with the mammoth clearance task they faced. This group was followed by a contingent from the Morris Arboretum of the University of Pennsylvania who between 13 and 18 November 1987 also supported the Wakehurst Place staff. Their efforts weren't just appreciated at the garden but in the local hostelry, the Ardingly Inn, where their prodigious consumption of English beer is still spoken of in hushed and deferential tones. Final support at Wakehurst Place came from David Paterson, of the Royal Botanic Garden, Edinburgh, and six of his staff.

As the cold winter of 1988 stuttered into a late spring a full national postmortem on the Great Storm was being conducted. Not only was the performance, or perceived lack of it, of the Meteorological Office being scrutinised in withering fashion, but other matters, more pertinent to Kew, were also being examined. A strong and reasoned voice was that of the ecologists, who took a dispassionate view of events. Environments are subject to continuous change, they argued; destruction and regeneration are inseparable companions, and climatological phenomena, no matter how extreme, are part and parcel of an ongoing dynamic to which all plants are subjected: the Great Storm was merely an example of such forces at work. More controversially, they recommended that the best course of action was to do nothing, that, given time, nature would do whatever repair work was needed. This at a time when everybody else thought they should be doing a great deal—clearing away smashed trees, removing their roots, cultivating the ground, planting saplings. Time has revealed that much of their advice—scientifically based and objectively considered—was right. I have too often seen examples of expensively produced and diligently planted nursery trees outgrown by self-sown seedlings.

Such opinions, and others ventured by a whole host of vested interests, were being digested at Kew into the summer of 1988 as longer term development plans were being laid. A key realisation, which began to drive much of what followed, was that, on the conclusion of clearance work, what *remained* in the arboreta at Kew and Wakehurst Place was now much more important than what had been lost. Further, that a concerted effort should be made to investigate the changed composition of the arboreta in terms of their taxonomic make-up—what species had survived—and geographical representation—where these plants were from. This coincided with my move from Kew to Wakehurst Place, where I took up the job of supervisor of the Gardens Unit under Tony Schilling. My immediate concern was the recovery work, which was vigorously underway, and in this I was ably assisted by David Marchant, a Sussex man through and through, born and brought up on the Wakehurst estate and practical to the core. As time allowed I began to analyse the battered but unbowed collection in the exotic woodlands. Schilling's planting work had injected a large amount of first-rate natural source plant material, much of it grown from his own collections in Nepal; nonetheless, huge areas of the world were barely represented in an arboretum that purported to display a wide geographic spectrum of temperate trees. There was very little from the extreme edge of eastern Asia, Japan and Korea for example; a tiny representation of the unique flora of Taiwan; a smattering from temperate South America—even the rich woodland of the eastern United States was underrepresented. In short there were big gaps in the representation of the world's temperate woodlands. Also, a good deal of the remaining plants hadn't been collected in the wild at all; the origin and identity of such material was uncertain, which did little to enhance the scientific value of the collections.

Not surprisingly the geographical omissions identified at Wakehurst Place manifested themselves in taxonomic gaps in the family-based arrangement in Kew's arboretum. Within the extensive collection of *Rosa* species, no Taiwanese roses were to be found; in the Oleaceae (the olive family), Korean material of *Syringa pubescens* subsp. *patula* was absent. Much of the Celastraceae (spindles) was composed of nonnatural source material of dubious value.

Fortunately, thanks to the Great Storm, huge physical gaps in the landscape provided the space to accommodate any new material which might be obtained. This situation pointed the way to a path that would guide the recovery of the arboreta at Kew and Wakehurst Place: a plant collecting programme needed to be developed that would target areas of the world which were underrepresented in Kew's collections. In addition it was decided that Kew staff, as part of their own professional development, should themselves acquire this material. Once collected it could be brought back to England to be raised in the nurseries at Kew and Wakehurst Place, and thus would begin the repopulation of the ravaged arboreta in southwest London and the Sussex Weald. Now, there was a challenge, and an undertaking worthy of the effort.

CHAPTER 2

The Garden of the World

AS THE SUN BROKE over the mud flats to the east, the archaeopteryx stretched its wings, catching the first warming rays. Shafts of light pierced the cold, lingering mist of early morning and lit the surface of a broad, slow-moving river. With the sun, the archaeopteryx rose from its overnight roost in a tall magnolia tree and began a slow circling ascent above the dense tree canopy. In the distance a bay, azure in the sunlight, revealed itself as an out-fall for the river, which snaked its way lazily through the unending forest.

On the forest floor other creatures began to stir, strange and frightening creatures whose world—they knew no other—was the trees. Trees that millions of years later would be called redwood, swamp cypress, sweet gum, umbrella pine and a hundred other names by humankind. Trees that provided an unbroken forest in a land humankind would call England.

Forgive my flight of fancy and the liberties I have taken with scientific facts. This is a mental picture I have carried since I first learned the incredible story of the evolution of the temperate forests of the Northern Hemisphere. My passive tutor was the great dendrologist Alan Mitchell; I say passive, because these gleanings were garnered from a book rather than firsthand from the great man. As a novice horticulturist a close friend, John Tinsley, bought me a copy of Mitchell's recently published *Field Guide to the*

Trees of Britain and Northern Europe. It was a Damascene revelation—so many trees, so many new concepts. I devoured the contents and was soon putting the book to its intended use as a field guide. I still have the book, dog-eared, full of pressed leaves from vaguely remembered summers and expanded to twice its original size following one particularly wet field trip to the west coast of Scotland in the company of my longtime field confederate Alan Fones. Within this great book is a section about the origins of trees, a story that still exercises my mind and has a great bearing on what is to follow. Far from an unending, biologically diverse forest, the landmass of England is now sparsely forested and has a depauperate woody flora. The lack of forest cover can be explained by millennia of human activity, but how to explain the lack of species? If the original forest cover was so diverse, where have all these tree species gone?

Not surprisingly the answer to this question is much debated in scientific circles. The timescales involved are almost unimaginable, the evidence scanty and the analysis of data open to many different interpretations. What is not in dispute is the fact that the forest over much of what is today the Northern Hemisphere was very different twenty million years BP—not so much in the types of trees which were present (this ancient flora contained many genera we would recognise today) but in their distribution. Perhaps as recently as three million years ago a great temperate forest extended virtually unbroken across the landmass of Eurasia and North America; it was remarkably homogeneous, without the regional variations we see today. How do we know this? The fossil record tells us so; classic studies, in the nineteenth and early twentieth centuries, of deposits that lie beneath the south and east of England, particularly at Cromer in Norfolk, revealed the remains of trees which were no longer part of the European flora, let alone that of the British Isles. Hickories, magnolias, *Sequoiadendron* and *Sciadopitys*, genera now restricted to North America and eastern Asia, flourished during the time that these deposits were being laid down from about fifty million years ago. More recent studies in North America have yielded plants that are now strictly Asian in distribution.

Of course all these trees can still be found in eastern Asia, where the diversity of tree species is staggering. In the woodlands of central and western China we can gauge what the prehistoric forests may have been like as

Ginkgo from the Palaeocene of Almont, North Dakota, U.S.A.,
circa sixty million years BP (photograph courtesy Peter Crane)

many relictual genera, eliminated from Europe and North America, are still growing there, and the head count of tree species very closely matches that presented by the fossil record. Excepting a few North American endemics such as *Oxydendrum* and *Planera*, the forests of eastern Asia have a full suite of temperate tree and shrub taxa, many of them extremely ornamental. Not for nothing is eastern Asia considered by many horticulturists to be the natural garden of the world.

When we look across the temperate floras of the Northern Hemisphere today we see great diversity in China and the East, a rich though reduced assemblage in North America and notable paucity in Europe and particularly in the British Isles. So I return to my earlier question. What happened to the rich forests which once grew in England? Scientists agree on the single most important factor: what brought catastrophe to the ancient temperate forests of the Northern Hemisphere were the successive glaciations of the Pleistocene era. As the Earth rapidly cooled, four glaciations are known to have occurred, the last retreating north as recently as eighteen thousand years ago, a blink of an eye in geological time.

With the onset of glaciation conditions worsened in the higher latitudes and the plants growing there retreated south. As each summer dwindled in length and winter lingered longer, conditions became more and more uncongenial for the growth of forest trees. As the glaciers advanced so the climatic zones moved before them—what had been temperate became arctic, what had been subtropical became temperate. Thus the forest temporarily relocated southwards. In North America the forests made an orderly retreat as the mountain systems, running north-south, provided no barriers to this movement. During the height of the Ice Age the temperate flora took a furlough in what is today Central America, to return as conditions improved. In Asia, the evidence suggests that the advance of the glaciers was more modest and the temperate forest largely escaped unmolested. In Europe, by contrast, not only were the glaciations severe and unrelenting but the routes to the south were by no means assured. Physical barriers in the form of east-west mountain systems—from the Pyrenees in the west, through the Alps to the Tatra mountains in the east—made migration more difficult. Once through, the retreating vegetation was then faced with the Mediterranean Sea and literally had its back to the wall. Only the hardiest and most adaptable species survived. The warmth-loving magnolias, hickories, wingnuts and catalpas perished as did the primitive and nonadaptive katsuras, ginkgos and many conifers. For those with the imagination to hear, their death throes scream to us down the aeons.

Again and again the glaciers advanced and retreated. With their final retreat recolonisation northwards began. In Europe the flora that recolonised was drastically reduced; gone were key elements of the preglacial flora. No magnolias, no hickories, no sweet gums, no katsuras, no tupelos, no catalpas—the head count is a long and depressing one, like the roll call of fallen soldiers in some forgotten battle. For the British Isles one further factor dealt a final blow. The land bridge connecting the archipelago at the extreme northwestern edge of the continent was cut as sea levels rose with the melting of the glaciers, thus creating the English Channel. What had failed to colonise this far north would never reach the British Isles under natural circumstances. Today fewer than forty woody plants are native to Britain. China has more species of woody plants on the single peak of Emei Shan in Sichuan Province than the entire British Isles can muster, and by some way.

Rich temperate forest in China

The great irony in all this is that the present climate of the British Isles is eminently suitable for the growth and development of temperate trees. With sufficient rainfall and a lack of temperature extremes these maritime islands offer the right conditions for broadleaved plants to flourish. What geological events took away humankind set about restoring. Today the gardens of the British Isles are the most diverse in the world—diverse in their design, the styles which they employ and, most importantly, in their plant content. The country's leading arboreta once again provide a home to long-extinguished trees. The location where my imaginary archaeopteryx took to the air is today the 140 ha (300 acres) which make up the Royal Botanic Gardens, Kew, containing an arboretum which boasts more hardy, woody plants than any comparable area on the planet. For this we have one man in particular to thank, William Jackson Bean, better known when his given names are reduced to initials.

W. J. Bean working
in the herbarium at Kew

(photograph courtesy The Library & Archives,

Royal Botanic Gardens, Kew)

Ernest Henry Wilson

(photograph courtesy The Library & Archives,

Royal Botanic Gardens, Kew)

W. J. Bean, curator of Kew between 1922 and his retirement in 1929, began his long association with Kew's arboretum in 1900. A more auspicious date is hard to imagine as at just that point in time Ernest Henry Wilson was working his way into the central Chinese province of Hubei in search of the fabled dove tree (*Davidia involucrata*). Wilson, a Kew man himself, was on the verge of achieving greatness. Over the next ten years he brought back over a thousand different taxa of woody plants and was almost single-handedly responsible for embellishing Western gardens with the hardy trees and shrubs that we now take for granted.

As Wilson's labours began to yield their fruits so other collectors, working for other gardens and patrons, entered the biologically diverse areas of eastern Asia. George Forrest, Frank Kingdon Ward and Joseph Rock shared their harvests with Kew and W. J. Bean, a harvest that Bean made full use of. The arboretum was bursting with new plants, and Bean's own studies of

The original tree of *Aesculus indica* 'Sydney Pearce' by the Nash Conservatory at Kew

these plants soon led to the seminal publication, *Trees and Shrubs Hardy in the British Isles*, two volumes that would provide Bean with horticultural immortality. Bean was followed by a whole succession of talented horticulturists who were decidedly 'woody' in their professional inclinations: Arthur Osborn, author of the influential *Shrubs and Trees for the Garden*; Charles Raffill, responsible for a wonderful magnolia hybrid that carries his name; Sydney Pearce, another prolific writer and for whom the majestic *Aesculus indica* 'Sydney Pearce' is named; and George Brown, whose *The Pruning of Trees, Shrubs and Conifers* (now in a second edition, revised and enlarged by Tony Kirkham) is still the standard work on the subject. These men provided continuity and cemented Kew's reputation as a centre for excellence in all matters pertaining to hardy woody plants.

On Brown's retirement in 1977 Kew had a famous arboretum with an unrivalled collection of trees and shrubs. Unfortunately, spectres were gathering on the horizon. Amongst gardens managers and scientists it was widely felt that the boundaries between horticulture and botany had become blurred. In botanic gardens horticulture is the craft that serves the needs of botany rather than an end in itself; in the early years this was clearly understood. Kew along with other botanic gardens was a place for science, and science used other disciplines to promulgate its business. When Kew's arboretum was laid out in the 1870s it was done so as a living scientific representation of the plant families of hardy woody species. W. J. Bean had continued and expanded this process into the twentieth century; however, when during the middle decades of that century political developments closed many of the collecting grounds in eastern Asia, increasing numbers of plants of dubious origin were added and increasing numbers of purely ornamental features created. At Kew a new curatorial team led by the ambitious John Simmons, who took up his post in 1972, recognised the shortcomings of this approach.

Nonnatural source plant material has little to offer science; it is undocumented and often of hybrid origin or, having been propagated vegetatively, of limited genetic diversity. A new way forward had to be found. Opportunities and funding were limited, and travel to the key areas of the wild for trees and shrubs was still difficult. John Simmons seized a chance to collect in the Elburz Mountains of Iran in 1977 as a demonstration of his personal commitment to bringing science back to the arboretum. It was a hugely successful visit; Simmons's team were able to bring back good seed harvested in a botanically important area, underpinned by accurate field notes. Other members of the horticultural staff were also encouraged to undertake fieldwork. Tony Schilling made several journeys to the eastern Himalaya during the 1970s and '80s and brought back hundreds of new introductions; deputy curator Ian Beyer spent six weeks in South Korea in 1982 with Charles Erskine, assistant curator in the arboretum, and herbarium botanist Jill Cowley.

As opportunities for travel increased the whole initiative gathered momentum, with mainland China targeted for expeditionary work. John

Simmons followed up a 1979 exploratory visit to China by organising a plant collecting trip to Guizhou Province, in the southwest of the country, in 1985. John and his companions—Kew colleague Hans Fliegner and James Russell of Castle Howard in North Yorkshire—achieved a great deal on this trip, which included a visit to Fanjin Shan, a mountain unknown in the West; and they were amongst a small group of botanists and horticulturists who were then carrying back the first significant amounts of germplasm, including new species, to reach the West from China in almost fifty years. The unusual and recently named birch, *Betula austrosinensis*, for example, was introduced to cultivation by this 1985 expedition.

More important, however, was that John made contact with influential and strategically placed Chinese officials, amongst them Liu Zhaoguang of the Institute of Biology in Chengdu, the capital of Sichuan Province, who was willing to engage with Kew in setting up a series of trips to key areas of this biologically rich province. John had deliberately identified Sichuan as the area to major on; historically the collections of E. H. Wilson and others from Sichuan had proven to be most amenable in cultivation in England. Additionally, other institutions, notably the Royal Botanic Garden, Edinburgh, were becoming active in the neighbouring province of Yunnan, and John was anxious to avoid overlaps.

Things moved fast. The post-storm review undertaken at Kew and Wakehurst Place continued to point to eastern Asia, with its great wealth of flora, as a key locus for overseas collecting efforts. It became clear that other gardens were interested in pushing the Chinese door as wide open as possible. Charles Howick of the Howick Arboretum, Northumberland, in the northeast of England, was anxious to become involved and had already established contact with Jane Davenport Jansen, who was developing a new botanic garden in Sonoma, California—Quarry Hill Botanical Gardens—and who herself wanted to be at the forefront of any new opportunities in the East. Furthermore Jane had, in Bill McNamara, a young man who was likewise straining at the leash. John Simmons put together a joint expedition to Sichuan in 1988, truly a modern landmark for all concerned. This consortium and its partnership with the Institute of Biology in Chengdu was to see eight subsequent expeditions to Sichuan and the introduction of over two thousand collections of plants and seeds.

But John Simmons and his able deputy, Ian Beyer, were equally anxious to ensure that other parts of temperate Asia were not neglected. They well knew that the countries which neighbour China were also rich in suitable plants, and the review conducted at Kew and Wakehurst Place was identifying big gaps in both the taxonomic and geographic representation of woody plants in the arboreta from these areas. The visit to South Korea in 1982 had left much unfinished business, and Charles Erskine was charged to take this matter forward. But Charles had also been asked to join the team heading to Sichuan. He therefore turned to his number two in the arboretum, Tony Kirkham, to step up and take his place. Here was a golden opportunity, an opportunity not to be missed. With a good deal of trepidation, but driven by a huge sense of excitement, Tony began to make arrangements for the expedition to South Korea. But, we're getting ahead of our story!

CHAPTER 3

Land of the Morning Calm

I WAS SUMMONED TO IAN BEYER'S OFFICE on a chilly autumn morning in 1988. As deputy curator of Kew's Living Collections Department, Ian enjoyed a formidable reputation and the respect of the botanic garden world. Many at Kew feared his no-nonsense approach but grudgingly acknowledged that he ran a tight ship—firm but fair was the consensus. With Ian's reputation in mind I was more than a little apprehensive as I climbed the staircase of Aiton House in the Lower Nursery; named in honour of William Aiton, the first curator of the original 4-ha (9-acre) botanic garden started by Princess Augusta in 1759, this building acted as the curatorial nerve centre of Kew. I knocked lightly on the outer office door and was invited in and offered a seat looking out over the River Thames. Ian, a balding, portly man, came straight to the point. 'We want you to lead a seed collecting expedition to South Korea and begin the post-storm fieldwork programme'. Dumbstruck I searched for a response. I hadn't ventured into the field since a near fatal seed collecting trip to Chile with colleague Stewart Henchie in 1985. The memory of my brush with death—a combination of salmonella typhoid, a military coup and a massive

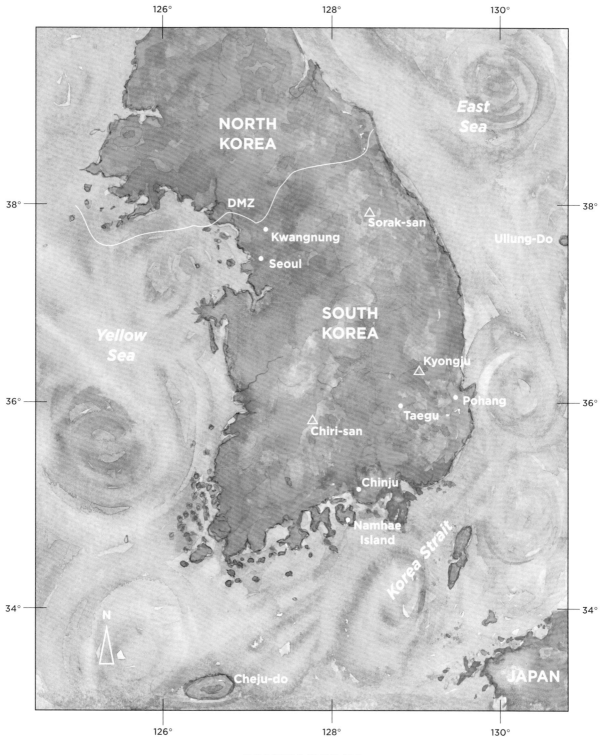

SOUTH KOREA

earthquake in Santiago—was all too fresh in my mind, but here was an offer too good to miss and I was eager to oblige.

Most collections from the 1982 Living Collections Department trip to South Korea, led by Ian Beyer, were now growing well in the arboretum and herbaceous section, but many areas on the mainland had not been visited and several collections failed to germinate or were not successfully established in the gardens—the unfinished business. I therefore was to organise and lead a follow-up expedition next autumn, in 1989. I had to choose a colleague, which wasn't going to be too difficult, as there was really only one candidate who would be suitable: Mark Flanagan, a fairly new lad to Kew from Manchester, trained at the Royal Botanic Garden, Edinburgh, who had recently moved to take a manager's post at Wakehurst Place.

Ian made a telephone call to Tony Schilling, and the green light for Mark to participate was given. The invite was put to Mark, who didn't need much persuading. This was the start of an association that would make a significant impact on the future woody collections growing in the arboreta at Kew and Wakehurst Place.

At the request of Grenville Lucas, keeper of the herbarium and chairman of the Fieldwork Committee, a third member would join us: Peter Boyce, an assistant scientific officer and Araceae expert in the herbarium who required real fieldwork experience. Our hosts would be the Korean Forestry Research Institute, who successfully administered the 1982 expedition jointly with the Korean Horticultural Society. Contacts were made with Mr Jo Jae-Myung, the director general in Seoul, and once again he and his colleagues kindly offered their valuable help and assistance, which Mark and I gratefully took up. The offices of the Forestry Research Institute also arranged for all the collecting permits and permissions needed to collect officially in the national parks, national forests and other natural monuments in South Korea. The following months were spent in the two arboreta, at Kew and Wakehurst Place, and the herbarium, compiling a target list of plants to collect and an inventory of equipment we would need for a six-week field trip.

On 21 September 1989 we check in at Heathrow Airport for a Korean Air flight to Seoul via Anchorage in Alaska. I say goodbye to Sally, who is six and a half months pregnant, and Mark to Lesley and their six-week-old son Callum. Our timing for an expedition to far-flung places is impeccable!

As well as our rucksacks we have a large blue suitcase, carrying expedition equipment and gifts for our hosts, which puts us well over our baggage allowance. A long discussion with the duty manager follows, and a gift of a 1990 Kew calendar and an explanation about the nature of our trip (complete with buzzwords like 'conservation', 'genotypes' and 'germplasm') help to oil the wheels. We get away with paying a modest charge for excess baggage, which doesn't eat too much into an already small expedition budget.

On 22 September 1989, after a monotonous yet nerve-wracking eighteen-hour flight via Anchorage in Alaska (over the Kamchatka Peninsula, where on 31 August 1983 the Soviet Union shot down Korean Air Flight 007 after a supposed air space incursion), we finally arrive in Kimpo International Airport, Seoul. Rebuilt for the 1988 Olympic Games, the main airport arrival area is an impressive cathedral-like piece of architecture.

We are met by Mr Kim Un-Cho, founder of the International Gardens Foundation in Korea, and Mr Oh Jeong-Soo, chief of the forest ecology section at the Forestry Research Institute, and feel a little more relaxed being in capable hands in foreign parts. We load the institute jeep with our baggage and are driven to the Mammoth Hotel in Tongdaemun district, where we are to spend the first three nights of our duration in South Korea. It feels expensive, and Mark, who is treasurer for the expedition, starts to mentally juggle figures and conversion rates and announces to Peter and me that he intends pulling in the purse strings on day one. It later turns out that the Forestry Research Institute have special rates, and Mark's fears are somewhat allayed.

Following a short discussion with Mr Oh about the trip, we are taken out to sample the delights of Korean cuisine. Bulgogi, a dish that we are to become very familiar with over the next six weeks, is at the top of the menu, and no meal would be complete without a portion of the national dish, kimchi. Bulgogi consists of thin strips of beef marinated in soy and a strong chilli sauce with copious amounts of garlic, barbecued at the table on a cast iron pan over red-hot coals. Rather more of a culinary shock to Western palates is kimchi, a pungent, fiery hot sort of Eastern coleslaw consisting Chinese cabbage, sometimes with radish or carrot added, fermented for long periods in earthenware jars with exotic spices, red pepper, garlic and ginger—and I can vouch that it is an acquired taste. On the way back to the

Tongdae-mun Sijang market

hotel we are shown a place suitable for breakfast and are told what to ask for, hae chang kuk. We all feel relaxed and comfortable at the close of this first day and with the way in which our hosts have been so helpful.

The following morning we awake to the roar of traffic and people going about their daily business. We venture out, dodging bicycles overloaded with cardboard boxes and speeding motorbikes, to the eating house recommended by Mr Oh last night and confidently ask for hae chang kuk. When it arrives, it's not what we would have expected for breakfast: a bowl of eel heads, complete with teeth, staring out of a broth of congealed blood and rice with another bowl of kimchi as a side salad. All around us Koreans pick out the fish heads with their chopsticks and drink the soup whilst taking in mouthfuls of kimchi at the same time. We all quietly prod and poke at the contents, pushing them round the bowl, waiting for someone to say something and finally unanimously decide that we are not hungry and should forego breakfast. This was to be the most difficult mealtime for us whilst in Korea and nothing could have prepared us for this experience—we don't make this mistake again!

Peter, a supposedly ardent traveller to the far east of tropical Asia in search of arisaemas for his monograph in the herbarium, has arrived in Korea with an empty suitcase with the intention of procuring clothing here in a Seoul (rather unusual I thought, but it certainly helped ease the excess baggage problems at Heathrow). This called for a trip to the Tongdae-mun Sijang market at the Great East Gate, one of several large markets in Seoul that sell everything from silk to fruit and, for the not-so-faint-hearted, any form of meat or fish from dogs to sharks and much, much more. It is said that if you can't find what you are looking for here then you won't find it anywhere. In the spice market it will be possible to collect most of our target list without even venturing out into the field. However we are here to top up Peter's wardrobe and this we do with an array of cheap, top-brand designer reproductions that would make any of the trendy sports companies livid.

In the afternoon we are picked up at the hotel and taken to the Research Institute at Chongryangri-Dong. We are to have a meeting with several senior staff to discuss our itinerary further. Mr Oh introduces us to Mr Choi Myoung-Sub, a dendrologist at the Kwangnung Arboretum (the institute's base just north of Seoul), a well-built Korean with hard facial features dressed in denim jeans and a short fishing vest. 'He will be your guide, bodyguard and interpreter for your trip', explains Mr Oh. We introduce ourselves and get a wry smile from Mr Choi; we are then told that he doesn't speak English. We all look puzzled, and Mark breaks the silence by saying '*Acer okamotoanum*'—a rare maple uncommon in cultivation in the West, now recognised as a subspecies of *A. pictum*, from a Korean island in the East Sea. Mr Choi responds by opening a map and stubbing the island with his index finger, saying 'Ullung' several times. Mark is happy, as he believes that Mr Choi knows his plants and will be a great field botanist. We all shake hands and celebrate with a cup of ginseng tea complete with pine kernel floaters.

Mr Oh advises that the institute's accommodation in Kwangnung Arboretum in Pochun-Gun will be made available to us as a base to stay and prepare collections between trips out in the field. A walk round the Kwanak

Arboretum, attached to the institute, completes our afternoon before we return to the Mammoth Hotel for what will be one of our last Western meals for several weeks. A 10-m (32-ft) specimen of *Firmiana simplex*, the parasol tree, is growing outside the main offices; the large maple-like leaves and fruits with broad papery wings make this a striking species. This is one of the few hardy species in the Sterculiaceae, which is primarily a tropical family, and if it can survive a winter here in Seoul it must be hardy enough for the south of England. With permission a few seeds go in the bag to start the collection.

The following day is spent visiting British Ambassador Lawrence Middleton at the embassy, where we dispense horticultural advice in the embassy garden in exchange for their monthly quota of tinned Spam luncheon meat and corned beef. This addition to our field ration supply would later prove to be a valuable resource to us. We leave the embassy to visit Pagoda Park by way of the Secret Garden and observe thousands of maidenhair trees, *Ginkgo biloba*, growing as street trees. The majority are females, showing the familiar symmetrical fastigiate habit, and the apricot-like fruits, just beginning to ripen, are giving off that strong smell of rotting flesh that seems to fill and linger on the air. At present the leaves are green, but by the time we return to Seoul in late October they will be a fantastic butter-yellow colour. The other common street tree is *Zelkova serrata*, grown as a multi-stemmed tree, a rather unusual habit for an urban tree but one that seems to work.

We exit the park onto the main highway and are confronted by thousands of students being contained by riot police dressed in full combat outfit. The tear gas in the air is starting to have an effect on our eyes when some of the riot police recognise us as Western tourists and quickly escort us into the subway, advising us to leave the area on the next train. We take their advice and return to the Mammoth Hotel for our last night in Seoul before leaving for Kwangnung Arboretum. We spend the evening at a bar next to the hotel drinking OB, Korean beer, before retiring to our beds for a much needed sleep.

The next morning is bizarre to say the least. I am awakened, I think, by a telephone call from the Forestry Research Institute: our meeting time has changed from 9.00 a.m. to 7.00 a.m. and we will be met in the reception downstairs. I quickly call Mark's room and then Peter's, explaining the

Administrative buildings at Kwangnung Arboretum

change of plan whilst half-asleep. It's already 6.30 a.m., so there is a sense of urgency as I wash and pack. We gather in the lobby, all looking the worse for wear, slightly hung over. 'Who telephoned this morning?' asks Mark. I cannot recall, and it soon becomes apparent the whole thing was a dream and I have deprived Mark and Peter of an extra two hours sleep!

Mr Oh arrives at 9.00 a.m., as planned, and takes us for a meeting with the director general of the Forestry Department before our departure for Kwangnung. But there is a hitch in the itinerary—Mr Choi, our guide, cannot join us until later, so our first field trip will be delayed. The good news is that we can collect in the foothills surrounding the arboretum. After an hour's drive we arrive at Kwangnung and are shown the two rooms that are to be ours for the trip.

There are only two beds between the rooms and whilst I am busy making conversation with our hosts and trying to apologise for the weight of

Deciduous woodland on Sori-San

the blue suitcase, which has left two Koreans with bad backs, Peter chooses one room and Mark the other. They both quickly fall onto the beds, attempting to make up for the lost time this morning. Mark is supine and asleep within seconds, and it looks like I'm on the floor. I settle down, about to drift into some badly needed sleep, when there's a knock at the door, followed by another and then another. Clearly I'm not going to catch up on any bonus 'shut eye'.

Our first day is spent on our own in the forests surrounding the arboretum, collecting on the flanks of Sori-San, a relatively small mountain of some 536 m (1715 ft). This is mixed deciduous woodland, the climax species being oak and hornbeam, *Quercus mongolica* and *Carpinus laxiflora*, with occasional specimens of Korean white pine, *Pinus koraiensis*, and Japanese red pine, *P. densiflora*. The autumn colour is just starting to turn, with the cloudless blue sky as a backdrop, and there is no shortage of fruit.

The understorey comprises *Styrax japonicus*, *Clerodendrum trichotomum*, *Aralia elata* and *Viburnum dilatatum*, plants that are very familiar to us as exotic specialities in our gardens back at home. The temperature is very warm and by the time we get back a cold Korean beer in the bar across the road from the arboretum is a welcome sight. Mr Choi and his colleague Dr Kwang-Woo Park, another dendrologist at the arboretum who will be accompanying us as a guide later on into the expedition, soon join us. They check our herbarium specimens and agree with our determinations. Today has been a good day to try out our field equipment, and we naturally assign ourselves roles for the smooth collecting process in the field. I will be responsible for the seed, Peter the herbarium specimens and Mark the field notes. When we are all up to speed with these respective duties in the evenings, we will all get on with the seed cleaning, which is possibly one of the most important aspects of a seed collecting expedition, as seed can deteriorate very quickly if left wet or dry in sealed bags. It can be deprived of oxygen and rot or dry out too fast, reducing the viability of the seed by the day.

We have an early start next morning in order to prepare our bags for our first trip. The water in the washroom is bitterly cold and there appears to be no hot water, but we brave a cold shower before a homemade breakfast with leftovers from yesterday's meal. Feeling cleansed and well fed, we gather outside the offices to wait for Mr Choi. I am amazed at how quickly the weather has changed. It has been raining hard through the night; the forests we were collecting in yesterday have disappeared under a shroud of mist, and the temperature has dropped considerably.

Our aim is Sorak-san National Park. Sorak-san ('snow-peaked mountain') is a series of peaks in the mid section of Taebaek Sanmaek (Great White Range) situated in the northeast of South Korea, just south of the DMZ (demilitarised zone) that separates North Korea from South Korea. But first we head south, boarding a forestry lorry for a lift to Seoul's central bus station, whence we embark on an uncomfortable five-hour bus journey northeast across the country following the South Han River through poor weather that steams up the windows, denying us any views of the country. I am sitting next to a young boy aged about nine who is chewing on a piece of dried squid, and the fishy aroma gets stronger as the journey goes on. He kindly offers me a piece, but I decline the offer, sticking to conventional Western chewing gum. I offer him a piece, which he tries; he turns up his nose and decides he prefers the squid. I fall asleep. I awake at about four o'clock in the afternoon as we arrive at our destination, a small town called

View across the mountains in Sorak-san

Yong-Dae-Lee. Mr Choi finds us a yogwan, a type of traditional inn providing bed and breakfast; it is dry, warm and comfortable, but very noisy with the sound of car and bus horns sounding off every few minutes and dogs constantly howling.

Once settled in we take a short walk and recce to the park entrance. The weather has started to clear and there are now patches of blue sky breaking through the cloud, but as the sun goes down dark comes in very quickly. We return to town and eat some noodles in a small bar before retiring to our yogwan for an early night. This is our first night on and under traditional yo and ibul, a thin mattress and form of duvet, respectively, which gets too warm in the night, as the floors are very warm from underfloor heating.

We awake in the morning to sunshine beating through the windows and mist rising up from the river valley, revealing the spectacular granite

Roof detail of Paekdam-sa

The striking bark of *Betula davurica*

mountains. I take a cold-water bath in the communal bathroom before breakfast, which consists of noodles, bread and coffee, and at 7.00 a.m. eagerly head once again for the park entrance. It is not long before we start collecting, as every plant is new to us. However, we have to be well disciplined and ensure that the plant features on our target list; otherwise, we will be duplicating the collections made in 1982 and wasting valuable time. We climb steadily through the day to 620 m (1984 ft), past Paekdam-sa, a charming, colourful Buddhist temple in Inner Sorak.

I am delighted to find *Lindera obtusiloba* with its butter-yellow autumnal leaves and the Dahurian birch, *Betula davurica*, my favourite of all birches, with fingers of light from the midday sun shining through and highlighting the wonderful loose, pale-coloured flaky bark. The tree with the greatest presence is *Acer pseudosieboldianum*, showing strong hints of bright scarlet autumn colour from its small palmate leaves through the rest of the surrounding vegetation. However, disappointingly, there is not a sign of a samara to be found.

The going is tough, as this is the first real day in the field. It's starting to test my fitness, and Mr Choi encourages us to head back. Before we do, we take in some of the splendid rugged scenery that surrounds us, with the sharp columns of granite pointing up from the river bottom. Despite the harsh nature of the rock, plants still seem to thrive on them, including naturally bonsaied, in all shapes and sizes, *Pinus densiflora*, the Japanese red pine, closely resembling our native Scots pine with its red bark. We start to make our descent to Yong-Dae-Lee and finally arrive as the sun disappears behind the mountains at 6.00 p.m., foot-weary and hungry.

Fiery autumn tints of *Acer pseudosieboldianum*

The following morning we catch a bus and leave for another small town about 5 km (3 miles) down the road in order that we can enter Sorak-san from another direction. The trail today is a lot more difficult than yesterday with much climbing, following the river up into the mountains across great slabs of smoothly worn granite. We pass many hikers on their way down and are greeted with continual smiles and 'kamsa hamnida' (Korean for 'thank you'); I have never met a friendlier people. Growing out over the edge of a gorge above the torrent of water is *Magnolia sieboldii* clothed in red fruits with orange-coloured waxy covered seeds exposed. We saw this plant yesterday, barren of fruits, but today with some precarious climbing above the steep gorge, we manage to make a good collection of seed. This species of magnolia was first introduced to the arboretum at Kew in 1893 by the Yokohama Nursery Company from Japan and later by E. H. Wilson from

Magnolia sieboldii collected in Sorak-san flowering at Kew

Korea in 1918. With its fragrant nodding white flower and bright red sta-
mens, it bears a close likeness to *M. sieboldii* subsp. *sinensis*, which was first
found in the mountains of western Sichuan in China and introduced into
cultivation by E. H. Wilson in 1908 but not introduced into English gardens until later in 1928. The flowers of both plants are best observed in the
garden from beneath the pendent flowers.

Growing with the magnolia along the river is *Betula schmidtii* with its dark
brown bark and lenticelled trunk, and beneath it is *Callicarpa japonica* with a
profusion of purple berries. The surrounding forest contains two large
stately conifers, the Manchurian fir, *Abies holophylla*, and *Pinus koraiensis*, with a
deciduous element of *Acer pseudosieboldianum* and *Quercus variabilis*.

We pass 700 m (2240 ft) elevation, higher than we reached yesterday,
and the autumn colour is well and truly set in here. We are climbing a magnificent natural monument known as Nam Gyo Lee (Twelve Nymph Pools),
a series of large pools gouged out of the granite bed rock by millions of
years of water cascading down the mountain from one pool to another. We
stop for lunch, Embassy Spam and bread by the riverside. Mark spots an
eye-catching climbing plant on the opposite bank and whilst leaping across

Silvery underside of *Thuja koraiensis* foliage

to photograph a flowering and fruiting *Clematis koreana* gracing a shady, mossy slope, his camera slips from his shoulder and lands in the river. It is fished out, but both camera and film are ruined. Luckily we have a spare.

We reach the last pool at 3.00 p.m., and it's a good two-and-a-half-hour nonstop trek back, leaving us an hour to collect anything we see. On the forest floor is Korean arbor-vitae, *Thuja koraiensis*, with a strange growth habit. It appears to reach about 4 m (12 ft) high, falls over and begins growing upright again, making a dense, impenetrable thicket. Some old brown cones are attached, but we struggle to find only three seeds, which we carefully bag and record.

Growing amongst the arbor-vitae is *Deutzia coreana*, one of the earliest flowering and in my mind most beautiful deutzias, producing small, graceful white bell-like flowers before the leaves appear. Mr Choi is getting fidgety and eager to begin the return hike, knowing how quickly the night will set in and how tired we will all be after a long hard day in the mountains. Our daysacks are packed with a good collection of seed, and the plant press is full and heavy from the day's herbarium voucher specimens, so we take turns carrying the press as we trot back down the track. At the village Mr

Choi has lined up some well-earned liquid refreshments that quickly quench our thirst and a sit-down to rest some tired feet whilst we wait for one of Mr Choi's friends to join us. He is apparently a keen hiker familiar with tomorrow's location. Mr Kim arrives and drives us over the mountains to our next overnight stop, a town called Osaek Yaksu. At 900 m (2950 ft) altitude we drive through the Han'gye Pass, where we get some spectacular views of Sorak-san in the fading evening light.

Our accommodation tonight is a single room that the three of us will share, but it has hot water and the floor is so hot I can hardly stand on it, which is great for drying the herbarium specimens. As we dine lavishly tonight on bulgogi with heaps of garlic and good kimchi we begin to get to know Mr Choi, who is pleased to hear that we have had a good day and are very happy to have made some interesting collections.

It is Saturday morning, and after a walk round Osaek Yaksu to find breakfast we return to the yogwan to pack our bags for a long day in the mountains, culminating with a climb to the peak of Jum-bong. We manage to find a lift to the start of the trek, below the Han'gye Pass, where we stopped to take in the view last night. The climb starts straightaway, and immediately Mark is excited by the wealth of herbaceous elements here; *Lychnis cognata*, *Aconitum carlesii*, *Caulophyllum robustum* and *Ligularia fischeri* all make up the rich community in the dappled light of the forest floor. The tree species include a walnut, *Juglans mandshurica*, and the Mongolian oak, *Quercus mongolica*, but unfortunately there are very few walnuts or acorns to find.

We are climbing a smaller mountain named Mang Dearm Bong to reach the foot of Jum-bong. Despite its modest height, the going is tough, and we need the tree climbing rope to help us scale a few rocky outcrops safely. We are soon in a heavily wooded valley of Mongolian oak with ground vegetation of pure *Sasa borealis*, a bamboo up to my chest. Walking is difficult as it is impossible to see obstacles protruding from the ground, and it's not long before we lose Peter, who, propelled by the weight of the plant press on his back, has tripped over an unseen tree stump and into the bamboo. Mr Choi and Mr Kim are highly taken by this and show it in their uncontrollable laughter, but Peter is clearly not amused. As we climb higher, the bamboo gets shorter, until it is only ankle deep, and the diversity of plant material begins to get more interesting again. After about another two hours of hard

E. H. Wilson in Korea, 1917

(photograph by E. H. Wilson courtesy Photographic Archives of the Arnold Arboretum, copyrighted by the
President and Fellows of Harvard College, Harvard University, Cambridge, Massachusetts)

climbing and several arguments in Korean between Mr Kim and Mr Choi
about directions and positions on the map, we reach the summit of what we
think is Jum-bong, only to find that we are still on the smaller peak of
Mang Dearn Bong. Mr Choi points to the west, and in the far distance,
peeping through the shimmering haze that has now started to form in the
heat of the day, is the elusive peak of Jum-bong. Mr Choi insists that we
press on if we are to reach our destination before dark, and with every plant
we collect, he nervously encourages us to get a move on.

We climb steadily through a dwarf alpine forest of *Betula ermanii* and
Taxus cuspidata with occasional dwarf shrubs of smaller habit, more *Magnolia
sieboldii* and *Berberis davurica*, *Rhododendron dauricum* and *R. schlippenbachii*. The
higher we ascend the more free-fruiting everything is and the more tired I
become. We eventually reach the summit at 1424 m (4557 ft); the
panoramic view is breathtaking with huge drifts of the magnolia and rhododendron running riot in the afternoon sun. I take time to remove my

heavy boots and socks to air my tired feet and reflect. When the great plant collector Ernest Henry Wilson visited and explored these mountains in 1917 he wrote, 'Not even in the richest parts of China or Japan have I seen such extensive displays of pure pink and white as on the Diamond Mountains, where *Rhododendron schlippenbachii* and *Magnolia parviflora* dominate the undergrowth for miles and bloom to perfection'.

Today *Magnolia parviflora* goes under the new name of *M. sieboldii*, and how I would love to be here in the spring to see the colours that Wilson witnessed so many years ago. Mr Choi produces two enormous Chinese pears from his daysack, peels and chops them and distributes them amongst us all. This is the most delicious, juiciest pear I have ever tasted in my life and I relish every piece as I take in the scenery and help to tidy up the many herbarium specimens we have managed to collect today. The vegetation, including the trees, grows right to the very top of the mountain—when Mr Choi talks about alpine plants, he means any herbaceous plants, not what we perceive as alpines.

I don my socks and boots once more; there is a fresh spring to my step as we begin to make our descent off Jum-bong. But this renewed energy does not last too long, and soon I am pushing my legs to their limit—oh, what I would do for a lie-down on a Korean mattress! I am lagging at the back of the team now, and whenever I can I stop to ponder the mountains that surround me. I use a photograph moment as an excuse for a break, but there are only so many photographs you can take of one mountain!

Three hours later we reach Osaek Yaksu and, heaven, Mr Choi has already got the ice-cold beers in, which I drink whilst resting my aching body. It's not long, however, before we leave for the outskirts of town, a small village called Kwan-Dae-Lee, where Choi finds us a small minbak, a type of granny flat attached to a private house. The landlord has moved granny and everything else, including all the furniture, out, and we move in with all our belongings, including the seed and herbarium specimens. This is the smallest of rooms so far, and it takes some time to organise the layout for maximum efficiency. Anything would suffice after today's exertions, and the bedroll on the floor is looking more and more inviting. Still, like all yogwans up to now, it is warm and dry, with its own fire outside and the chimney is channelled under the floor to provide the heating. We stoke this up,

Mark and Peter pressing herbarium specimens on Jum-bong
whilst Mr Choi looks on

as the weather is looking to take a turn for the worse, and head back to Osaek Yaksu once more in search of dinner.

As we pass a table outside the minbak Mark points to a large, dead snake coiled on the surface and asks Mr Choi, 'Why?' We think his reply is that it is being prepared for dinner; later we find out that there are snakehunters in the village, as snake meat is highly prized for food and as an aphrodisiac. We find a small food place in town and thankfully snake is not on the menu! However, there is very little else on offer, and we eat a type of hamburger as a last resort to stave off our hunger until morning. As we are settling down to a much deserved sleep, Mr Choi comes in with some huge Chinese pears from the landlord which we eagerly consume before trying to get to sleep. Despite my tiredness, I am struggling to fall asleep because of the noise (many screaming children, barking dogs, the buzz of heavy traffic on the main road), an uncomfortably hot room and the stale, sweet stench of sweaty socks and wet boots, not mine of course, that are now steaming from the heat of the floor.

I wake to the sound of heavy rain; Mr Choi's weather forecast last night was right. I try to brave the latrine-type toilet but decide in the end to go for a walk despite the downpour. When I return I let Mark know that the snake is still on the table.

Over a cup of coffee, Mr Choi suggests that we try an area in the east of Sorak-san, as the vegetation will be new to us. It is also a touristy place so it will be easy to access and to explore, especially given the bad weather, which would make it foolish to attempt any serious mountain work. After yesterday's hard slog this sounds ideal to me, and I agree wholeheartedly with our guide. We pack our daysacks with Goretex jackets and trousers and catch a bus to Naksan, a small coastal fishing town on the East Sea. We walk along the main street past the many restaurants with fish tanks bubbling away outside, displaying their catches of the day: live squid, lobster and other unappetising species of fish and crustacea.

The waves of the East Sea crash onto the main street as we head for Ulsan-bawi, another spectacular granite formation that dominates this region of Sorak, just south of the Diamond Mountains. The rain is unforgiving, and yet it appears that every Korean family in Sorak has descended upon this tourist feature, all donning clear plastic macs complete with hoods. Even Mr Choi wears one over his short fishing vest, and we struggle to contain our amusement in front of him. He soon gets his own back when he sees Mark wearing his brand-new, bright red 'Yeti' gaiters, which look like slippers, over his boots.

Despite having permission to collect seed in this resort, the weather is so bad that we decide to call it a rest day and sightsee with the rest of Korea. We leave Mr Choi alone in a seedy bar at the bottom of the mountain drinking coffee and climb about 3 km (2 miles) to the Kejo Hermitage. This is a small temple, partly built into a granite cave, and a subsidiary of the world's oldest Zen temple, the Sinhung-sa, built in its present location lower down the mountain in 652 AD. Unfortunately, when we finally reach it the cloud is so low it is difficult to see any of the beautiful artwork that graces the entrance or the trees that frame the temple with their would-be scarlet hints of autumnal colour. We take our turn to have a touristic photograph in front of the Rocking Rock, a huge granite boulder precariously balanced on the edge of an outcrop in front of the temple, before a final steep and bracing climb to the peak of Pison-dae. Here, in this remote area, we are greeted by a hardy, weather-beaten Korean man selling Buddha medals to tourists eager to prove that they had conquered Flying Fairy Peak. We chose the wrong day: a Sunday when every Korean family takes to the hills and the worst weather we have experienced on this trip. The one saving grace—closer inspection reveals there is no fruit on any tree, so we have not wasted a potential collecting day.

We make a quick descent and find Mr Choi comfortably dry, still drinking coffee where we left him. That he knew more than we did was clear from his grin, and I am sure he has a Buddha medal from an earlier trip. We take a bus back to Osaek Yaksu via Naksan without a stop and walk along the road to our tiny minbak, struggling against persisting rain that even the Goretex is finding tough. The sodden snake is still on the table!

The following morning we rise early, feeling hungry, and pack our bags for our return to Kwangnung. 'We're ahead of the game' is Mark's saying whilst we patiently wait for Mr Choi to get ready. The landlord of the minbak invites us to eat breakfast, quite a nice tasty broth full of large chunks of meat, until Mark remarks with horror that the snake has finally gone from the table! Before we depart, the landlord invites us to collect seeds from the small woodland at the rear of his garden. We make a good collection of *Diospyros lotus*, the date plum, a small tree with yellow fruits resembling a cherry tomato, and *Castanea crenata*, the Japanese chestnut—both possibly planted many years ago as orchard trees but still worthy of a collection for our gardens. The terrain is steep, and Mr Choi takes a nasty fall finishing up at the bottom of the slope; the empty husks of the spiky chestnuts cover him, sticking him painfully through his clothes. It is time to leave, and we finally arrive back at Kwangnung at about 7.00 p.m. after another long bus journey.

A glorious blue sky and warm autumn weather greet us next morning, just what we need to get on top of washing, field notes, seed cleaning and drying herbarium specimens. Mrs Fu, the forestry workers' in-house cook, cleaner and laundress, shouts 'bali' from out of the kitchen—washing time. Mr Choi has asked her to do our clothes, but Mark is getting twitchy about Peter's purchases from the market in Seoul being included in the same wash as ours. He spends the next ten minutes explaining to Mrs Fu the difference between hot and cold washes and colourfast cotton and noncolourfast synthetics, in what could be perceived as a new international language with lots of hand gestures, which she seems to understand and take on board. He was right to worry. Not long after, what was a white polo shirt with red hoops is now hanging on the line (the multiuse kernmantel tree-climbing rope), a pink polo shirt, flanked by several pairs of pink underpants.

The next three days are spent resting whilst cleaning seed and preparing herbarium specimens on the south-facing balcony of our arboretum accommodation. The main priorities with the seed are to cross-check all the collection numbers against the field notes and herbarium specimens to ensure there is no mix up, put as much seed as possible into the most practical drying bags and begin to clean the fleshy drupes. The viburnums, callicarpas, vacciniums, berberis and arisaemas need to have the flesh removed and the seed washed and dried before packing them away safely. The best and most efficient wash technique begins in the field, where the fruits are squashed in the polythene bags to extract the seed from the fruit. Everything is then placed in a washing basin from Mrs Fu's kitchen and mixed with fresh water under pressure from the tap. As the water is tipped out, the floating debris is washed away with the water, and the good viable seed is left to fall to the

Fruits laid out prior to cleaning

bottom in a neat pile ready for air-drying on newspaper in the sun before packing. Depending on the age of the fruit and the species, several washes may be required to reveal perfectly clean seed. This is a highly rewarding task on the expedition, despite the hard work, and we spend many hours into the night accomplishing it, as we exchange stories about our families back home and exploits of the past days in the field whilst consuming a dram or two of a single highland malt.

In the evening we walk a few kilometres into the nearest village, Uijongba, to dine on a traditional meal, be-bim-bap, and, of course, kimchi. Be-bim-bap is a sort of eastern risotto—rice with parboiled fern, soybean sprouts, spinach and red pepper sauce, garnished with a fried egg and, occasionally,

Kwang-Woo Park

roasted ginkgo nuts. It goes down very well with a cold beer. Whilst strolling back to continue seed cleaning, we spot a shrub on the side of the road covered in small dark red berries. None of us are quite sure what it is and later, from the herbarium voucher, the specimen is identified as *Lonicera maackii*. To this day, I have never seen such a free-fruiting example of this species in England.

On Thursday, 5 October, the rain drumming against the windows awakens us, so we have a lie-in as most of the work is done and the cold water in the washrooms is not an inviting thought. At 2.30 p.m., Dr Kwang-Woo Park arrives to discuss the itinerary for the following six days, in the south; he suggests a 9.30 a.m. start. The institute's jeep complete with driver are to be loaned to us, giving us much more flexibility and the ability to make short trips into different collecting regions. We are very grateful to the director of Kwangnung.

It is a fresh Friday morning, the sky is clear and bright with no sign of rain. We pack away all the seed that has been drying and wait outside the offices for Dr Park and the jeep, which is late from Seoul due to heavy traffic. We eventually leave the arboretum, and it is about 12.30 p.m. by the time we quit the suburbs of Seoul after a gruelling drive through rush hour, which incidentally lasts all day! Our steady driver, another Mr Kim, is very surly; unbeknownst to him, 10,000 Korean Won from the expedition funds will go to the first person to make him smile. Peter is trying desperately, but to no avail. We continue to drive south along the Seoul-Pusan Expressway, passing endless paddy fields with everyone working hard to harvest the ripe rice crops before winter sets in. With every day that passes now, the night temperature drops a degree, and winter gets ever closer.

At about 8.00 p.m. we arrive at Chinju City and pay a courtesy call to the director of the southern branch of the research institute. The director and his colleagues are delighted we are collecting in their region, and following a cup of ginseng tea, we are taken out to dinner at one of their favourite restaurants. We all dine Korean style, in our own separate room with a raised floor, cross-legged on cushions at a low table—not too uncomfortable, despite our Western bodies' being unaccustomed to sitting for long periods in this position. In come the cast iron barbecues, filled with red-hot glowing coals and carried by asbestos-gloved waiters, who drop them into large holes in the table. This is true Korean bulgogi, and it turns out to be one of the very best we have eaten to date—tender strips of marinated beef, onions and lots of garlic cloves, and it just keeps coming. Even the kimchi tastes good tonight. What we don't know is that we still have another one-and-half-hour's drive ahead of us before we reach tonight's accommodation, which is closer to our next destination, Chiri-san National Park, and we are all feeling very weary upon arrival. The yogwan is comfortable and warm but again there is no toilet, hot water or washing facilities. Worse, it is coming up to a bank holiday, and to our dismay there are many screaming teenagers shouting throughout the night in neighbouring yogwans. We are grateful to Mr Kim, who eventually tells them to shut up. This is the first time I have heard him speak, and it is a pity that it's in anger, though I am pleased that it was not directed at us.

We are up early this morning and make our own breakfast and sandwiches for lunch with the supplies brought with us—more delicious Embassy Spam. We board the jeep and drive what would have been a two-hour walk along a monotonous concrete road to the entrance of the National Park. Today we are to collect in the southerly part of the Sobaek

Mountains on the flanks of Chiri-san. If possible we will climb to the summit, Chong-yang-bong, which at 1915 m (6128 ft) is the highest peak on mainland South Korea, second to Halla-san on the southern island of Cheju-do, which is 1950 m (6240 ft). Whilst we are on the mountain, Mr Kim will go in search of a yogwan for the night and arrange for somewhere to eat. As this is a bank-holiday weekend, in a popular hiking location, it will get very busy with tourists, making it difficult to find anywhere to stay locally tonight.

Immediately we leave the jeep, we are confronted with a very different flora to what we have become familiar with on this trip. A large shrub with bright, glossy red fruits showing clearly above the leaves, growing amongst large boulders washed down by the river, is the first collection of the day: *Lindera erythrocarpa*, a deciduous member of the family Lauraceae. Higher up the trail we find *Fraxinus sieboldiana*, the finely pinnate leaves purple in full autumn colour. By lunchtime we reach a large rock bluff and decide to stop to eat in the warm midday sun. This is a bad idea, for as we sit down to eat, we begin to spot more gems that need checking and end up collecting instead of eating and resting. Within the reach of one spot up on the rock, it is possible to collect from several plants, including *Phellodendron amurense*, the Amur cork tree, so called for the corky bark effect on older trees. The sun is penetrating through the leaf canopy, lighting up the autumnal yellow, pinnate leaves, the small black fruits at the ends of the branches highlighted against the leaves. Next to it is a charming multi-stemmed Amur rowan, *Sorbus amurensis*, with autumn-tinted leaves, clusters of berries on the very tips of the growing points and large purple, almost black dormant buds ready for the winter that is fast approaching.

After lunch we push on to Popkyesa Temple, one of the many small Buddhist temples that are found tucked away in the valleys of Chiri-san. This temple, built in 541 AD, has a small pagoda outside and is surrounded by *Acer pseudosieboldianum*, resplendent in full scarlet autumn colour. We are frequently passed en route by jogging Buddhist monks on their way to the various temples, with their shaved heads and naturally coloured blue-grey robes dyed from the black berries of *Rhamnus davurica* or the bark of *Fraxinus chinensis* subsp. *rhyncophylla*, both of which can be found growing wild in these

Foliage and fruits of *Sorbus amurensis* on Chiri-san

mountains. The unexpected thing about the monks' attire is the modern training shoes that can be seen peeking from under their traditional robes.

At 1000 m (3300 ft) elevation pure stands of the Korean silver fir, *Abies koreana*, a relatively small fir with needles dark green above and silver on the underside, start to appear. Most of the trees bear the violet-purple cones, and as I climb the most symmetrical tree in the area to collect them, I get covered in a sticky resin. In cultivation, this species of silver fir can bear cones at a very young age and on trees no taller than 1 m (3 ft 3 in) high, which make it an attractive horticultural plant for the garden with winter

A contemplative Buddhist monk taking
a rest after a long jog to his temple

interest. Whilst I am collecting the cones, Mark and Peter collect an interesting dwarf variety of the rock birch growing close by, *Betula ermanii* var. *saitoana*.

The final hour of our eight-hour climb is a hard pump to the summit of Chong-yang-bong over rough terrain and boulder-strewn tracks. We take time to stare at the remarkable view south—rolling mountain peaks clothed in vegetation to their very tops, like a piece of green baize draped over many vases on a table-top. The Korean flag (t'aekuk ki), featuring symbols for yin and yang, is flying from a pole in a cairn at the top; we surprise Dr Park by revealing a Union flag from our pack and fly it alongside. There are loud cheers and clapping from the many Korean hikers, who seem to enjoy this ceremonial performance as much as we do and want their souvenir photographs taken with our flag.

Looking north is a different story. The vegetation is dried, wind-scorched and bleak. As our warm, sweat-soaked shirts begin to cool down, we notice a dramatic fall in temperature and believe it's time to make our descent along another route, but not before collecting from a free-fruiting *Rhododendron schlippenbachii*. This exquisite deciduous azalea, rightly called the royal azalea, is as distinctive as it is beautiful. With leaves in whorls of five it produces pink or occasionally white flowers in great profusion, often before the leaves have unfurled. Add to this its reliable autumn tints of red and orange and you have a winning combination. The royal azalea is also very hardy, revelling in a continental climate such as that of the eastern and central states of America. Often considered exclusively a Korean plant, *R. schlippenbachii* can also be found in neighbouring parts of northeast China and, it is said, the Ussuri region of Russia.

On the summit of Chong-yang-bong

It does not require much working out that we are going to have to move fairly quickly, with no stops for collecting, if we are to reach the awaiting jeep and Mr Kim before dark. A drink and a light snack sustains us before we start our descent, a steady trot that plays havoc with the knees. We stop for a brief respite and refreshment at a large stone-built communal refuge divided into large dormitories and bunks, where it appears that every Korean on the mountain is spending the night. We press on. The light is fading fast now, as with some urgency, we climb and leap from one giant boulder to another along a dried-up riverbed, where there appears to be no path. We find the track as the light finally disappears and darkness descends. Luckily we all have head torches in our bags, which we quickly put into action, freeing up our hands and allowing us to negotiate the rocks safely. We can see other torchlights flickering through the trees as Korean hikers head up the mountain to the refuge for the weekend. At 8.00 p.m. we find Mr Kim where we left him, in the jeep—such a welcome sight; he informs us that he has found a minbak in a neighbouring village, a few kilometres away.

We arrive not knowing what to expect, but as we approach our spirits drop as what we find is the worst so far, the pits—and expensive! For a price, a family have kindly moved their children out of a room for us to move in. There is no lighting, toilet or bathroom, no washing facilities and several families share an outside cold-water tap, with no drainage, about 20 m (65 ft) away round the corner. I am tired, hungry and not amused and whilst Mark and Peter sort the day's collections out, I go in search of some food. I let Dr Park, who accompanies me, know of my disappointment and disapproval. 'What's the driver been doing all day?' I ask him. He explains again about the difficulties posed by a bank-holiday weekend, with many people in the mountains needing accommodation for the night. I'm still not happy, and as we return to the minbak, Mark can hear me reiterating this to him. Dr Park apologetically promises us better tomorrow night.

All I could find in the way of food was a small bar in the village offering pindatok, an omelette of bean flour and mixed vegetables, cooked quickly by an old woman on a filthy gas ring cooker. I fetch Mark and Peter to eat this meagre meal and we return for an early sleep. The room is very dirty, and I choose to sleep fully clothed, whilst guarding seed from a family of marauding rats that seem to be wearing heavy boots whilst traversing the

Korean women harvesting rice in the paddy fields

ceiling for most of the night. I don't sleep much and rise early to use the communal tap before it gets busy and muddy.

By 8.00 a.m. we are packed, washed and back in the village, where we eat more pindatok from the same woman who was making them last night. I wonder, did she ever actually go home? or did she stay up all night making lots of omelettes for the many hikers descending upon Chiri-san? She is nevertheless pleased to see us again, imagining we cannot wait to try her speciality again, and we are soon tucking in, with a can of cold tea from a vending machine. Not the best way to start the day.

Mr Kim is sulking, having been told by Dr Park that we were not happy with last night's situation, and drives on to our first stop like a man possessed, leaving a dust trail behind as we roar up a dirt track into another part of Chiri-san National Park. On either side of the road the paddy fields, yellow with ripened rice, are full of women harvesting the crop and others threshing it to remove the seed before it is made into stoops to dry in the heat of the day. Some work bent over double with babies strapped to their backs, without a murmur from the child. This is real teamwork, but where are the men? As we drive into the village at the end of the road, dispersing tables and chairs in the slipstream of the speeding jeep, several children run to greet us, clamouring for our sweets and for their photographs to be taken with us. In a small café we find all the men squatting round low tables playing ch'anggi, a Korean version of chess, obviously awaiting the delivery of harvested rice from the fields.

We leave the village on foot, Mr Kim staying behind to look after the jeep again, and head for the mountains along a forest track leading to Seisuk-Pyung-Chun. The first collection is *Pinus densiflora*, followed by a shrub resplendent in its crimson fall colour through the surrounding greenery, *Sapium japonicum*. This small, rare, deciduous tree, about 5 m (16 ft) high, is the first recording of this species, a member of the family Euphorbiaceae, in this locality. We are all excited, especially Dr Park, who is not keen to move too fast through the forest today, as he didn't manage to get much sleep last night either.

We are stopped for lunch in a forest clearing adjacent to the river when Mark starts gesticulating wildly (mouth full of Spam): there in the canopy is a large specimen of *Kalopanax septemlobus*, a member of the ivy family, Araliaceae, with lobed leaves closely resembling those of a maple. It's got ripe black fruit on, which is unusual, as plants in this family do not usually bear ripe fruit until later in the season. As I am the official tree climber, I don the climbing harness and with the rope begin to climb the trunk and main branches, which are covered with cutting prickles. By the time I get down, I need some surgery to repair the puncture wounds in my calves and arms. What we do in the name of science!

This is an interesting piece of forest with *Pyrus ussuriensis*, one of the wild pears used in the hybridisation of the large Chinese pear that we see in all the markets and are regularly eating on this trip. With it we find *Syringa pubescens* subsp. *patula*, a medium-sized lilac bearing delightful, elegant pale violet flowers in spring. 'Miss Kim', a choice cultivar of this species, is a selection from seed-raised plants collected in South Korea in 1947; with fragrant

Syringa pubescens subsp. *patula* from Sorak in flower
in the Oleaceae collection at Kew

purple flowers fading to pale blue, it should be included in every connoisseur's garden.

We decide to finish early in the field today, as we have to drive to Chinju City to find accommodation. As we make our way back, we come across a family picnicking on a rocky bluff; they offer us some pindatok and a drink of beer that has been cooling in a bucket of water, which we share with them gratefully. Amongst the group are two beautiful little girls aged about seven years old, dressed in their Sunday best. Each has a gentian; one has tucked it in her hair, the other holds the flower carefully. Mark jokes that he would like to take one home for Lesley, and I'm not sure whether he means a gentian or a little girl. Reluctantly we take our leave of the family, thanking them for their kindness.

At the village we find Mr Kim waiting in the jeep, and the men in the café are still playing ch'anggi, looking a little more worse for wear than when we saw them this morning. Judging by the number of empty bottles strewn around the table, they have spent the day consuming soju, a pretty potent

Young girl with gentian

liquor made from distilled grains. As we drive along the road, we notice the hedgerows are full of *Platycarya strobilacea*, an interesting member of the family Juglandaceae, closely related to *Pterocarya* but with erect cone-like fruits instead of the wingnuts.

Back in Chinju City Dr Park finds us a good hotel, with the luxury of hot water and a toilet. The bedding is crisp, clean and dry, and we are all happy—this lifts our spirits, which have taken a tumble over the past few days. He also says that we can call England tonight after dinner. We eat more bulgogi, have a couple of beers and try to get through to England on the telephone, but with no joy, despite calling from the main post office. We have an early night after a game of cards, as we are all very tired. I don't sleep much; Peter is snoring very loudly, and Mark rears up in his sleep at one point, shouts 'Is there a dog in the room?' and goes straight back to sleep. I wonder what he's dreaming about and what's going to happen next? In the morning no one believes what I say or what went on in the night.

It's Monday, 9 October—Hangul Day, the celebration of Korea's indigenous alphabet, invented in 1446. When Korea was liberated from Japan in 1945 it was declared a national holiday for everyone in Korea, except Dr Park and Mr Kim today. We celebrate by having a Western breakfast in a coffee bar followed by a walk round Chinju Castle, a walled fortress built in the Koryo Dynasty on the highest ground in the city. We buy a few souvenirs, including some vases turned from the wood of *Fraxinus mandshurica*, the Manchurian ash, with Hangul characters carved into them. Mark goes into bartering mode and gets a good price, much to the disgust of Dr Park, as this is not the done thing, and then we head off south across a bridge to

Cleaning freshly harvested rice on Namhae Island

A fruiting branch *Neolitsea sericea*

our final collecting area this week, Namhae Island. At Meejo-ri Dr Park has taken the precaution of prebooking our yogwan, because of the holiday; Meejo-ri is normally a small fishing village right on the end of the island, but this week it has been taken over by the rice harvest, and every free square metre of hard surface is covered in the yellow husks of the drying rice. The women rake it repeatedly to speed up the drying process, and several small teams of women dehusk and remove the unwanted chaff by taking advantage of the light breeze, a technique that we use on a smaller scale to clean our dry seed.

We leave our main bags and, without wasting any time, drive to a small natural monument, a piece of remnant evergreen forest on the coast just by Meejo-ri. As we walk along the coastal road toward the preserve, we are joined by a group of inquisitive young boys with fishing rods; they are highly amused when we take their rods and immediately catch a small fish from the sea. The children follow us to the woodland but soon decide that fishing beats botanising and leave us. I am debating whether or not to join

Tetradium danielli with developing fruits in September by Kew Palace

them, especially as it is a bank holiday, but before long we are in the fenced woodland and adding numbers to the bag.

The woodland is made up of *Neolitsea sericea*, *Ligustrum japonicum* and *Euonymus japonicus*, all evergreen elements, with an interesting deciduous tree on the woodland edge which I have been struggling to grow in the arboretum for the last few years, *Carpinus coreana* var. *major*. At Kew this makes a scruffy, shrubby tree with an untidy habit; it does not grow with a leader and central stem like any other hornbeam. Despite lots of time spent trying to train it, I have just about given up, and I am pleased to see that here in its natural habitat it grows in exactly the same way. Found growing with the hornbeam is *Tetradium daniellii*, another deciduous tree that in my view is underplanted in UK gardens, as it is one of the few hardy temperate trees that flowers during late summer and early autumn. Here it has flowered and now bears the full reddish-purple fruits and their shiny black seeds.

We return to our yogwan, where we are told we can have a bath. Much time is wasted waiting for the water to run hot, to no avail; we give up and comfort ourselves with bulgogi in a nearby bar just before everything shuts down for the night. After another bad night spent listening to the roar of Peter's snoring, I prepare for a day on the mountain, which we can see in the distance from our window. The weather looks promising as the sun makes its way up above the trees into the sky, and I can hear the chugging of small fishing boats leaving the harbour for a day's fishing amongst the thousands of tiny islands in the South Sea. We drive into the forest on the lower flanks of Kum-bong; everything has been cut and the secondary regrowth is very young. However, there is lots of new material, and with seed, so we begin the collecting almost immediately with a plant that has us all baffled, including Dr Park. It has pinnate leaves and strange bright red fruits resembling polystyrene packaging material which contain black seeds. Dr Park suggests *Sambucus sieboldiana* var. *pendula*, but we are very doubtful (it is later identified as *Euscaphis japonica*; wait until chapter 7 for the anticlimax!). Further along the track we find a wonderful *Sorbus alnifolia*, normally a tree in cultivation, but here it is a shrub, bearing very large red fruits, dangling in large, lax trusses. It's not on our wanted list, but it's too good to walk past and it's soon in the bag—Mark and Peter both promise to give it the cultivar name 'Tony's Dangler' as soon as it fruits in the garden back at home!

We next come upon a tree we are all excited about, and the happy expression on Mark's face sums it up: a lone specimen, only about 4 m (12 ft) tall, of *Quercus dentata*, the daimio oak. Mark cuts a piece with several large leaves intact; the lobed leaves on this species can be up to 35 cm (14 in) long and these aren't far off that. We have to scratch around for acorns, but finally find enough for a collection and move on. Before entering Hallyo-Haesang National Park, we pass two familiar climbing roses in full fruit, *Rosa wichurana* and *R. multiflora*, but hesitate to make a collection as we have many growing well in the species rose garden at Kew and these need plenty of room in cultivation.

Dr Park shows his ID card to park officials, and we are allowed entry free of charge, much to the treasurer's relief. The road we are now on was cut through the forest within the last three years to give the monks quicker access to the Boriam Temple, at the top of Kum-bong. Growing at around 400 m (1300 ft) elevation in this deciduous woodland we see *Cornus kousa*, the Japanese strawberry tree; the tiny flowers and larger white pointed bracts that make this plant a winner in early summer are long gone to be replaced

The marbled trunks of
Stewartia pseudocamellia var. *koreana*

by masses of fruits. These are pendulous, red and strawberry-like, and it's easy to see how the common name came about. Growing with it under the dark canopy of the oaks is *Viburnum erosum*, with its red fleshy fruits, and *Photinia villosa*, another red-berried shrub.

As we climb higher in elevation to around 650 m (2080 ft), the oak forest changes to ash with the occasional red pine, and amongst these appear the magnificent decorative trunks of *Stewartia pseudocamellia* var. *koreana*, straight, with flaking lace markings, resembling pythons climbing into the canopies. There is plenty of seed; the wide-spreading white flowers must have been a show earlier this year. A second show is about to begin as the leaves are beginning to turn yellow, and as this is one of the better autumn-colouring species of *Stewartia*, the overall effect will bring these forests alight in a few weeks time. Carl Linnaeus founded the genus *Stewartia*, honouring John Stuart, the 3rd Earl of Bute and Princess Augusta's horticultural advisor, at Kew. What a superb ornamental genus to have named after you!

We finally reach the Boriam Temple and are treated to an overwhelming view out to the East Sea and the tiny fishing boats between the many islands. As we leave the temple to make our way down the south-facing flank of the mountain, Mark finds Dr Park's white bush hat on a step and quietly hides it under his sweater. He then asks Dr Park where his hat is. Park pretends not to be too bothered by the loss but offers to buy the beers tonight if anyone finds it. A few minutes later Mark dons the hat and carries on looking at plants until Dr Park realises that he's wearing his hat. He takes it in stride, enjoying the banter and leg-pulling, and we all have a good laugh.

We need to collect seed from the black pine, *Pinus thunbergii*, which is starting to creep in on the maritime side of the mountain, but we are having great difficulty distinguishing it from the red pine, *P. densiflora*, as they seem to be intermediate in characteristics. Judging there is possibly some hybridisation between the two species, we make a collection that best matches the description but also decide to make another collection from the pines growing right on the coast to satisfy ourselves that it is true, as it is a maritime conifer that grows at sea level. We eventually make the bottom, where the jeep is waiting, and leave for Sun'chon City, but not before collecting the pine and a shrubby *Malus toringo* growing in a ditch by the roadside. We make it just in time; the heavens open as we leave, and the rain makes driving very difficult.

Tonight after a bath Dr Park takes us to meet his father-in-law, who lives in a small town renowned for its wonderful seafood and as the home of the long-necked turtle fishing fleet. We are to dine out at an exclusive restaurant highly recommended by Dr Park. Before entering the restaurant, we choose the live fish we'll later eat from large tanks on the street outside, pointing them out to an adept netsman, who catches them and places them in a large bowl bound for the noisy kitchen. We all play safe, settling on creatures known to us back home, but Dr Park and his father-in-law are unfortunately a little more adventurous. Some odd-looking sea creatures that would be more at home in the seaworld aquarium join our humble selections, and the meal looks to be deteriorating rapidly. As we sit at our table, Dr Park enters carrying a tray of beers, holding true to his word on Kum-bong this afternoon; he recounts the hat story for his father-in-law's benefit, and we all share another laugh about it. The chefs soon follow, serving up the creatures we selected: first the crabs and other shellfish with quail eggs, crayfish and kimchi—very nice—and then a huge pile of finely chopped white cabbage covered in finely chopped live squid and octopus tentacles, still writhing over the cabbage. We have to show our host that we are enjoying this special banquet, but it is difficult. The twisting seafood latches on to my chopsticks as I move in to try it, and I cannot release it into my mouth without using my teeth to pull it off the end of the stick. I swallow. I can feel it sliding down, attaching itself to my throat, and seeing the expression on my screwed-up face Dr Park tells me to drink some soju to wash it down. It doesn't help. I gesture to the others that it tastes good and for them to help me out, but all take a sudden liking to the kimchi, for some reason. We return to our hotel in Sun'chon City, a thirty-mile drive, and collapse onto our mattresses to enjoy a badly needed good night's sleep.

This morning it is foggy with showers—a good day, I suppose, for driving back to Kwangnung. We leave around nine o'clock and arrive at the bar opposite the arboretum in the early evening, where all the arboretum staff are waiting for us to find out how the trip went. Mr Choi is there to discuss the proposed trip to the island Ullung-Do and the arrangements he has made for us. It all sounds great, and the evening turns into a sort of celebration, complete with the bar's finest bulgogi. Mr Choi, with loud cries of 'Ajimah!' (Korean for 'lady'), has the waitress running backwards and forwards for more food and beer. Just before midnight Dr Park leaves to catch the last bus home and Mrs Choi arrives to find Mr Choi (who was only to have popped out for a few minutes to greet us) a little worse for wear; she is not happy and sends him home.

The following three days are spent cleaning seed and carrying out all the other usual and necessary domestic chores associated with an expedition. I arise early one of the mornings; it is still dark outside and looking at my watch, I make it 6.00 a.m. I can hear someone chipping away at ice frozen in a washing bowl outside—Mrs Fu, getting things ready for washing. I snuggle back into the warmth under my duvet and go back to sleep. The sun streaming through the window and the noises of forestry workers eagerly eating downstairs in the staff canteen, preparing for their day's work ahead, waken me again later. The thought of that cold shower is no encouragement to get up, but there is work to do and people to meet, so I face it. It is exceptionally cold this morning, as Mrs Fu breaking the early morning ice from her bowls reminded me, and I literally run in and out before drying off. It develops into a beautiful autumnal day, and as the clouds lift from the valley bottoms, the forested flanks of Sori-San, which I have not seen in over a week, come into view. The change is quite remarkable—autumn has really moved in, and the colours are dazzling. The grass is white with frost, and it crunches under my feet as I walk across to the offices to see Dr Park. 'There are problems in the office', he tells me. It seems Peter used the telephone to call England yesterday, and it has caused some bad feelings. In future every communication must go through Dr Park. I apologise and assure him it will not happen again.

After lunch Mr Choi stops by to see our work and notes and offers to take us across to his office to use his library. I find Krüssmann's *Manual of Cultivated Conifers* and check the information on *Pinus thunbergii* in relation to *P. densiflora*. It turns out the two species do indeed hybridise in the wild, producing *P. densi-thunbergii*. Luckily we have made several collections on Kumbong and are sure that we have the hybrid. Mr Choi enters the office carrying a large bowl of fruit, and we are treated to a feast of peeled and chopped Chinese pears and the fruits of the Chinese persimmon or kaki, *Diospyros kaki*. This is a much larger fruit than that of *D. lotus*, which we saw in Osaek Yaksu, about 7 cm (3 in) across, resembling a tomato but bright yellow. When ripe, they are very juicy, but when hard and unripe they dehydrate your mouth with a single bite. We have seen these fruits being sold in markets throughout our travels in Korea, and growing on trees in small orchards around rural dwellings, but this is our first taste and they are delicious. Later in the afternoon, Dr Park and Mr Choi take us into Seoul to change our Sterling travellers cheques into Korean Won, as there are no banks on Ullung-Do. We have also arranged to meet Mr Kim Un-Cho again for dinner, this time at his home; apparently he has some news for us.

I have never met anyone so pleased to see us. We tell him tales of our experiences over the past few weeks in Korea, taking care not to embarrass our hosts, and list the many plants we have seen and have safely stowed in the collection bag. He is elated and on the spot offers Mark and me jobs in his new arboretum, which we both decline. So what is the news that Mr Kim has for us? He whispers as though the room is bugged. 'There are four Americans also in South Korea collecting woody plants, headed by Sylvester March from the National Arboretum in Washington, D.C.' He slips me a piece of paper across the coffee table. 'This may be of use to you on Ullung-Do'. It is the full itinerary of the American party, who had visited South Korea in the spring and marked up flowering plants with high horti-cultural merit as part of a USNA programme to develop ornamental plants sufficiently hardy for the United States. Their next collecting area is on Ullung-Do, where they are to arrive two days later than us. We thank Mr Kim for his news and hospitality and make our way back to Kwangnung—by train, bus and taxi. I am so tired when we get back, I fall into bed and go straight to sleep.

We spend the next day sorting and packing cleaned and dried seed and placing herbarium specimens in clean, dry newspaper, as it will be several days before we get back to check and change things. We are well on top of seed cleaning, and there is very little outstanding from our previous field-work. To be ahead of the game, we pack our rucksacks with the bare mini-mum, literally a change of clothes and a couple of luxury items each, as we will have to carry everything with us on public transport and we are uncer-tain about the accommodation facilities on the island. Once we are on top of everything, I have a power nap, as tonight will be a long one.

At 8.30 in the evening, we wait for Mr Choi at the entrance to the arboretum. It's a clear night, the sky bright from the stars and a full moon; the temperature is already well below freezing, the grass crisp beneath our feet. Mr Choi arrives with his wife and two children, the younger a baby on her back in a homemade papoose. As the bus for Seoul pulls up, the young boy gives Mark and me a present, two sweet chestnut seeds for good luck. Today is 16 October, the second anniversary of the 1987 storm that has provided us with the opportunity to be here seed collecting.

The main railway station in Seoul is pandemonium, even at midnight, with people shouting above the noisy departure announcements of the Tannoy system. About fifty percent of the men appear to be drunk, either lying around on any available floor space or attempting to make their way through the concourse, stumbling and bumping from one person to the other. One intoxicated person falls into Peter, who has already had a bellyful of this by now. Peter fires a string of verbal abuse at the man, which sobers him right up, but we are too quick for him and are soon in the ticket office, booking on the overnight train to Taegu.

The train journey is very comfortable, and we manage to get some sleep in the reclining seats. At four o' clock in the morning we arrive in Taegu, the third-largest city in South Korea and home of the country's most famous and largest Buddhist temple, Haein-sa Temple. We are met by Dr Yong-Shik Kim, a lecturer in landscape at Taegu University, a close friend of Mr Choi and an aide of the 1982 expedition. Given the hour, he takes us back to his home, where we have coffee and talk about life in general. He is very excited about us coming to Taegu, albeit for a short stopover (before we take a bus to Pohang, where we are to catch a ferry to Ullung-Do). Yong-Shik has made many trips to Ullung-Do in the past as part of his studies on *Camellia japonica*, and after looking at our wanted list gives Mr Choi lots of advice on routes and collecting stations to help the trip run more effectively. Before embarking on a short field trip we are treated to an American breakfast of ham and eggs in a large hotel—a real indulgence but none of us really enjoy it: we would prefer pindatok with a side dish of kimchi instead.

Yong-Shik and Mr Choi flag down two taxis, and we drive to the outskirts of the city to natural monument number one: a sheer cliffside, completely fenced in for protection, with the naturally occurring small tree *Platycladus orientalis* (previously known as *Thuja orientalis*) growing out of every available crevice. I am reminded of the wall separating the Duchess Border from the Duke's Garden back at Kew, where three plants of this, the Chinese arborvitae, grow successfully out of joints in the brickwork. We attempt to collect seed from them, but to no avail. Most are out of reach without the safety of the rope that we have left at Kwangnung to save weight, and the trees that we can get to have long since shed their seed, leaving only empty cones.

We take a bus back to Taegu, collect our bags from Yong-Shik's flat and, after farewells and thanks, catch another bus for the long ride to Pohang. We have timed our arrival in Pohang to coincide with the departure of the ferry, but when we check in to the booking office there is bad news. No sailing today—a typhoon in the East Sea has whipped up the seas and no ferries will be leaving until further notice. We were warned back in Seoul that when you leave for Ullung-Do at this time of the year, you build in spare time and take enough provisions to last at least ten days. It is not uncommon to be stuck on the island for several days longer than anticipated because of bad weather; little did we know it would be the other way round.

We decide to find a comfortable yogwan close to the ferry terminal and settle down to a beer whilst discussing what we should do until the ferry sails. Mr Choi suggests a site not far away that may be of interest to us; he'll arrange for permission to collect there. If the ferry does not sail tomorrow, we will make an excursion to a forest surrounding a temple on the lower slopes of Naeyon-Bong in nearby Kyongju National Park. In the hotel I have a hot bath with Body Shop Raspberry Ripple bubble bath and lemon soap—what a luxury—and after dinner (bulgogi), I write a letter to Sally before having an early night, which I need so much.

At nine o'clock next morning, Mr Choi comes by to say he'll check the state of sailings at the ferry terminal before breakfast. He returns with a look of dismay on his face: although the weather looks good here in Pohang, it is bad out at sea; the ferry is going nowhere, and there is nothing we can do about it but sit tight. Mr Choi thinks it will almost certainly sail tomorrow, however, so Plan Two, collecting in Kyongju National Park, will kick in after breakfast.

The park entrance is a short bus ride from Pohang, and after a brisk walk of about 300 m (960 ft) we are at the magnificent and imposing Posong Temple. Every roofbeam and rafter is hand-painted in an array of bewildering colours and decorated with Buddhas in meditative poses staring out at you with scowling eyes. Here, many nomadic Buddhist monks take time for prayer and rest before moving on to one the other thousands of temples in the Korean mountains.

The surrounding vegetation is as interesting as the temple, with some of the largest trees of *Zelkova serrata* and *Sophora japonica*, the Japanese pagoda tree, that I have ever seen. All these specimen trees are protected by high metal railings with informative labels identifying them; they too are under the natural monument scheme that preserves so many of Korea's natural beauties. After a brief respite we leave the temple and head up into the park, following a steep, winding track to a tremendous waterfall that cascades from the side of the mountain into a large deep pool. We leave our daysacks with Mr Choi, who uses this opportunity to rest and cool his feet in the cold water, and move off into a steep gorge in search of new collections. Amongst the oak canopy we find the occasional *Celtis sinensis*, standing out by its glossy foliage, but the collection of the day has got to be *Lindera glauca*, a deciduous shrub about 3 m (10 ft) in height, bearing a few fruits: we have to search and sample every plant we can find in order to make a reasonable collection. The wood of this plant is used in the production of incense sticks in China.

As we push through the thick vegetation, climbing higher up to a scree visible from below, we come across a deciduous shrub growing on the edge of the woodland understorey in granitic spoil, *Rhododendron mucronulatum*. This is a popular plant in the winter garden at home, with its bright purple flowers appearing before the leaves between January and March; this hillside must have been alight early this spring with the wealth of fruits on all of the plants. We head back and find a plant of *Cornus walteri* growing in remnant forest close to the temple; we think it is planted, but Mr Choi insists it is wild so we attempt to make a collection. All the fruits are high in the canopy, out of our reach—until Mark climbs onto Mr Choi's shoulders and is able to pick several of the black globose fruits. By the time we return to Pohang, the temperature has fallen dramatically and you can see your breath in the sea air. The saving grace is the thought of another hot bath in the yogwan before dinner.

We wake up early the next morning to a stiff breeze blowing off the sea; chances of our catching a sailing ferry are not looking good. There is a loud knock on the door, and Mr Choi enters the cluttered room with a huge smile on his face. He has been to the ferry terminal—the boat will sail at midday. We all punch the air in delight and promise Mr Choi the best bulgogi on Ullung-Do tonight, with as many beers as he can drink.

We pack quickly, as though the ferry is about to depart immediately, leaving us with almost five hours to kill. As we return from breakfast, I spot a mini people carrier parked by the side of the road. We look through the window and spot several plant presses and a copy of *The Vascular Plants of Ohio* on the back seat; this must be the transport of the Americans—who else would have plant presses and such bedtime reading? The bad weather and delayed sailings mean that they have caught up with our itinerary.

We make our way onto the ferry, find comfortable seats below deck and right on time we set sail, bound for the elusive Ullung-Do, a small volcanic island about 268 km (166 miles) northeast of Pohang, no more than 10 km (6 miles) wide at its broadest point and rising steeply from the storm-ravaged East Sea between Korea and Japan. By order of Korea's King Yeji it was captured from pirates during the Shilla Dynasty, and until 1884 it remained a military outpost; since then there has been some migration to the island, which now boasts a population of some twenty thousand people. The mountains on the island—overshadowed by the highest peak, the extinct volcano Songin-bong, at 984 m (3149 ft)—play host to over forty species of plants that occur nowhere else, including two maples. Ernest Wilson and Dr Takenoshin Nakai visited this island several times in 1917, when it was known as Dagalet Island. Since then there have been many other forays by eminent plant collectors, but few of the plants indigenous to the island have found their way into cultivation in the Western garden. We hope to put an end to that.

As soon as we are on the sea, we go in search of the American team; it doesn't take us long to find them. I've met Paul Meyer, director of the Morris Arboretum in Pennsylvania, several times before in England and clearly remember that he is well over six feet tall; he will definitely stand out from the shorter Koreans by towering above them all. The other members of their party are Sylvester (Skip) March from the National Arboretum in Washington, D.C., Peter Bristol from the Holden Arboretum, Bill Thomas from Longwood Gardens in Pennsylvania and their Korean guide. We meet up on deck, engage in greetings and introductions and swap stories and plant names from the previous four weeks on the mainland. It's good to talk and get news from the West, but before long we are forced below for shelter and safety, as there is a real swell building up from the remnant typhoon.

Approaching the remote island of Ullung-Do in the East Sea

Many sorry-looking passengers sway from side to side, trying to hold themselves together on their way to the bathroom. We, on the other hand, enjoy several English-language films that are being shown in a cinema below deck then catch up with the Americans again before we reach the island. We plan to meet up for a drink in the next few days before we leave for our return journey to the mainland, leaving the arrangements to our guides.

Seven hours after departing Pohang we are coming up on Todong, the capital and largest town of Ullung-Do. It is hidden away on the southeast coast, in a very steep-sided valley between two forested mountains, resembling a small fishing village on the Pembrokeshire coastline in Wales; it is not until we are almost there that we can see the harbour and the *Han II Ho* speedboat ferry, which must wait for the seas to quell before it can return to Pohang. We say good luck and goodbye to the Americans and quickly disembark; they are amazed that we are carrying everything we need on our backs, including plant presses, with no vehicular support. Mr Choi finds us

The picturesque harbour of Todong

a very comfortable yogwan, clean with piping hot water, and we retire to the Boo-me-rang bar for dinner, a few celebratory beers and a discussion about the next few days' itinerary.

We are up with the larks and packed ready for the field by 7.00 a.m. We go in search of breakfast, eventually finding a café open, and ask the lady preparing the stoves if we can have pindatok. She seems to understand what we want, offers us a table and begins to cook. Lots of small pickle-type dishes begin to appear, and, worried, Mark returns from a quick glance into the desperately dark and dirty kitchen, his nose turned up in horror. 'It's the congealed blood and eel heads broth!' he shouts—and leaves. The Seoul experience has left him badly scarred and he's decided he cannot face it again. We all follow him out, and as we hurry up the street, we can hear the lady shouting Korean abuse at us. No other food place is open this early in the morning, so, missing out altogether on breakfast, we head for Songin-bong, which translates as 'mountain of the good people'.

We leave Todong along one of a few miles of metalled road on the island and then head up a steeply grooved track, flanked on either side by a tall grass, *Miscanthus sinensis* var. *purpureus*, through rough agricultural land. We are temporarily forced into the grass to make way for a farmer struggling to control a huge brown bullock being led by a ring in its nose down into town. Pointing to the beast, Mr Choi shouts, 'Bulgogi!' The mere thought has our mouths watering.

We continue along the track. There is the occasional tree on the edges of a degraded, mixed woodland—a lime, *Tilia insularis*, and the Japanese raisin tree, *Hovenia dulcis*, with shiny foliage and an abundance of what appear to be the gnarled, shrivelled-up fleshy fruits from which it gets its common name. Under these trees we find the self-clinging *Hydrangea anomala* subsp. *petiolaris*, climbing the tree trunks and scrambling over rocks through the vegetation. It is good to see this popular garden plant growing here, in its natural habitat, rather than in its usual spot on a north-facing wall back at home. At about 450 m (1440 ft) elevation we move into rain and secondary woodland made up primarily of *Acer pictum* subsp. *okamotoanum*, one of the two indigenous maples on Ullung-Do, the other being *A. takesimense*. The latter species is very infrequent, and we manage to find only one small specimen; its leaves have begun to turn orange and it bears no seed. We search every specimen of *A. pictum* subsp. *okamotoanum* frantically, however, and begin to feel pretty dejected when, after about an hour, we have not found a single seed, nor any sign that there has been any.

Peter is excited about a herbaceous plant with a large orange fruiting head, growing in the dappled light of the maples; he initially thinks it is *Arisaema heterocephalum*, so we take time to collect seed and a herbarium specimen. He promises to confirm its identity on return to Kew. This is a good time to stop and don the Goretex before we get too wet, as the rain is starting to become a bit more persistent now and visibility through the trees is extremely low. We all decide that we are in need of some sustenance, so break out the emergency ration kit, Embassy Spam and some slightly mouldy rolls that we brought from the mainland. Mark sets up the kitchen in the shelter of the largest maple and begins to prepare lunch, finely slicing through the luncheon meat with his Swiss army knife and scraping the mould off the bread before making up the sandwiches. How little we knew the importance of these tins of Spam when the ambassador so kindly proffered them five weeks ago in Seoul. Even Mr Choi is getting to like it and pulls three cartons of milk out of his daysack as a token contribution to the picnic, ensuring himself a roll in the bargain.

After lunch the going is difficult; the rain has turned to hailstones that sting my face on their way down, making the track very slippery. We nevertheless reach the summit of Songin-bong, where growing all around us is a small, tough, multi-stemmed tree, the Japanese rowan, *Sorbus commixta*, on the very brink of winter dormancy with only a handful of yellow leaves still intact. Again we struggle to find seeds, and looking up into the crowns is painful with the driving hailstones. Out of the corner of my eye I see a very large, bedraggled rat run across a small clearing in the low bamboo, quickly followed by another. I look on the ground where the rats first showed themselves and find partly decomposed red rowanberries, which the rats have been collecting for their winter larder. Inspection determines the seed inside the rotting flesh is good, so we spend the next ten minutes along with the rats, collecting from the ground around the summit. Mr Choi surprises us all by pulling the Korean flag out of his bag, Peter pulls out the Union flag again and surprises Mr Choi, and Mark surprises Peter by pulling a pair of his still-white Y-fronts out of his bag for a photo shoot. What a pity that the weather is so bad today—the view from this vantage point must be stunning.

Mark is soon concerned about Peter's health and well-being, as his water-proof clothing is not really up to the elements we are now facing here on Songin-bong. We decide to make our descent and head down into shelter and a more hospitable climate at lower elevation. We hike a different way back to Todong, past the Pong-nae waterfall to Jeodong, another fishing village just around the coastline, with the most incredible smell—never to be forgotten—of thousands of dead squid, threaded onto bamboo poles and drying on racks in the sun. Once back at our yogwan, we process the meagre collections from our fieldwork before taking a bath and some light refreshment. Mr Choi joins us to discuss the day; we tried not to show our disappointment in the lack of seed on today's plants in front of him, but our morale, which had taken a bit of a tumble, must have been clearly apparent. He suggests a two-day trip to the other side of the island, where the trees may be more freely fruiting. He did warn us back at Kwangnung that seed might be lacking on the island, but we had not really taken that on board. Anyway, we are here now, and we must make the best of it. Mr Choi's idea of going across to the north side of the island sounds good, and we will plan something along these lines for tomorrow. Mr Choi goes in search of ferry information whilst we dine alone in Todong, avoiding the café where we almost breakfasted this morning, followed by an early night.

We wake to a beautiful day on Ullung-Do: blue sky and little wind, which means that the sea must be calm—essential if we are to save time getting around the island. Given the nature of the terrain, there are virtually no interlinking roads between towns around the west or east coastline. Breakfast is skipped again, as we are in a hurry to catch a small ferry in the fish market. The harbour is full of large motorised fishing vessels, their masts strung with large mercury lamps ready for the evening squid fishing expedition. The squid boats leave Todong for the depths of the East Sea in darkness of night and attract the squid by the intensity of these lights. It is believed that this fleet of squid boats, like the Great Wall of China, can be seen from outer space.

We board a fishing boat-taxi arranged by Mr Choi and make ourselves as comfortable as possible on the coiled-up nets; the skipper fires up the

Squid fishing boats with the mercury lamps in Todong harbour

inboard engine, raising a plume of black smoke into the air, and sets sail. We chug steadily counterclockwise around the island, passing several fishing boats returning to Todong or fishing with lines closer to the coast. After about twenty minutes we dock on a small quay where, remarkably, there is a single-decker bus waiting to take us to Chonbu, the small village which is to be the start of our trek.

We make our way into the centre of the island, the huge crater, Nae-lee-bong, which was left from the once active volcano; now tilled and farmed, its fertile soil is home to a huge herb-growing industry. Once across the crater we enter a beech forest of *Fagus japonica* var. *multinervis*. Disappointment again: there is no seed, just thousands of seedlings on the forest floor from last year's heavy seed mast. Normally we would not lift plants but take only seed; however, as there are so many and this is an important tree on our target list, we carefully lift about ten plants and wrap them in damp moss to take back to England with us. We push on, finding two evergreen shrubs in fruit, *Camellia japonica* and *Daphniphyllum himalaense* subsp. *macropodum*, a strikingly beautiful plant with leaves resembling those of a rhododendron. We drop down into Chusan and walk the northern coastline, heading for Tae-wha in the northwest corner of the island. Mr Choi assures us that a bus will be along soon, but it fails to show. We stop for refreshments and a rest and carry on, finding a massive landslide that has dropped everything including the road into the sea. We attempt to traverse it but finally give up as the sea makes it impossible to pass, leaving the only option: to turn around.

Back along the road we find an alternative route and decide that we must hurry, as it is now 5.00 p.m. and it will soon be dark. We are all feeling very weary and take a few minutes' rest under a small, isolated, spreading tree by the side of the road. It turns out to be *Zanthoxylum ailanthoides*, and it has plenty of ripe fruit on it, about to shed the seed, which we collect. Suddenly we hear the sound of a vehicle approaching; Mr Choi flags the long-wheel-base jeep down as it comes into sight—it appears to be a taxi running between Chusan and Tae-wha. After speaking with the driver, Mr Choi announces, 'One thousand Korean Won each to Tae-wha'. The treasurer replies, 'That's far too expensive, we'll walk'. Peter, who is looking pretty fatigued by now, goes straight into a turn, desperately wanting a lift for the rest of the journey. But Mark has already jumped in the back, laughing, shouting, 'I'm joking'. Peter is not amused as he climbs in the back to join him, and we head off over the mountain, finally arriving in Tae-wha as it begins to get dark.

Mr Choi finds us an excellent minbak overlooking the sea, which we can hear clearly but not see. It is clean and warm, and the family who own it are very friendly. The mother asks if her son and his friends, who are gathering outside, can meet us, as they are intrigued by our visit and would like to practise their English with us. We agree, and in double-quick time they are in our room, giggling and smiling, practising the rudimentary phrases they have recently learnt at school. They follow us to the only restaurant in the village and watch us through the windows all night. Mr Choi apologises in advance to us: the owner has no bulgogi and after several days of squid, beef sounded inviting. 'They only have Chinese food', says Choi shrugging his shoulders, 'and they only have sweet and sour pork and chicken in black bean sauce left'. We can't believe it, coming all this way to be treated to a feast of Chinese food. 'Four portions of each and lots of rice', we reply. As fast as the food comes out, we clear the plates, making up for all the missed

Squid hanging up to dry in the small port of Tae-wha

breakfasts and packed Spam lunches. The chef is flattered and cannot believe how much we have eaten so quickly.

We return to our minbak to watch a World Cup football qualifier on the television. South Korea beat China by one goal to nil. We then have a few problems with the lights, as, for some reason, the master lightswitch for the house is in our room, and we keep switching off the whole house by mistake. Our hosts find it highly amusing.

This morning as I lie in bed, I can smell fish—outside, now in daylight, the entire seafront, as far as I can see, is covered in squid drying on racks. A quick recce of the area and we find there are two large deciduous trees on the neighbouring property, left over from remnant forest, and they are covered in seeds. One is *Acer pictum* subsp. *okamotoanum* and the other is *Celtis choseniana*, and after getting permission from the owner, we are soon climbing them and making two more valuable collections, now making the trip to the island well worthwhile. Celtis is not one of my favourite groups of trees, but this particular species seems to make an attractive medium-sized tree to 25 m (80 ft).

We leave Tae-wha in good weather for the final leg of our journey on the island to climb over another mountain, T'aeha-dong, situated on the southern coastline. On the summit of T'aeha-dong occur two conifers more associated with the Japanese flora, *Pinus parviflora*, the Japanese white pine, and *Tsuga sieboldii*, a Japanese hemlock.

A short journey around the coast on a fishing boat taxi followed by a short bus ride and we are back in Todong, after what seems like a week's travel. We are all exhausted, but there is still one location to visit before we call it a day on Ullung-Do. On one of E. H. Wilson's visits to the island he found a small cotoneaster, with arching branches and an abundance of matt, crimson-coloured berries, which was later named after him—*Cotoneaster wilsonii*, Wilson's cotoneaster. It grows with *Abelia insularis* on the hills above Todong, in a small, dedicated reserve.

Despite our weariness, we make one final climb to the summit of a promontory between Todong and Jeodong to search for it amongst the ground vegetation and grasses. We are out of luck and fail to find it; however, we do find a terrific, tagged specimen of *Sorbus commixta*, with signs of a previous visitation from our American friends. On the way down, after a pause to watch the hustle and bustle of Todong from above, we come across several paper mulberries, *Broussonetia papyrifera*, a wonderful economic plant in the family Moraceae. It has orange globular fruits and rough, hairy leaves that vary in shape from simple to unusually lobed, and its bark is used for making paper in Japan. This is the last collection of the trip.

Tonight we take Mr Choi for dinner and a celebratory drink in the Boome-rang bar before looking up the Americans in the five-star Todong Hotel. We find Peter Bristol cleaning seeds on his own, whilst the rest of the team are out for the evening; it appears from our short chat that they have had the same problems as we have, with a shortage of good seed. We leave him to his seed cleaning and go in search of his fellows to say our goodbyes, soon

Cotoneaster wilsonii, an endemic species to Ullung-Do

finding them in a noisy, smoky nightclub having a whale of a time on the dance floor. They obviously haven't walked around the island, as we have today. Mr Choi is very uncomfortable and uneasy and I can't say that I am surprised, so we leave to have another quiet drink in the peace of the Boo-me-rang bar on the way back to our yogwan.

At 1.00 p.m. the following day we catch the *Han II Ho* speedboat ferry, and after a superb cruise of less than four hours, we are on the mainland at Hupo, just north of Pohang. The next twenty-four hours are spent travelling, through the night, back to Seoul and then Kwangnung on a series of buses and trains. We are physically and mentally exhausted when we finally arrive at the arboretum, but there is no time to lose. Once Mrs Fu leaves for home, Peter heads for her kitchen and serves us up a mouthwatering egg and chips. Now is the time to begin reducing the levels of garlic in our bodies in preparation for our return home to our wives!

We have much to do now, following a very successful expedition, in preparation for our return to the UK. There is work needed on the seed collections and herbarium specimens (both the ones just brought back with us from Ullung-Do and the ones we left back here); there are preparations for a lecture to the arboretum staff about Kew Gardens and, the best of all, a farewell party in the bar opposite the arboretum with all our new friends. It's a great party that goes well into the night, with lots of OB beer, soju, and an opportunity for me to sing the theme song from *The Beverly Hillbillies*, 'The Ballad of Jed Clampett'. Dr Park has a dance with a dried squid, and I present Mr Choi with my flashing red bow tie, which he has admired so much on this trip.

It's the early evening of our last day in Kwangnung, and the temperature is a good ten degrees below freezing as we walk across the grounds, the white grass crunching beneath our feet. This feels like the right time to be leaving Korea; winter is literally just around the corner, with temperatures that regularly drop to -32°C (-25°F)—not the time to be taking cold early morning showers in the Kwangnung bathroom. Before we leave for Seoul next day, we take in the surrounding scenery one last time. Spectacular is an understatement—there is not a single shade of green amongst the yellows, reds and oranges of the deciduous elements on the mountainside. It seems so long since we were in the mountains of Sorak-san yet the time has passed quickly, and we will soon be back at home with our families, looking forward to a fairly mild English winter, compared to what's in store here in South Korea.

CHAPTER 4

Atop the Jade Mountain

'WILSON!'—AND AGAIN, 'WILSON!' The name reverberates across the mountains and echoes through the valleys all around us. 'I feel better for that', says Tony. His passionate cry is a spontaneous gesture to the memory of the great man and an acknowledgement of what he achieved. We are on the summit of Yushan, the Jade Mountain, Taiwan's highest point. It is 30 October 1992, almost seventy-four years to the day that Wilson himself stood here. This moment lives in my mind as a highlight of my plant hunting career, perhaps the apogee of my time in the field. To the first European colonists, the Portuguese, Taiwan was 'formosa'—'beautiful'. A fitting soubriquet as we discovered.

With the visit to South Korea successfully concluded it was time to take stock, not just of what had been achieved but what needed to follow. Before this could be done, however, I had to undertake a collecting trip to Turkey in the autumn of 1990 with another Kew colleague, Mark Pitman, Tony's counterpart in the West Arboretum. Planning for this trip had actually pre-dated the South Korean expedition. The conduct of the visit to Turkey doesn't concern us here, though Mark and I spent a wonderful month in the mountains in the west, south and north of the country, enjoying the breath-taking scenery, plant life and hospitality of what is a compelling part of the

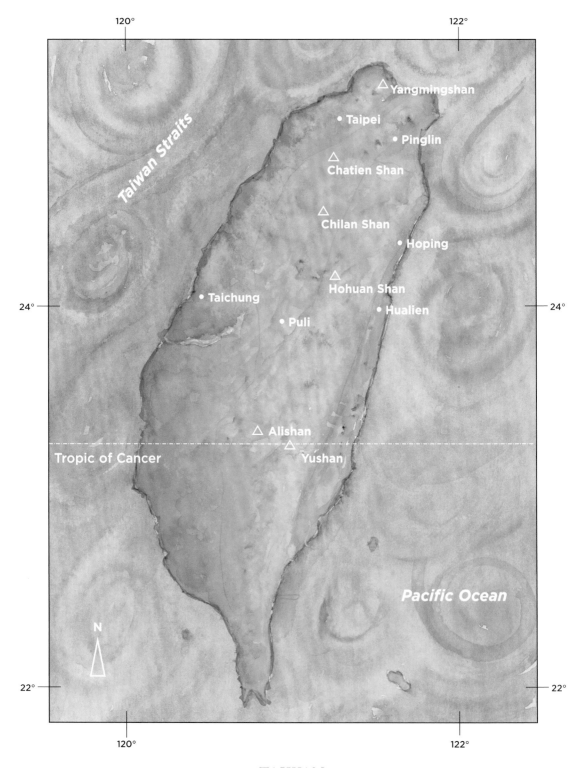

TAIWAN

Yushan, Taiwan's highest mountain

world. Though the trip to Turkey was something of a diversion, in the context of the developing programme in eastern Asia and on a personal level, it was important in honing the field skills that make for a successful collector.

Back in England, during the winter of 1990–91, Tony and I began serious discussions about what direction our fieldwork should take in order to maintain some sort of momentum. Our evaluation of the needs of the woody collections at Kew and Wakehurst Place continued to point, clearly, to eastern Asia as the necessary focus for our efforts; the China programme, spearheaded by John Simmons, was forging ahead, but with many other institutions and individuals planning visits to the temperate parts of China, it made sense to look in other directions. The concept of targeting countries in the extreme east of the Eurasian continent began to strengthen, but it was important for Tony and me to make an informed decision as to our next destination. Fortunately, the unrivalled botanical library at Kew and the presence of so many knowledgeable and experienced horticulturists and botanists were invaluable aids in this regard.

This was a satisfying if demanding period of my career. Having always had an interest in history and a penchant for geography, I enjoyed discovering the rich tradition of exploration that resulted from the efforts of botanists of many nationalities, but it was also necessary to gain an understanding of the content and distribution of the native floras of these far-off places and to attempt to assess their suitability for cultivation in the British Isles. I discovered that many of these plants had been introduced before. Why, then, were they no longer in cultivation? Had they found the climatic conditions in England uncongenial? Had they proved to be difficult to propagate? All these questions had to be answered before a destination could be selected. Equally, the choice of destination and the reasonings behind it had to stand up to the close scrutiny of Kew's Expeditions Committee, whose remit was to vet the many applications for funds to travel and collect overseas put forward by Kew staff.

By the spring of 1991 our studies were complete. Our conclusions were bold but, we felt, well researched, logically derived and, most importantly, certain to contribute to the renaissance of the arboreta at Kew and Wakehurst Place. In the end, I wrote the proposal (the rather long-winded and prosaic title of which was 'A Programme for Collecting Expeditions to Support the Development of the Floristic Collections at Wakehurst Place') that went 'upstairs' for consideration. Fortunately, it dovetailed neatly with the developing arboretum policies at Kew and gained the strong support of the curatorial team of John Simmons, Ian Beyer and Charlie Erskine, who were continuing to develop the expeditions profile of the Living Collections Department, Kew's horticultural arm.

Our thesis: we wished to pursue a series of trips in what we termed the temperate loop of eastern Asia. This loop included an area from Sakhalin Island and the extreme southeastern corner of Siberia in the north, through Japan and the Korean peninsula to Taiwan in the south. We envisaged that three further expeditions, in addition to our Korean visit, would assure a strong sampling of the floras of these areas, a sampling that would greatly augment Kew's collections and better balance its taxonomic and geographic representation.

With support from our superiors, we identified Taiwan as the next destination. This subtropical island had for centuries hid its floral wealth from visitors. The mountainous nature of the island and the savage tendencies of the aboriginal peoples—head hunting was still practised well into the twentieth century—discouraged detailed exploration. Many prominent collectors, amongst them Richard Oldham and Augustine Henry, had been largely confined to the coastal areas, and it fell to the Japanese to undertake the compilation of a botanical inventory following their cession of the island in 1895.

A government-sanctioned botanical survey was placed in the hands of Takiya Kawakami in 1906; to conduct the actual inventory, Kawakami employed young Japanese botanists, most notable amongst them Bunzo Hayata, Nariaki Konishi and Ryozo Kanehira, who undertook many exploratory trips into what was dangerous country. After studying at all the key European herbaria in 1910 Hayata began the exploration of Taiwan, eventually identifying and describing more than a thousand new species from the collections made on the island. These descriptions, published in ten volumes as *Icones Plantarum Formosanarum*, form the basis of our understanding of Taiwan's flora.

A Taiwanese aboriginal
with his trophy in 1918

(photograph by E. H. Wilson courtesy Photographic Archives of the Arnold Arboretum, copyrighted by the President and Fellows of Harvard College, Harvard University, Cambridge, Massachusetts)

Botany received very little attention over the next sixty years, however: the exigencies of the post-war situation—with the Japanese being expelled in 1945 and the Nationalist administration of Chiang Kai-shek assuming control—rendered scientific research a luxury that could be ill afforded. Economic progression was the only priority for the Taiwanese people. As matters improved, a joint venture between the National Scientific Council of Taiwan and the National Science Foundation of the United States saw the publication of the first comprehensive Flora of Taiwan in 1975. Horticulturally, however, virtually nothing of interest emerged from Taiwan. As we have seen, the peerless E. H. Wilson made an important visit to the island in 1918 and introduced a few key plants, but he was severely restricted by the lack of communications at the time.

In modern times a tantalising glimpse of the wealth of the Taiwanese flora and its suitability for cultivation in England was provided as a result of a brief visit undertaken by Paul Meyer of the Morris Arboretum, Pennsylvania, in 1979. Paul introduced several plants that showed promise as first-rate garden plants, including a wonderful skimmia. This plant, *Skimmia japonica* subsp. *reevesiana*, with its heavy crops of sealing wax–red fruits and attractive red-flushed leaves, made such an impact on Tony Schilling, custodian of the UK National Collection of skimmias at Wakehurst Place, that he named it, by agreement with Paul Meyer, 'Chilan Choice' (Chilan Shan being the mountain where Paul first encountered the plant). Tony's judgement has been amply vindicated: 'Chilan Choice' has proven its worth in many gardens in North America and the British Isles, and it also plays a part in our story, as we were to discover a very similar plant on our own travels in Taiwan.

The Expeditions Committee at Kew initially expressed surprise at our choice of destination. Wasn't Taiwan too far south to yield hardy plants? Though bisected by the Tropic of Cancer, Taiwan is extremely mountainous with over two hundred peaks of 3000 m (10,000 ft) or more. The highest point, Yushan (previously known in the West as Mount Morrison), reaches 3952 m (12,900 ft) and is the highest mountain in Asia east of the main massifs of the Himalaya and western China. Indeed, to the occupying Japanese it was Niitakayama, 'big new mountain', a reference to it being of a greater height than Mount Fuji.

We provided the committee with a comprehensive list of target plants that included all the familiar deciduous, broadleaved genera—*Acer, Alnus, Carpinus, Fagus, Juglans* and *Quercus*, though surprisingly no native birches. In addition Taiwan boasted several 'specials', plants found nowhere else, not least the remarkable *Taiwania cryptomerioides*, a conifer purported to grow up to 80 m (260 ft) in height and a serious rival to the redwoods of California. In fact, of a total native vascular flora of 4120 taxa, up to forty percent

occur only on Taiwan. After a
demanding meeting of the
Expeditions Committee towards the
end of 1991, with Charlie Erskine
fighting our corner, we were granted
the funds necessary to continue our
planning.

Dreaming up such a visit is one
thing; turning it into reality is quite
another. Happily, we had one of
those strokes of luck that make you
feel something is meant to be. Tony
received a call from the office of the
director of Kew—Professor Prance
had some important visitors from
Taiwan, could Tony spare some time
to take them around the arboretum?
Could he just! The visitors were key

Fuh-Jiunn Pan

officials in the Taiwanese government, Yu Yu Hsien and Frederick P. N.
Chang, chairman and senior special assistant, respectively, of the Council of
Agriculture; and lo, the door to the Taiwan Forestry Research Institute
(TFRI) in Taipei, the island's capital, swung open. Following protracted
negotiations during the early summer of 1992, we were placed in the hands
of Fuh-Jiunn Pan, and things really began to move. In no time Dr Pan had
'translated' our hit list of plants into an itinerary. The dates for our trip were
agreed, 4 October to 8 November, and a team to assist us was pulled
together.

The time until October seemed to vanish, not least because Lesley and I
were making preparations for our second child, due in December. As can be
imagined I was anxious to have everything ready—the nursery, prams,
clothes and all the other myriad equipment a new baby needs—before leaving, as I knew there would be precious little time on my return. Not to be
outdone Tony and Sally announced Sally's second pregnancy, with their
baby due the following April.

Departures are always difficult, but with a lively toddler and expectant wife this time it seems doubly hard. Nonetheless at 6.00 p.m. on Sunday, 4 October 1992, we take to the air on a Cathay Pacific flight to Taipei, via Hong Kong. As we enter the arrivals hall we are greeted by a huge sign— 'Mrs Kirkham & Mark'! A wizened old man looks blankly at us from below the sign as we introduce ourselves; not a good start. Immediately, however, a younger man steps forward and announces in fluent English—'Mark, Tony, how are you? I'm Fuh-Jiunn Pan'.

In no time we are installed in a four-wheel-drive vehicle, heading into the city. During the small talk on the way we quickly warm to Dr Pan. We stop for food and Taiwan beer before completing the journey to the hotel; and, after a refreshing night's sleep, we are off to the bustling modern headquarters of the TFRI. After the inevitable, though necessary, glad-handing with forestry officials, we are in Dr Pan's office, where he outlines the detail of our forthcoming journeys. We are joined by Allen Chen, one of Dr Pan's students, who is to remain with us for the whole trip. Like Dr Pan, Allen also speaks very good English, with a discernible American accent and peppered with American expressions. A third man, Chang Nai-Hang, a seed technologist, joins us. The driver, Chen Kau Chang, completes our group, and we are assisted in carrying our luggage to the waiting short-wheel-base Isuzu Trooper.

Unfortunately, Dr Pan cannot join us at the outset but will journey down by train and meet us on the way. We drive south on a smooth, multi-lane highway to Taichung, Taiwan's second-largest city, cleaner and more spacious than Taipei, where we stay with friends of Allen's; everyone is courteous and helpful. We collect Dr Pan and his research assistant, Li-Ping Ju (an attractive girl, soon to be called Julie), from the station at 8.00 a.m. the next day and, after stocking up with food from a local supermarket, we begin the journey to the mountains on the Cross-Island Highway. The Taiwanese are justly proud of this road, which cuts through the mountains from the west coast to the east, a distance of over 200 km (120 miles). Climbing above 3000 m (10,000 ft) at its highest point, it is marked by long tunnels, innumerable hairpin bends and countless steep gradients. It was principally built by veterans of Chiang Kai-shek's Kuomintang army after their ignominious retreat from the mainland; some four hundred men are said to have lost their lives during the construction process.

As we begin to climb, the intensively cultivated fields either side give way to a very rich evergreen, broadleaved forest with a scattering of conifers. Everything is exciting—*Gordonia axillaris*, the majestic *Schima superba* in full flower, *Rhododendron formosanum* and the Taiwan black pine, *Pinus taiwanensis*. Later we see *P. armandii* var. *mastersiana* and huge numbers of evergreen members of the beech family (Fagaceae). Our first collection is *Viburnum luzonicum* var. *formosanum* made at 1750 m (5740 ft). This attractive member of the genus is widely distributed on Taiwan and is very variable. A deciduous shrub up to 6 m (20 ft) in height, it has the flat heads of white flowers typical of the genus followed by masses of red shiny fruits. This variety is also found in the southeastern provinces of mainland China. A second variety, var. *oblongum*, is endemic to Taiwan; it has narrower, less sharply toothed leaves and occurs up to 3000 m (10,000 ft) in the central mountains. Though the flora is interesting, we are concerned that we are operating at a low elevation: our pre-expedition researches had suggested that material hardy in the British Isles will only be found above 2600 m (9000 ft). Soon, however, we are amongst one of our target species, the Taiwan incense cedar, *Calocedrus formosana*. Old trees with enormous boles and heights to 25 m (80 ft) are easily reached from the road. High up in the canopy we can see masses of fruiting cones.

Tony dons a climbing harness and, panting and blowing, hauls himself up a trunk into the crown of a tree. I glance slightly to the left and find a small sapling, no taller than 4 m (12 ft), loaded with ripe seeds. Tony's expression when he descends exhausted to the road can be imagined. This genus comprises only three species. The well-known incense cedar of California is *Calocedrus decurrens*, which is widely grown in Western arboreta, including the famous group at Westonbirt in Gloucestershire. Less well known, and certainly not well established in cultivation, is the Chinese incense cedar, *C. macrolepis*, from Yunnan and Sichuan provinces, Hainan island and Myanmar (formerly Burma). This interesting disjunction is a feature of the Taiwanese flora and confirms our initial studies, which indicated

Tony ascending a *Calocedrus formosana*

Calocedrus decurrens growing at Westonbirt

a close relationship with western China and a somewhat more tenuous link with North America.

From this point good things continue to flow; we are aided considerably by Chang, who proves to be a good field botanist as well as a seed technologist. We collect until dusk is gathering and then head for the night's accommodation. Deep valleys and huge precipitous slopes surround us, and as the sun sets behind the high peaks to the west of us it sends shafts of light into the inky black depths between the mountains. Journeying beyond the town of Chiayang, we leave the metalled road behind and in the darkness speed along a rough forest track, eventually ending up at a somewhat run-down forestry hut. It is empty but spacious, though a little dirty; with a kitchen, a rudimentary toilet and rooms at the back that serve as bedrooms. Pan organises things whilst Tony and I begin what is to become our nightly routine, sorting through the day's collections. I write up the field notes, working from the Dictaphone, on which I record my observations during the day, whilst Tony goes through the herbarium specimens. Afterwards we both work through the seeds, disposing of extraneous matter, such as stalks and leaves, to ensure that excess weight is kept down and material that might rot is removed. In the kitchen we can hear the hiss of woks as Julie prepares dinner. In no time our meal is brought through to the main room—rice, fish, tofu and an unidentified leafy green, followed by a sweet corn soup. Everything is delicious and is speedily devoured. Next is a most important task, to teach our new friends the simple game of three-card brag, an effective way both to build bridges across the cultural divide and wind down after a day in the field. The Taiwanese pick up the rudiments very quickly, too quickly, and much to our chagrin Allen ends up the winner!

I endure a fitful night's sleep, rising before 6.30 a.m. Outside a warm, sunny morning promises much for the rest of the day. A simple breakfast and we're on our way. We continue to climb. Though the vegetation is still dominated by evergreen broadleaved trees and shrubs, deciduous elements begin to appear. The number of lauraceous plants (members of the family Lauraceae) is bewildering—*Litsea*, *Lindera*, and *Machilus* are strongly represented—likewise the beech family Fagaceae: tall trees of *Lithocarpus amygdalifolius* join *Quercus morii* and *Castanopsis carlesii*, forming a dense canopy. Taiwan is a regional centre of diversity for the beech family with over thirty species from various genera recognised. Sadly none of these majestic trees are hardy in cool temperate climates such as the British Isles and eastern North America. Vines weave their way up towards the light; everywhere ferns luxuriate. On the forest floor a strange twilight world exists, the dense, leathery leaf litter and lack of light precluding all but the most shade tolerant of plants. The ground is punctuated by the spikes of *Balanophora spicata*, a strange parasitic plant whose inflorescences push through the leaf litter like angry red fingers. The overall aspect is funereal and not at all to Tony's liking; he grumbles that he finds this vegetation type tedious.

Soon however, the appearance of two deciduous maples adds more interest. *Acer caudatifolium* is a small graceful tree, here no more than 8 m (25 ft)

Attractive autumn tints on *Acer rubescens*

tall, with narrow, barely lobed leaves and a decidedly greenish cast, quite different from the second species, *A. rubescens*. A distinctive snake bark maple, *A. rubescens*, has broader, shiny leaves with red petioles and red shoots and an altogether more substantial presence. Both maples are extremely rare in cultivation; the latter was for many years represented in English gardens by a single specimen at Trewithen in Cornwall. Both have a reputation for being tender; certainly they need cosseting in their early years. In arboreta in the south of England, including Kew, trees have proved hardy once established.

Also appearing amongst the broadleaved trees is *Cunninghamia konishii*. Again little known in cultivation, this conifer is far less seen than its mainland relative, *C. lanceolata*, the Chinese fir. So valuable is its timber that old

The giant *Cunninghamia konishii* at Puli

trees which have survived felling are rare and prized. Perhaps the most famous example is the huge specimen by the roadside close to Puli, midway along the Cross-Island Highway, which is estimated to be more than two thousand years old.

As the day develops Dr Pan proves to be a patient and supportive companion, and we are grateful for his forbearance. Plant collectors are notoriously slow and methodical, stopping frequently, examining everything minutely and moving at a snail's pace. Jack Cawdor, who accompanied Frank Kingdon Ward to southeast Tibet in 1924, famously erupted in his diary, 'If ever I travel again I'll make damn sure it's not with a botanist. They are always stopping to gape at weeds!' At the conclusion of a tiring day our tally of plants has risen to forty-two, and we end on a real high as we encounter another conifer on our hit list, the Taiwan red cypress, *Chamaecyparis formosensis*. This particular specimen is small but well fruited, and Dr Pan comments on how puny it is compared to the giants he has seen in the mountains to the north—giants that we are to see under very frustrating circumstances later in the trip.

It is growing dark, the temperature is dropping, and we return to the forestry lodge. By 6.00 p.m. the clear sky overhead is a beautiful carpet of stars. The day is marred only by comments from Tony that he feels unwell; nonetheless, our work continues. We process the day's collections, and by 10.30 p.m. I'm wrapped up in my sleeping bag and asleep in moments. The following day is bright and sunny again, but over breakfast Dr Pan reminds us that later in the day he must return to Taipei with Julie to meet scientists from the U.S. Department of Agriculture who are undertaking a soil survey in the south of the island. We take this news hard, as Dr Pan is a marvellous field companion.

We all head out, descending to the main road at Chiayang. We have hardly left the village when Pan stops the vehicle: he has spotted seed on a tree of *Liquidambar formosana*. The genus *Liquidambar* has an eastern Asia/eastern North America split but also includes a species, *L. orientalis*, which grows in Turkey and neighbouring parts of the Near East. In cultivation this latter species rarely develops into a tall tree, typically forming a broad shrubby specimen. Autumn colour can be as impressive as its better known North American relative, the sweet gum, *L. styraciflua*. I particularly recall a specimen in the Jubilee Arboretum at the Royal Horticultural Society's garden at Wisley with exceptional autumnal colours of a rich burgundy. Wisley's curator, Jim Gardiner, tells me the tree was received in 1979 from a private donor who lived near Epsom; discussions are underway to give this outstanding plant a distinct cultivar name.

The Taiwanese taxon is the typical form of a tree that ranges onto the Chinese mainland, whence it was introduced to Kew in 1884. E. H. Wilson also collected seed in the central Chinese province of Hubei in 1907, and it is from this introduction that trees became established. Wilson and Alfred Rehder, the senior botanist at the Arnold Arboretum, assigned this collection to the variety *monticola* on the basis of its glabrous shoots and leaves. It was soon recognised, however, that this character could be found on specimens in other parts of its range. Indeed *Liquidambar formosana* is remarkably uniform in its appearance across its wide, though scattered distribution, and it is difficult to pick out distinctive forms. Horticulturally there is an important difference between the species as found on Taiwan and on the mainland, particularly in central China, as the latter is much hardier. We realise that our elevation is perhaps too low, but encouraged by Dr Pan, who suggests that we might not see another tree in fruit, we gather the seed anyway. Pan is right: not only do we never see another tree in seed, we never see another tree. (The seed we collected germinated readily, but the trees were killed by the English winter before they even left their nursery rows.)

We head along the Cross-Island Highway towards Lishan. The road is noticeably busier than two days before—it is Sunday, the one day when the majority of the population are not working. Many people who pass us wind down their windows, in response to seeing Tony and me. Tony's ginger hair seems to be a real novelty, and it is obvious that this is the main talking point. Nevertheless, everyone is friendly, calling out 'Hello! How are you?' in rudimentary English. 'Ni hao' ('hello') we respond, in even more rudimentary Mandarin. We have an excellent lunch in Lishan, six separate dishes accompanied by rice. Tony eats sparingly and is looking increasingly forlorn. By mid afternoon Dr Pan and Julie are on their way back to Taipei, and our group of five heads back to the forestry lodge above Chiayang. Tony looks pale and complains of stomach pains and diarrhoea. Once again he eats little and without enthusiasm. Allen offers to use a traditional Chinese massage technique to help alleviate Tony's discomfort. He probes the inside of Tony's forearm until he decides he's located the right spot; for fifteen minutes he gently massages Tony's arm, ending by pronouncing that Tony will be cured by morning. We look at each other doubtfully. 'How do you feel?' I ask. 'Lousy!' We are shamed by our scepticism the following day when Tony springs from his sleeping bag and consumes his breakfast with all the eagerness of a starving dog.

We drive east again, following the route we traversed the previous day; soon we are further than the point at which we finished and at last the road is climbing significantly. New and interesting, and hardy, plants begin to arrive in greater and greater numbers. Huge, solitary specimens of Taiwan spruce, *Picea morrisonicola*, remnants of a once majestic forest are encountered, along with Taiwan hemlock, *Tsuga chinensis* var. *formosana*. Underneath the trees are a bevy of attractive shrubs—*Viburnum parvifolium* with tiny leaves and clusters of big, shining red fruits, *Rhododendron oldhamii* forming uniform, rounded shrubs and the Formosan elder, *Sambucus formosana*, with masses of cascading tiny orange fruits.

A key frustration of the plant collector is a poor seed harvest; all the great collectors have suffered to some degree from a shortage of good, viable seed. The variables affecting seed set are manifold and complex, and the collector has no control whatsoever over this natural phenomenon. But it is becoming increasingly clear to us that the summer and autumn of 1992 has produced a bounty of seeds and fruits on Taiwan. Our burgeoning collections attest to our good fortune; not only are we gathering a wide range

Viburnum parvifolium with Alishan in the background

of plants, but the quantities we are able to collect are prodigious. This trip was meant to be.

We continue due east, passing into the Taroko Gorge National Park. Almost immediately the scenery seems to become grander still, and towering peaks quickly swallow up the setting sun. Having reached 2600 m (9000 ft), we are conscious of a significant fall in temperature. Allen and Chang look for accommodation for the night in Tayuling, but the student guesthouse they know of is closed. We push on several miles up the road to Kuanyuan, where a similar hostel is open. It looks rather unpromising in the darkness—squat and uninviting. Both Tony and I are delighted to find our room clean and warm with an abundant supply of hot water.

We leave immediately for a nearby eating place familiar to Chang, who promises us the best noodles in Taiwan. Not put off by finding it closed, with substantial metal shutters protecting it from the outside world, he proceeds to bang vigorously on the shutters, at which point all hell breaks loose. A cacophony of barking dogs erupts inside, and a voice calls out in terms that—even we understand—are less than impressed. Eventually, with much cursing on both sides of the shutters, an old man appears, and after animated negotiations we are invited to enter. Inside it is rather grimy, but the old man quickly and expertly prepares bowls of delicious steaming noodles. By this time his ill-temper seems forgotten, and, with Allen interpreting, he tells us that he inherited the recipe from his mother. His family originates on the Shantung peninsula in eastern China; he escaped to Taiwan with the Kuomintang in 1949. He longs to return to his original home but fears that he never will. We reluctantly leave the old man to his memories and head back to the hostel. It has been a long day, but we still have work to do. Our growing collections keep us occupied late into the night, but the welcome compensation of a hot bath—the first in over a week—keeps our morale high.

The next three days are spent in the vicinity of Kuanyuan. Above the town mountains rise dramatically, culminating in the summit of Chilaichu Shan, at 3800 m (12,500 ft) not much below the island's main peak, Yushan, some way to the south of us. Our first day targets the accessible mountain of Hohuan, which offers an easy road to the top as it is a winter ski resort. It has been raining all night, and the fine weather we have been enjoying is gone. The mist is swirling about and visibility is poor. Despite this Tony and I are in high spirits; he is feeling one hundred percent again, and as we climb we are offered the promise of new hardy plants. As we pass the 3000 m (10,000 ft) mark we spot one of our important target plants, *Sorbus randaiensis*, the Taiwan rowan. This tree is closely related to the better known Japanese rowan, *S. commixta*, and though already in cultivation (courtesy of Hugh McAllister of the University of Liverpool's Ness Botanic Gardens), it is extremely rare. One remarkable quality the tree possesses, at least in English gardens, is that it comes into leaf in late February and seems impervious to late frosts. The whole hillside proves to be rich, and for the next two to three hours we are engaged in a steady bout of seed collecting. *Rosa transmorrisonensis* follows the rowan into our seed bags, as does an

Sorbus randaiensis in the mists of Hohuan Shan

The summit of Shihmen Shan, clothed with *Yushania niitakayamensis*

interesting viburnum, not unlike the familiar *Viburnum furcatum*, with large pleated and strongly heart-shaped leaves.

We drive to 3200 m (10,500 ft) and stop the car before proceeding on foot to the secondary summit of Shihmen Shan, which lies north of Hohuan Shan. By now the weather has closed in considerably, and squally blasts hamper our progress. With adequate clothing Tony and I are comfortable and happy to proceed; not so the Taiwanese, whose lightweight garments are clearly unsuitable. Allen returns to the warmth of the vehicle, though Chang continues on with us to the summit. Once there we can see little of value. A ubiquitous species of low-growing bamboo, *Yushania niitakayamensis*, forms a dense green carpet on the ground, which disappears into the mist in all directions.

As the wind rises to a shriek, we return to the car and head for the shelter of a ski lodge. Two other groups of shivering people are already there; they generously offer us some of their food, which consists of two evil-smelling pots of cabbage and some seafood. Tony and I politely decline, though our companions consume with evident relish. We venture back out again and though the wind has moderated, the mist and drizzle remain. We labour on manfully but largely in vain and eventually cut our losses, heading back to the hostel at Kuanyuan, which we reach by late afternoon. We use the time gained to thoroughly update our collections. It is gratifying to see that everything is in good order.

That night begins a strange phenomenon that I have experienced many times when travelling and living in overseas countries, namely bizarre, though not disturbing, dreams. Whether these are a result of the psychological dislocation that occurs when assimilating into unfamiliar cultures, or a consequence of the extreme tiredness brought on by hard, physical activity I don't know. It would be interesting to have them analysed. Tonight my dream features Margaret Thatcher, who provides me with a very creditable haircut. Subsequent nights see me scuba diving with Jacques Cousteau and preparing a banquet for unknown guests with Abraham Lincoln!

Fine, bright conditions greet us next morning, and with time in hand we decide to retrace our journey of the previous day. Things could hardly be more different; in good light the hillside on which we collected the rowan reveals a great yawning chasm, which had been completely obscured in the mists. Likewise the majestic peak of Hohuan Shan and that of Chilaichu Shan to the east are now both asserting their splendour. By afternoon we return to the Cross-Island Highway and drive east towards Puli. By the roadside is the aforementioned specimen of cunninghamia; it is difficult to take in the sheer size of this old tree; photographs certainly do not do it justice.

On Thursday, 15 October, we leave the comfort of our hostel in Kuanyuan, where we have enjoyed a three-night sojourn. An attempt to breakfast at the old man's noodle house, which we have patronised several times since our first visit, proves abortive. As usual all the shutters are down, and the place looks deserted. But this time no amount of banging and shouting can raise him, although his dogs are carrying on shamefully. Our Taiwanese companions are noticeably disappointed to miss their morning meal, and they drive reluctantly eastwards into the upper reaches of the Taroko Gorge. Straightaway it is evident that this is a special place. We are still at 2600 m (9000 ft) and can see the gorge falling away ahead of us, a

The upper reaches of the Taroko Gorge

huge V-shaped gash in the landscape. Early morning clouds are clinging to the hillsides, and we can hear water rushing in a river bed far, far below. We rapidly descend by a series of hairpin bends, the walls of the gorge closing in as we lose altitude.

'*Quercus!*' Chang shouts, and the vehicle screeches to a halt. An endemic oak, *Quercus tarokoensis*, a tree unknown in cultivation, grows in the gorge. Undoubtedly this is it. The tree is perched on a large boulder overhanging a sharp drop to the river 100 m (330 ft) below. Intrinsically this tree is valuable for its rarity, but ornamentally it is disappointing, with smallish evergreen, bristle-edged leaves, resembling certain Mediterranean or Californian live oaks. The acorns are tiny and difficult to spot at first. Indeed it seems there is very little seed. But after a good search and a rather hair-raising stretch over the gaping precipice, we secure a reasonable collection. Jumping back in the vehicle, we continue the rapid descent, eventually arriving at Tienhsiang, a tourist town at the eastern entrance to the Taroko Gorge National Park. At last, and much to their relief, our friends are able to eat breakfast. An attractive pagoda sits on the hillside above, and it is warm and sunny again after the cool of the mountains. All around the vegetation is lush and green, with palms and tree ferns in abundance. Driving on again we encounter the most spectacular parts of the gorge. Sheer marble walls rise for hundreds of metres and the landscape has a tortured feel, reflecting millennia of conflict between the force of water and the immovability of rock. Eventually the scenery becomes more serene, and we emerge into the low, flat floodplain of the river, before the industrial suburbs of the major east coast city of Hualien intrude on the primacy of nature. It is hard to believe that less than three hours before we were high in the mountains.

What remains of this day and the whole of the following are spent in Hualien, which gives us time to work on our collections, write up field notes and have our clothes, which are in a pretty shabby state, laundered. Having been charged £18 for the service, we are distinctly miffed when one of Tony's T-shirts comes back three sizes too small and I get someone else's underpants and socks!

Driving north from Hualien, we hug the narrow coast road, which is set high on the cliffs and affords exhilarating views over the raging Pacific Ocean. The eastward bias of Taiwan's mountain systems makes the topography of the west and east coasts completely different. The coastal plain of the western seaboard is broad and gentle, gradually rising into the mountains. In the east, by contrast, the high mountains fall rapidly into the ocean losing hundreds of metres of elevation over a relatively short linear length and producing spectacular cliffs for nearly 100 km (60 miles). We arrive at the town of Hoping around 10.45 a.m., at which point our companions decide it might be a good idea to eat. Tony and I decline, partly because we're not very hungry but mainly because pig's ear is the main feature of the menu. Allen eats with gusto, chewing hard on the rubbery flesh, which seems to have the consistency of knicker elastic. His vigorous mastication is

The precipitous cliffs of Taiwan's Pacific coast

punctuated by occasional approving nods of his head—this is obviously a favourite dish of his.

From Hoping we continue northwestwards, stopping at Pinglin, the centre of tea growing on the island, of which a celebrated form of oolong (black dragon) tea is the principal product. At one of the many tea houses lining the main road, we enjoy a delicious and refreshing drink of green tea from delicate bone china cups, ornamented with dragons and phoenixes and other mythical creatures. All around are neat landscaped hills with terrace upon terrace of hummocky camellia plants, typical of tea stations the world over. We can see the tiny figures of workers beavering away, their heads covered by broad-brimmed bamboo coolies' hats.

More important to us is the reported presence of another of our target trees, the conifer *Keteleeria davidiana* var. *formosana*. Chang guides us to the stands, where several of the trees are bearing their characteristic elongated cones, visually intermediate between those of the spruce and the silver fir. Tony climbs into one and starts happily collecting; he spots a huge hornets'

nest several branches above but continues despite the interest of the
hornets in this large intruder. Chang
comments, almost idly, that he read
about a schoolteacher who was
killed by multiple hornet stings
whilst taking a school party into
these woods. Quick as a flash Tony
descends from the tree. A nearby
tree provides just as much seed without the attendant dangers.

A coning branch of *Keteleeria
davidiana* var. *formosana*

Our journey back to Taipei continues, and long after nightfall we
are returned to the hotel we occupied when we first arrived on the
island. This marks the end of the
first phase of the trip, and Tony and
I take stock of what has been
achieved. We have 108 collections in
hand, many from our target list and all of good quality and quantity. Each
collection is accompanied by detailed field notes and herbarium specimens.
Just as important, we have managed to develop a good rapport with our
companions despite our very different backgrounds. Our health is good,
and we have had some wonderful experiences. We look forward to the next
part of our travels with relish. (That night I dream that Babe Ruth, the
famous American baseball player, is my long lost brother.) The following
day is spent at the TFRI. We decide to leave all our collections here whilst
we travel south again to try and find the Taiwan beech, taking considerable
care to instruct the technician who is to look after them.

In the late afternoon of Monday, 19 October, we drive south to Ba Lin.
The night is spent in a hostel sharing a room with our team—Allen Chen,
Chang Nai-Hang and Chen Kau Chang—and three other strangers (my
bizarre dream that night cannot be committed to paper). Next morning
begins an important part of the trip.

The Taiwan beech, *Fagus hayatae*, is a little-known species found only in the mountains of northern Taiwan at elevations between 1300 and 2000 m (4000 and 6000 ft). It occurs at two separate, though adjacent, locations. The largest population is on Chatien Shan with a secondary centre on Sanhsing Shan. Rarely referred to even in detailed textbooks, the Taiwan beech is unknown in cultivation and is regarded as an endangered species. For this reason the Chatien Shan area is a designated nature preserve, with the strictest conservation policies applied. Not surprisingly, this tree is high on our hit list of plants to collect during our visit to Taiwan.

The main mountain chains on Taiwan are arranged as a series of parallel ranges running in a southwest/northeast direction. The Taiwan beech is found in the Hsueh Shan (Snow Mountains) range in the north-central part of the island. Numerous spurs are thrown off from the main range, and it is on one of these lateral ridges that the beech occurs. Though close to some major population centres, the area is difficult of access, as we soon discover.

We rise by 6.00 a.m., allowing plenty of time to find our quarry, and head into the village which, despite the early hour, is a hive of activity. Allen finds a shop and procures some lunch for us. Ba Lin is in two distinct sections, upper and lower, and it is through the former that we pass on our way to the trail that leads into Chatien Shan. By the time we disembark from the vehicle the sun is rising rapidly, and as we walk we are soon down to T-shirts. We gather one or two things along the trail but don't tarry, as our real objective is some way off. We are surprised by the continued activity around us: rather than leaving the crowds behind, we seem to be encountering more people. Chang explains that the trail we are on, at least in its early stages, is famous throughout Taiwan as it leads into groves of red cypress (*Chamaecyparis formosensis*) and yellow cypress (*C. obtusa* var. *formosana*), trees of giant size. The genus *Chamaecyparis*, unknown on mainland Asia, is native to Taiwan, Japan and North America. Many of the biggest cypress trees were felled during the Japanese occupation of Taiwan prior to the Second World War, leaving a few tantalising specimens of immense size behind. What the original forest must have looked like can only be imagined.

As the first trees come into view we begin to understand why they are so revered. They rise like great monoliths, not exceptionally tall (the largest are less than 50 m [160 ft] in height) but with enormous boles which almost

The enormous bole of *Chamaecyparis formosensis* near Ba Lin

Conifers in the 'foggy forest'

defy comprehension. The trail yields tree after tree, each more impressive than the last. Estimates of their ages range up to two thousand years. The trees occur in what is locally known as 'foggy forest'. The nearby Pacific Ocean sends in great billowing masses of saturated air that engulf the mountainsides, releasing huge amounts of precipitation and suspending the slopes in a ghostly, almost perpetual shroud of mist. With relatively warm conditions many of the trees grow to prodigious size. We realise how fortunate we are to have encountered them during such fine, clear weather. The two species occur in distinct strata on the mountainside. Our first encounter is with the red cypress, which can be found between 1500 and 1800 m

(4500 and 6000 ft). Two-hundred fifty metres (800 ft) higher is the domain of the yellow cypress; these trees have a still larger girth. Many are fenced to prevent access, but this detracts little from their majesty. Having admired veteran trees all over the temperate world, I am still left with a sense of wonder at the seeming immortality of these plants. Much as we wish to stay amongst these aged leviathans Chang reminds us of our real purpose; the Taiwan beech occurs higher still.

The trail leaves the last yellow cypress behind, but not before we are able to gather its small cones, replete with seed, and becomes steeper and steeper as we climb. A tall-growing form of *Skimmia japonica* subsp. *japonica*, with large obovate (spoon-shaped) leaves, is common in the understorey; this is also collected. As we push on, the temperature begins to drop noticeably and a breeze from the east brings clouds and persistent light drizzle. The fine conditions we were enjoying have disappeared with alarming speed. Despite the change in the weather we continue upwards; the trail has narrowed considerably, and the groups of people who started the day with us are left far below.

Chang tells us that the track has almost certainly been created by bears, and the broken branches, flattened fern fronds, frequent depressions in the mud (made by their paws) and occasional scats (bear droppings) lend support to his assertion. The Formosan black bear is now greatly reduced in numbers. Its traditional foraging area, the mixed forests below 2000 m (6000 ft), have been much depleted, and pressure on its habitat has meant a decline in its breeding success. With a characteristic white V of fur around its neck, this bear is very distinctive. Eschewing hibernation, the bear is active throughout the year and can be encountered in only a few remote valleys in the central mountains. The area that we are in is known as a key location of this beautiful creature.

By early afternoon the weather hasn't improved, and we're all cold and wet. Though we have seen many interesting things we see no sign of the Taiwan beech. The path we are following is now taking us down the mountainside rather than up onto the higher slopes. We agree to call it a day and head back down the hillside. We will clearly need more accurate information on the whereabouts of the beech trees, particularly as these mountains are obviously subjected to heavy rainfall with an attendant low cloud cover.

We spend the night at the town of Lotung about 8 km (5 miles) inland from the east coast. The next two days are engaged in securing more of our target species. On Taipingshan, a narrow-gauge railway close to a holiday resort gives us good access into the mountains where we collect an important tree, *Phellodendron amurense* var. *wilsonii*. This cork tree, so called for its thick furrowed bark, gives us another clue to the affinities of the high elevation woody flora of Taiwan. *Phellodendron* is known solely from eastern Asia and comprises three or four taxa in China, the Korean peninsula and Japan. They are deciduous members of the citrus family (Rutaceae) and have the pungent smell characteristic of the family, a consequence of the oil-bearing glands found in the leaves, which are transparent when held up to the light. They make tall, handsome trees, eventually with flat-topped, spreading canopies. Often producing rich, yellow autumn tints, they deserve to be more widely recognised. The Taiwanese tree doesn't seem to be in cultivation in the West, and we hope that the few seeds we manage to secure will rectify this. The bark of the tree contains significant concentrations of the alkaloid berberine and is utilised in Taiwan for the treatment of stomach upsets. Plantations have been established in many places to prevent stripping of the bark from natural stands, such as those on Taipingshan.

As we return along the train track our attention is caught by a commotion in the forest above. A large troop of Formosan rock monkeys, a species of macaque, are making their way through a dense grove of *Acer rubescens*; we catch the merest glimpse of their long brown tails before they are gone. Further along the track Chang points to some monkey droppings; within this waste matter, he insists, are the seeds of the Taiwan plum yew, *Cephalotaxus wilsoniana*. We collect them somewhat gingerly and with a degree of scepticism. The conifer flora of Taiwan is a rich and important one. Seven conifer families are represented, comprising twenty-eight species from sixteen genera. Of these fully seventy percent are endemic (found only on Taiwan) at varietal rank or above. The abundance of conifers on an island of only 35,000 km^2 (10,736 sq miles) is quite remarkable. Sadly many of these native conifers are under varying degrees of threat; the Taiwan plum yew itself is listed as endangered by the IUCN, an international conservation body. And yes, Chang is subsequently proven right: the seeds we collect are those of the Taiwan plum yew (though we should note that many conifer authorities merely regard *C. wilsoniana* as part of the more widespread main-land species, *C. fortunei*).

Once again the weather closes in on us, reducing visibility to less than 50 m (160 ft), and as we drive to our overnight stop the poor conditions make our progress difficult. We head to the town of Nanao to take stock of the situation, settling into a small, comfortable hotel. Our original plan was to drive to Hoping on the Pacific coast and then inland to see the best stands of the conifer *Taiwania cryptomerioides* on the island. Unfortunately, Chang has received word that the road from Hoping is blocked, and this won't be pos-sible. A mini conference ensues, as we are determined to see the taiwanias—of all the trees on the island, this is the one we must find. It seems that Allen knows the location of a smaller, less extensive grove of trees somewhat to the north, not far from Chilan Shan. We are told that this will also allow us to return to Taipei a day early. Whilst Tony and I are happy to take the alter-native location, we don't like the idea of returning a day early. On looking at the map it seems to us that we could continue north from Chilan Shan and try again for the Taiwan beech on Chatien Shan. We persuade Chang to telephone Dr Pan and get better directions to the location of the beech trees. Pan confirms that we were looking in the wrong place and gives Chang more explicit instructions, conceding, however, that the area is a difficult one and that the beech trees are by no means extensive in their occurrence. With all this agreed, we turn in—and a potentially good night's sleep is ruined by the constant howling of dogs from a kennel below our room.

The following morning we are on the road by 7.30 a.m.; it is a beautiful warm, sunny day. We drive through Suao before turning west to pick up the road to Ilan. We call in at the local forestry office, which, in addition to being the 'Vocational Assistance Commission for Retired Servicemen', has responsibility for the area where the taiwanias grow. After many introduc-tions and much shaking of hands and nodding of heads, we return to our vehicle followed by two guides, who climb into a four-wheel-drive and roar out of town, setting a breakneck pace towards Chilan Shan. The road is well surfaced, and we make rapid progress. Almost immediately we are into groups of huge red cypress trees, which form part of a forest recreation area. A sign tells us that this is the Chinese Men Memorial Garden: Chang explains that each tree is named after an important historical figure from

Taiwania cryptomerioides showing its
characteristic, clean straight trunk

Imperial times. As we climb, we catch breathtaking views through the big old trees, across the mountains and east to a deep valley. At 1800 m (6000 ft) the road peters out at a forestry hut. The hut is run by a redoubtable woman who provides for fourteen workers whose job it is to encourage the regeneration of taiwanias by removing competition from other plants; this they accomplish with evil-looking machetes.

After a light lunch we continue up the track on foot. The area has obviously been cut over several times, and we see the debris typical of a logging site. Many large trees are left standing, however, and they enjoy strategic positions on the hillsides, obviously with the intention of acting as seed sources. Red cypress forms the initial groups, with many trees rising to over 60 m (180 ft). Soon scattered examples of *Taiwania cryptomerioides* begin to appear. Higher still we can see the huge, spreading canopies of the Taiwan hemlock, *Tsuga chinensis* var. *formosana*.

The forest is not at all what I expected; I had hoped to see the giant boles of the trees rising like the columns of a medieval cathedral, similar to the stands of coast redwoods in Hendy Woods in California. I am confronted instead with individual trees widely scattered. Nevertheless, each tree is impressive, many with trunks of 30 to 40 m (100 to 130 ft) before the first branch and rising to a height of perhaps 70 m (220 ft). At first the area underneath the giant trees seems to contain little apart from the lop and top of a forestry site; however, on closer examination we begin to find a wealth of interesting understorey species. Prominent amongst this association is the Taiwan sassafras, *Sassafras randaiense*, a tree we had hoped to see and collect. Sadly, though numerous, the trees are not bearing seeds. This species is one of three in the genus; all are typified by having three quite distinct leaf shapes on the adult tree: a simple, unlobed leaf, a leaf which has one side lobe, somewhat in the manner of a mitten, and a third trident-shaped leaf. All three species—*S. randaiense*, the more familiar *S. albidum* from eastern North America and *S. tzumu* from mainland China—display this unusual pattern, to my knowledge unique amongst temperate trees. I have been asked many times what the purpose of this arrangement might be, but I have never been able to discover a plausible answer.

An old cypress stump provides our next surprise—an unfamiliar lax-growing rhododendron. It takes some time to work out that we are looking at *Rhododendron kawakamii*, unusual in being a member of section *Vireya* of the genus. A distinguishing feature of this section is the umbellate (umbrella-like) flower structure, which lacks a central rachis (stalk); another is that, unlike many temperate and alpine rhododendrons, the individual flowers of vireyas are never spotted. Comprising almost half the total number of *Rhododendron* species, section *Vireya* has its centre of distribution in the mountains of southeast Asia, particularly the island of New Guinea. *Rhododendron kawakamii* represents a northern outlier. We are able to gather abundant seed of this plant, which has a tenuous hold in cultivation. I have seen it at Peter Cox's garden at Glendoick, in Scotland; it produces yellow flowers in the late summer and is perhaps the hardiest of what is largely a frost-sensitive group of plants. A third plant of interest is a species of holly, later identified by Susyn Andrews, at that time Kew's horticultural taxonomist and holly specialist, as *Ilex hayataiana*. In common with many other Asian hollies it has small leaves without prickles and is therefore very different from the English holly, *I. aquifolium*. Here it forms a multi-stemmed shrub to about 4 m (12 ft) carrying abundant, though not showy, red berries.

We have agreed with Chang and Allen to leave by 2.30 p.m., allowing time for the long journey to Ba Lin. In our haste to reach the top we deliberately bypassed an interesting shrub we saw by the roadside, but we manage to persuade Chang to give us twenty minutes at the end to make a collection. The shrub turns out to be *Daphniphyllum glaucescens* var. *oldhamii*, a relative of the slightly more familiar *D. himalaense* subsp. *macropodum*, which we collected on Ullung-Do during the 1989 trip to South Korea. In the scruffy undergrowth we spot another species of rhododendron, quite different from *Rhododendron kawakamii*. This is clearly an evergreen azalea belonging to subgenus *Tsutsusi*. Before we are hurried along, I tentatively put the name *R. lasiostylum* to it. This collection proves to be a most interesting rhododendron, though we are not to find this out for some years; of this more later, in chapter 7.

Our road journey continues, and we arrive in Ba Lin around 8.30 p.m., tired and hungry. Despite our fatigue our mood is buoyant; we feel privileged to have seen the majestic taiwanias, and tomorrow holds the prospect of finally securing seed of the elusive Taiwan beech. That night we enjoy an uproarious karaoke evening with the locals, who are transfixed by Tony's version of 'The Ballad of Jed Clampett' from *The Beverly Hillbillies*—word perfect but hopelessly out of tune! Their amazed expressions remain with me to this day.

An early start, our musical antics notwithstanding, sees us driving up the road that leads from Ba Lin to the car park at the edge of the forest. Here we check the seed collecting and herbarium gear, shoulder our packs and set off with a determined stride. As before, we are soon amongst the cypress trees. Unfortunately, today is very different from our first visit; the sunny conditions we enjoyed then, at least during the early part of the day, have been replaced by a swirling mist. Visibility is poor and the first tree is upon us almost before we realise. In the near distance another can be seen, and then another. The mist yields tree after tree, each more impressive than the last. We leave the cypress trees by a different track this time. As we climb, the mist thickens and the temperature drops. A breeze from the east brings in more cloud and a persistent light drizzle; visibility is reduced to less than 20 m (65 ft). The slope is increasingly precipitous, and I glance down towards Tony, who is finding the going just as tough as I am.

Despite the difficult conditions, interesting plants keep our spirits up. We notice, in particular, the diversity of ferns on this hillside. The super-saturated conditions obviously favour their development, and they form a dense ground cover, which further impedes progress. Taiwan is particularly rich in ferns, with around six hundred species of which sixty are endemic. On the woodland floor numerous cobra lilies (*Arisaema* spp.) and *Paris lancifolia* jostle for position with the ferns.

By mid morning we are wet and cold, and though we continue to see many interesting things, Taiwan beech is not amongst them. It seems clear that Chang, who is leading, is not certain of the route despite the recent instructions from Dr Pan. The path begins to fall and we double back, taking an alternative way off to the left to continue the ascent; this too begins to fall, so we return to the original point of divergence. We try a third option, to the right, but within a few hundred metres Chang stops us, and we return to the first point. Chang explains that the directions he has been given specify a steady rise to a ridge were the beech trees occur, with no falls along the way. We set off left again and continue on. Still, the path falls steadily.

Through the trees ahead we see the ghost of a ridgeline, perhaps 400 to 500 m (1300 to 1600 ft) away—this looks promising. The path falls steeply to a streambed, which we ford, and then rises up the slope to the ridge. The ground vegetation closes in. It is cool and misty; the fern fronds are dripping wet; an unnerving silence envelopes us. Chang sets a sluggish pace and stops after a few minutes, looking pensive and unsure. Tony and I resolve to push on to the top, leaving Chang behind. Visibility what it is, we keep in touch by whistling to fix each other's positions. The going is hard, and we are soaked to the skin by the time we reach the ridge top. There is no sign whatsoever of beech trees. The atmosphere is eerie; the all-pervading silence continues. What stunted shrubs and trees there are are covered in moss and epiphytes. I'm in a T-shirt and begin to feel the cold creeping in as I stand stationary, looking around. Pulling on some warmer clothes, I exchange a few brief words with Tony; we decide to start down, resigned to foregoing the beech yet again.

I look at my watch—amazingly, it is little more than midday: it seems like many more hours have passed. As we descend we whistle and call for Chang; he is far below to the left, and we skirt diagonally down the hillside, finding him without difficulty. Together we carry on down but fail to pick up the trail we came in on, hampered as we are by the swirling mist. We all have a vague recollection of where the stream that we forded is, but when we arrive at a stream nowhere does it look familiar. We remain on the same side but continue our descent; still we see no evidence of a trail on the opposite bank. After about half an hour it is clear that we have gone astray. Our plan was to be back at the car park by 2.30 p.m. to allow for the long journey to our next overnight stay at Lotung. It is obvious we are not going to be back at the car park by this time. After a discussion we agree to follow the compass in a southwesterly direction, as we came in from that bearing.

We follow the stream for some distance, travelling to the southwest—an increasingly risky proposition as the depth and strength of the water increases. An additional hazard is the slipperiness of the rocks on the banks and in the streambed. I have to negotiate each step with great care to avoid falling into the water. Two problems develop: we have lost too much altitude and are now below the level of the car park, and the stream has veered to the north. We agree to leave the stream behind and climb the slope on the left bank to regain our southwesterly bearing. A further ridgeline is gained before, confusingly, we see another stream in the valley below us. The pattern repeats, as we descend to the water only to have to climb up the opposite slope in order to keep to our direction. The vegetation is almost irrelevant, indeed its density is impeding our progress. Chang spots the tall inflorescence of an arisaema emerging from amongst low-growing evergreen bushes. In other circumstances we would be delighted by its appearance; now, it merely receives a weary nod.

Still no sign of a path or trail. The rain is falling steadily, which adds to our discomfort. Exhaustion begins to gnaw at me though there is little choice but to continue on. Darkness is not far off, and still we are clueless about our location in relation to where the car is parked. Each person is wrapped up in their own thoughts, but there is no panic. With two hours of daylight left we have another discussion; Chang is obviously unnerved and looking to Tony and me for advice. We decide to continue southwest and are heartened when we hear the distinct, though faint, sounds of vehicles from that direction. Immediately we are forced to descend to the water again, by now a small, swift river. Progress is painfully slow, as the banks are densely vegetated and the water deep. Chang, who is wearing wellingtons, is keen to keep to the river, but Tony and I want to move up the hillside again as we are finding the job of negotiating the treacherous rocks tiring. I cannot dispel a small, nagging thought that we might have to spend the night, and perhaps much of the next day, in the forest with little food, inadequate clothing and only one lighter between us. I voice these fears to Tony, who nods gravely and says, 'What a fuck up'.

It is amazing how quickly the trappings of the modern world can vanish and an almost primeval reality take over—we are lost and there is no one to help us. We finally persuade Chang to leave the river and climb yet another ridge. As we climb higher the ascent becomes steeper until it seems almost vertical; we are in dense bracken and the climb is absolutely exhausting. At the top is just another featureless ridgeline—no track, no road, no view-point. Dejection! To the left the ridgeline becomes razor-like, and Tony suggests we continue along it to see if there is a way through. With no great enthusiasm we follow him. Suddenly he gives a great shout—'The road!' Chang and I race along and sure enough, the next ridgeline is topped by a road and the car park we left nearly ten hours before. The decision to go in a southwesterly direction is vindicated; we are within a few hundred metres of where we started. Our problem is that we are separated from the car park by a deep valley and will have to descend perhaps 200 m (650 ft) and reclimb 200 to 250 m (650 to 800 ft). We have an hour until darkness; already in the forest the twilight is gathering. Chang seems reluctant for some reason, so I force the issue, and we quickly descend to the stream, but not before Tony slips on the greasy trunk of a fallen tree, crying out in alarm as he careers downhill. A dense thicket of *Photinia niitakayamensis* breaks his fall, and he rises gingerly, apparently unhurt.

We cross yet another stream at the bottom and begin the daunting climb up the other side. Tony leads. Painfully slowly we make progress; again the ascent seems almost sheer, but we are spurred on by our proximity to safety. I track our progress on an altimeter. Finally we emerge right beneath a shelter adjacent to the car park. A group of bemused workmen watch us come out, sweaty, exhausted and filthy, our hands, arms and legs cut by the dense vegetation. Allen and Chen are delighted and relieved to see us—they were within a few minutes of reporting our non-return.

After a change of clothes and a quick wash we head on to Lotung as planned. By now it is dark, and on the journey Tony and I discuss how lucky we have been and how foolish we were to expose ourselves in the way we did. Only the compass saved us from a frightening and possibly dangerous night in the forest. At Lotung we take separate rooms and have deep, hot baths.

A delicious meal of steak and spaghetti further helps our recuperation. Back at the hotel I fall into bed exhausted and enjoy a deep untroubled and revitalising sleep.

Compared to this drama, the following day is tame and pedestrian. We enjoy a leisurely breakfast before departing for Taipei. Though a little stiff I feel none the worse for yesterday's ordeal, but it was a chastening experience. Tony suggests we treat the group to a seafood meal along the coast, as this will be our last time together. I agree, expecting it will be mid afternoon before we reach the restaurant, but we arrive a little after 11.00 a.m.—my breakfast has barely had time to settle! The restaurant is right above the beach, with the huge Pacific waves crashing below. As we enter we see big tanks full of all manner of sea creatures, some familiar, some not so familiar. Our experiences at the restaurant outside Sun'chon City in South Korea flash through my mind, but I needn't worry: Allen and Chang make the choice—crab, lobster and shrimps, washed down with pitchers of Taiwan beer. There is much good humour around the table and in looking at the faces of my companions I reflect that we have bonded well, enjoying many experiences in a short time and accomplishing much. Our collections have risen to over 140, fully documented and backed up by herbarium material. We have every reason to be satisfied by what has been achieved so far.

On a road we have travelled before, we soon reach the town of Pinglin, where once again we stop for tea. From here it is a short drive to Taipei and our hotel. Dr Pan is waiting for us, and we spend a good two hours debriefing him. He listens intently, occasionally asking pertinent questions, sometimes in Mandarin and directed towards Allen and Chang; a dark expression clouds his face when we cover the events of our second trip for the Taiwan beech. Pan takes his leave with an invitation to his office on the following day to plan out the next stage of the trip, and we and our baggage are helped upstairs.

We arrive at TFRI headquarters at 8.30 a.m. Our first stop is the laboratory where our seed and herbarium specimens are being held. Happily, they are in excellent condition; the papers have been changed on the herbarium specimens, just as we instructed, and the seeds have been kept in a cool and airy situation. In his office Dr Pan outlines our next objectives. We are to travel south again into the central mountains; our first port of call will be Alishan, a famous mountain known to all the early collectors, including E. H. Wilson, who photographed a famous old red cypress here. From there we will travel on to Yushan, Taiwan's highest mountain. As we will be working at such high elevations, this part of the trip offers us the likelihood of acquiring very hardy material. We are also delighted when Dr Pan offers, without any prompting from us, to help us make a third attempt to find the Taiwan beech. Despite our recent experience we are determined to finally see this tree and, if possible, collect seed.

Once again we are on the road early, accompanied by Allen Chen and Julie. Our driver is Lin Shih Hong, a small, pleasant, though rather reticent man. As before we make rapid progress on the well-surfaced road out of Taipei, and by lunchtime we have reached Chiayi. Once beyond Chiayi the road begins to climb, affording us a good view of the mountaintops rising above the late afternoon cloud. As Alishan is a favourite destination of the Taiwanese people, the road continues to be of excellent quality, and by early evening we are hauling our bags into the forestry lodge that is to be our base for the next few days. We spend the evening wandering around the tourist shops. As with popular holiday areas the world over, the goods are expensive and tacky, and we are soon retracing our steps to our accommodation.

Unfortunately, Tony has been reading the Taiwan guidebook, and I find myself, despite protestations to the contrary, rising at 4.30 a.m. to accompany him and Allen to the top of Alishan to view the sunrise over Yushan. Apparently this is a 'must see' event for anyone visiting the area. Luckily a narrow-gauge railway will take us a good deal of the way. I'm amazed to find how busy it is at such an ungodly hour; we are literally swept along in a tide of humanity. Allen purchases the tickets, and we board the train. By now it is 5.20 a.m.; sunrise is expected at 6.15 a.m. but already it is growing light. There are only one or two Westerners, in addition to ourselves; many of the rest of the overwhelmingly Oriental passengers, not their usual garrulous selves, are in fact falling back to sleep. At the end of the line everybody comes to life and hurries to the summit.

We are all greeted by hordes of traders hawking cheap souvenirs. Tony and I push past them in order to secure a good view. The gathered throng waits expectantly as the first shafts of light appear from behind Yushan (our position lies due west of the mountain). One particularly enterprising hawker is regaling the crowd with stories as he plies he wares; though we cannot understand what he is saying, he is obviously extremely amusing as everyone is in fits of laughter. Sadly one of the major elements of this dawn spectacle, the so-called sea clouds (formed by cold air condensing and descending into the valleys, leaving the mountain peaks exposed above), has not manifested itself today. The sun seems to rise quickly, and overall I'm left with a feeling of disappointment; I'm sure I've seen more impressive sunrises elsewhere.

As swiftly as they arrived the crowds disperse, leaving a handful of religious types who strip to the waist (males only!) and perform an arm-waving ceremony (something to do with the aboriginal peoples of Taiwan, I understand). We decide to

The famous red cypress,
Chamaecyparis formosensis, at
Alishan, 1918
(photograph by E. H. Wilson courtesy Photographic
Archives of the Arnold Arboretum, copyrighted by
the President and Fellows of Harvard College,
Harvard University, Cambridge, Massachusetts)

return on foot, taking the opportunity to botanise along the way. On a mossy outcrop we find a colony of *Ophiopogon formosanus* carrying masses of fleshy, blue-black fruits amongst grassy foliage. As we skirt along the side of the railway Tony notices the bole of a huge tree leaning out from the bankside. Having studied E. H. Wilson's black-and-white photographs of Taiwan, we know this to be tree that he photographed.

It is not exactly the same, however. On enquiring we are told it was struck by lightning many years ago and killed. Now a sapling grows out of its top: apparently the ever optimistic Taiwanese planted a young cypress in the old dead one as a means of securing its immortality.

The same tree in 1992

By now it is 8.30 a.m. and we return to our accommodation to join Julie and Mr Lin for breakfast. Allen has telephoned a friend who knows the area and has indicated that the best natural forests in the area are to be found at Ta Ta Chia, the hillsides above the Yushan National Park visitor centre. This certainly accords with our observations so far, as much of the vegetation in the tourist areas is exotic, with many North American tulip trees and plantations of Japanese cedars. Though there has been a good deal of tree felling and subsequent replanting (not all of it successful) at Ta Ta Chia, the understorey is well developed, and through a hot afternoon we collect *Codonopsis kawakamii*, a scrambling herbaceous species. In wet spots and depressions an astilbe with elegant spikes of reddish flowers is common; it is later identified as *Astilbe macroflora*.

The next day, our last in the Alishan area, we return to Ta Ta Chia. Mr Lin has shown us a path that leads away from the area where we collected the previous day. Visibility is very poor, perhaps less than 50 m (160 ft), and it is raining steadily. Despite this we gather a range of interesting things including *Pieris taiwanensis*. Regarded by many as merely a form of the variable *P. japonica*, this plant is certainly different horticulturally, having larger leaves and more upright panicles of flowers. Clambering amongst the pieris is a vigorous form of *Rosa multiflora*, carrying masses of small red fruits like childrens' marbles. *The Woody Flora of Taiwan* (Li 1963) distinguishes this plant as var. *formosana*, but we can see little difference between this and the familiar *R. multiflora* of cultivation, which was introduced from Japan in the nineteenth century.

In addition to the usual processing of seeds and herbarium specimens and writing up of field notes, we spend that evening preparing for the ascent of Yushan. Julie has to leave us tomorrow, but we are to be joined by two other TFRI officials who will accompany us on the climb. Tony and I are slimming our packs down as much as possible and find to our consternation that no sooner have we removed something than Allen is putting it back in. We have a minor disagreement before finally convincing him that only essential equipment, clothing and food, should be packed.

Thursday, 29 October 1992, dawns fine and warm, which is a relief after the poor conditions of the previous day. We are up by 7.00 a.m. and eat a quick breakfast. Mr Lin takes Julie to the bus station and returns with our two new companions, Ma Fuh Jing and Tze Wen Hsu. The former is particularly friendly and speaks fluent English; we warm to him immediately, and our first impression proves correct, as over the next few days he shows himself to be an intelligent, capable and efficient field guide. Mr Lin takes us by Land Rover to the point where the hiking trail to Yushan begins. The walk starts auspiciously: we collect a fine, strong form of the Taiwan lily, *Lilium formosanum*, by the trailside, its fat, elongated seed pods sticking prominently above the grasses and coarser vegetation. This lily is common throughout the island and occurs almost from sea level to 3000 m (10,000 ft). Not surprisingly with such a distribution, it is variable, mainly in the height it attains; flower size seems to be fairly constant. The dwarfer forms, occasionally referred to as var. *pricei*, were originally collected by English botanist and explorer William Robert Price in 1912, near to our present location. Modern botanical opinion does not support maintaining these genotypes as separate entities as any number of variants between the extremes exist, and thus it is impossible to segregate out consistent characters by which they might be recognised. In the north of the island, however, a very unusual lily with narrow leaves and small flowers occurs; it can be found on dune slacks by the seashore. These distinctions and the isolated position of this plant, therefore, make it well defined; to my knowledge this *L. formosanum* var. *microphyllum* is not in cultivation.

By 10.30 a.m. we are well on our way. The trail starts some way below 3000 m (10,000 ft), and the distance to Paiyun Lodge, where we are to spend the night, is 9 km (6 miles). A steep grade makes the going quite

A view on the ascent of Yushan, just below Paiyun Lodge

tough initially, and the heat of the day adds to our discomfort; within an hour I'm sweating profusely. The path soon levels off, however, allowing a steadier pace to be set and enabling us to catch our breath. Visibility is excellent, affording us marvellous views across the mountains. As we gain height, ridgeline after ridgeline retreats into the distance, each clothed in a green baize of vegetation. We break for lunch at 3010 m (9900 ft) and enjoy half an hour's respite from our efforts. The second half of the climb is harder, as I am tired and the gradient has become steeper again. Fortunately, it is cooler, and this makes things a little more bearable.

Paiyun Lodge nestling amongst the silver fir forest

The kilometres continue to pass, marked by small, wooden posts, until at last I can see the lodge building above. I follow Allen inside and am pleasantly surprised; it has a kitchen, toilets and several dormitories of varying sizes. Though not exactly the Ritz it is quite comfortable considering its remote location. Paiyun Lodge has served the needs of climbers for over a hundred years and provides a profound sense of place, perched as it is high on the shoulder of this magnificent mountain. I wait on the deck for the others to arrive. The view is superb: the lodge sits at 3528 m (11,500 ft), thus my vantage point places me above all but the most prominent surrounding peaks.

Abies kawakamii forming the treeline on Yushan

The grandeur of the landscape is astonishing—I did not imagine that this small island could provide so expansive a panorama. It is late afternoon and the sun is dipping in the sky, casting giant shadows into the depths of the valleys and bringing everything into relief—razor-sharp ridges and craggy peaks cleanly etched against an indigo background. A few hundred metres above I can see the treeline, where the hardy Taiwan fir, *Abies kawakamii*, peters out. It traces a border across the mountainsides, at one point rising higher, perhaps where the shelter of an outcrop affords some protection from the elements, at another point dipping lower. Huge screes cascade down the flanks of the mountains, their shifting surface defeating all but the most tenacious plants.

Tony joins me within a few minutes, but it is another hour before Ma and Hsu turn up. Tony and I drop down the trail and help them with their packs. In short order two small gas stoves are lit, and we enjoy a meal of rice, eel, sausages, potatoes and beef. I am starving after my exertions and tuck in with relish. We have several cups of refreshing green tea before organising ourselves for the night. By now it is 8.30 p.m.; a low-power generator has been running since darkness fell an hour or so before, but it is due to be switched off in half an hour. We share a dormitory with another group of hikers. In the room are two large bunk beds; quilts and pillows are provided. I take a bottom bunk and, not surprisingly given the exertions of the day, fall asleep quickly. A scratching noise close to my ear wakes me up at 1.00 a.m. It is pitch black and cold. Above the snores I hear more scratching and scurrying about—rats. I reach for a torch and catch a pair of eyes twinkling at the end of my sleeping bag. Across the room I see Tony knocking one off the top of his rucksack, where it has been searching out a packet of sausages. The Taiwanese sleep on, seemingly oblivious to the rats' activities. It is hard to settle again; however, though the rats continue to scurry around, they don't climb amongst the sleepers again. At least I don't think they do. As soon as it starts to grow light, I'm up and about with Tony right behind me.

An unappetising breakfast of soggy rice and cold eel doesn't help to improve my mood. Fortunately, the rising sun and clear, crisp mountain air have an immediate therapeutic effect, and we leave the lodge in good spirits for the climb to the summit of Yushan. The path is good but steep, and our progress is steady rather than spectacular. The wonderful scenery affords us the excuse of photography in order to regain our breath. At the tree line the tenacious Taiwan fir finally gives way to low scrubby vegetation dominated by *Juniperus squamata*, here forming fantastic knarled specimens, and *Rhododendron pseudochrysanthum*. The rhododendron becomes increasingly dwarf as we ascend to the top. It was evidently a good spring as the bushes are loaded with ripe capsules, and we make several collections along the way. On the last stretch we have to negotiate an awkward shoulder of rock; a strategically placed length of stout chain aids our climb. The top comprises an area of about 50 m² (60 sq yds) of fairly level rocky ground surmounted by a statue of some pioneering administrative official, whose name now escapes me—I presume his importance was sufficient to give him pride of place at the highest point on the island. We have a tremendous 360° view, completely unhindered by cloud.

The sun is blazing down, and even at this high altitude it is quite warm. How fortunate we have been: when E. H. Wilson completed his ascent of Mount Morrison in October 1918 and stood at the very spot we now occupy, he did so during a tremendous storm and could see nothing, nor did his party dwell for any length of time. Of some concern is the UV effect, as we lack any kind of shelter. I decide to keep my shirt on and raise the collar to protect the back of my neck. Tony is down to his T-shirt and seems quite oblivious to the sun. We spend several hours combing the top; here *Rhododendron pseudochrysanthum* forms extensive mats no more than 10 cm (4 in) high, and with the abundant fruits we are able to make a large collection from the best examples. I know from previous collections of these plants that they retain their dwarf habit in cultivation; thirty-year-old plants in the Savill Garden in Windsor Great Park are no more than 15 cm (6 in) high. Sadly, they are very shy flowering,

Dense mats of *Rhododendron pseudochrysanthum* below the summit of Yushan

and I have not known these same shrubs to flower in the Savill Garden in the seven years I have been observing them. This lack of flowers is partly compensated for by their exquisite young foliage, which is covered with a silvery indumentum as it unfolds. This rhododendron has always been one of my favourite species, combining wonderful foliage with delightful pinkish white trusses of flowers. I first saw it as a student in the marvellous rhododendron collection at the Royal Botanic Garden, Edinburgh, and to see it now in its home environment set high on a magnificent mountain is a thrill indeed.

Nearby, bushes of a dwarf barberry, *Berberis morrisonensis*, yield a few red fruits, which are not easily seen amongst the scintillating oranges and reds of its falling leaves. The ripe capsules of a dwarf willow, *Salix morrisonensis*, are shedding masses of seeds with cottonwool-like appendages. A species of *Anaphalis*, distant relative to the Alpine edelweiss, makes handsome clumps amongst the woody vegetation. By mid afternoon our work on the summit is finished, leaving us time to collect several things we saw on the journey up, a white-flowered clematis being particularly attractive.

Back at Paiyun Lodge in the early evening, we are presented with a scene quite different to the one we left. The whole of the hillside is covered with tents, and people are milling about everywhere. Ma explains that the next two days are important Taiwanese national holidays celebrating the birthday of Chiang Kai-shek, the country's first president and leader of the Kuomintang army that was ousted from the mainland by Mao Zedong's communist Red Army. It seems that, though we are to sleep inside tonight, our berth for the next night is unsecured and we would have to pitch a tent outside. Such a prospect doesn't hold much appeal, and we agree with Ma to cut our visit short. Tomorrow we will make our way back, visiting the lower western peak of Yushan on the way. Once down, however, we will have to walk another 4 or 5 km (2 or 3 miles) to another lodge at Lu Lin, as our rendezvous with Mr Lin isn't planned until the following day.

My concerns about the sun were not misplaced; in the shade and cool of the evening it is clear we have both suffered from excessive exposure to the sun. Tony's face is beetroot red, much to the amusement of our companions. An application of Nivea, provided by Ma, helps, but it is a salutary lesson on the power of the subtropical sun at high elevation. Tony and I elect to prepare the evening meal, and despite the constraints of our situation—two small gas stoves, limited ingredients and an absolute press of humanity all around—we come up with what we think is a creditable sausage risotto and beef and potato stew, though, much to our chagrin, the Taiwanese turn their noses up at it. It is nearly dark now, and the stream of arrivals shows no sign of abating; we watch them from the deck—people of all ages, many completely exhausted and dressed in the most inappropriate clothing. By 8.00 p.m. the lights have been extinguished, and we retire to the dormitory. After last night's problems I elect to join Ma and Hsu on the top bunk; Tony concurs. As soon as this idea is broached, our companions decide they will sleep on the bottom; in the half light I see a knowing smile play across Tony's lips.

I sleep fitfully, sweaty and uncomfortable after the exigencies of the day and the exposure to the sun. I don't hear any rats, but there is a commotion in the main room: a gas stove starts up, pots and pans clang and the smell of fried onions fills the air. I assume it must be dawn, check my watch and find it is 3.30 a.m.! It turns out that a party making an early start on the summit has decided that some breakfast might be a good idea. I manage to fall back to sleep, but Ma wakes me at first light—our friends have had a torrid night with the rats. After a hurried breakfast of beef noodles we leave Paiyun Lodge for the west peak.

Already the sun is climbing high into a cloudless sky. I am hot and sweaty with the effort of walking, and in the pit of my stomach an awful bilious feeling begins to develop. There is little of interest on the west peak, and we begin our descent. I feel progressively worse; this hike is going to be difficult. Tony, by contrast, is in fine fettle, cracking jokes with Ma and Hsu and greeting people on their way up the trail with a cheery smile. His reddish hair and newly red face give rise to amazed looks, followed by roars of laughter. I become aware of a continuous buzzing, which seems to be coming from behind me, but as the trail twists and turns down the mountain, it doesn't abate. I imagine it is some mechanical process being undertaken in a nearby valley. It is unrelenting and becomes irritating—what's more, it seems only I can hear it. It is only when we arrive back at the road that I discover it is my Dictaphone, which got switched on somehow and has run to the end of the tape! I am grateful the descent is over; though I feel marginally better it has been a very unpleasant experience, probably as difficult a day in the field as I have ever had, and the prospect of a further walk to Lu Lin holds no appeal. Fortunately, providence lends a hand in my moment of need. Two men and a young boy who have followed us down have a van parked nearby—do we want a lift to Alishan? We don't need a second invitation. My relief, as we speed along the metalled road, is inexpressible.

By now a mist is falling, and as we arrive back at the tourist area we are greeted by a chaotic scene. The national holiday has brought thousands of people up into the area, and the road is choked with all manner of vehicles and pedestrians. A broken-down coach adds to the traffic jam. The driver is arguing with several policemen and gesticulating wildly; several other people join in, and it seems that Oriental inscrutability is about to be lost and blows exchanged. We disembark from our gridlocked vehicle, and with sincere thanks to our newly found friends, we continue on to the forestry lodge on foot. My spirits rise with a hot bath and a meal, and by the time I turn in I feel almost back to normal.

Taiwan beech scattered along the
ridgeline of Chatien Shan

The following morning we make the long journey back to Taipei; there is little to do other than watch the kilometres go by. As we approach the capital the traffic increases, and we spend the last few hours crawling our way through the early evening rush hour. In all, the journey takes eleven hours, and we are relieved to finally disembark at our hotel. The respite is brief, as next morning Dr Pan arrives to take us on our third attempt to find the Taiwan beech. He is accompanied by Julie and another Mr Chen. We are told that this Mr Chen is a nursery-man who knows the site of the beech trees very well; apparently our efforts so far have been too far to the north, and our starting position this time will be at the southern end of Chatien Shan. This will involve a day's walk in, a night under canvas and a morning amongst the beech trees, with a return walk during the afternoon.

We arrive at the Chatien Shan Forest Recreation area and begin the climb. Chen sets a spanking pace, and we're all winded in a very short time. At twilight we set up camp in a clearing amongst a Japanese cedar planta-tion. The area is strewn with dry fallen timber, and we soon have a fire going. We spend an interesting evening with Dr Pan by its flickering light; he gives us a detailed account of the natural history of the island and much else besides, and finally advises us to get a good night's sleep, as we will have an early start. By 9.00 p.m. we are all settled in our sleeping bags.

Up at 6.00 a.m. and away—it is barely light, and a low mist moves eerily through the campsite, where the last glowing embers of the fire cast a fee-ble light. The tent is left in place, as we intend to return and break camp in the afternoon. The mist lifts, leaving behind a dull, overcast day; the sur-rounding vegetation is dripping wet and our clothing is soon soaked. At

Mark amongst the trunks of
Fagus hayatae

Autumn leaves of the Taiwan beech

1600 m (4600 ft) the vegetation begins to change. So far we have been walking through the typical evergreen broadleaved forest we have become familiar with; now deciduous elements begin to appear. We are delighted to find the recently named *Enkianthus taiwanianus*, here forming a tall, narrow, flat-topped shrub of about 1.8 m (6 ft), its leaves turning a beautiful orangey-red colour. Ample seed allows us to collect and introduce, probably for the first time, this little-known plant. In common with several other plants on Taiwan, there is some disagreement as to the status of this taxon. Some botanists suggest that it is conspecific with the Japanese plant *E. perulatus*. Certainly they appear to be very similar.

A gap in the canopy shows a ridgeline above us topped by the telltale russet-coloured leaves of beech trees in their autumn garb. '*Fagus!*' Dr Pan calls out. I am dubious: given the difficulties we have experienced so far, it seems we have located our quarry too easily. But we have indeed finally reached the elusive Taiwan beech, *Fagus hayatae*. The trees are quite unlike the European beech, in that they do not form tall columnar trunks, with dense canopies, casting a shade that all but eliminates the understorey. Rather the Taiwan beech is a medium-sized tree, with a spreading canopy below which is an almost impenetrable shrubby layer. Whether the stature of the trees is genotypically fixed or is due to their environment is difficult to know. Certainly, though the ridgeline we are on is only at 1750 m (5740 ft), the climate here is a cool one, and the beech trees are exposed to winds coming in from both the Pacific Ocean and the Taiwan Straits to the west.

Though we have found it at last, the Taiwan beech has one more trump card to play: we are too late for seed collection. Even had we found the trees on our first visit, it is unlikely we would have gathered much seed anyway, as so few fruits have developed; and we are even hard-pressed to find any seedlings, such is the density of the understorey. It now becomes clear why this tree is in such a precarious position. The vegetation underneath is composed of broadleaved evergreens which are obviously colonising upwards from the hillsides below; unfortunately the beech are already occupying the highest reaches of the mountain range and can go no further. It seems to us that the Taiwan beech is likely to disappear without human intervention, and it is comforting to be told that the Taiwan authorities, led by the Taiwan Endangered Species Research Institute, have an active programme to conserve this tree.

Whilst considering the plight of the trees, we are still left with the immediate problem of collection. We decide to take a few scions from the trees in the hope that they might be successfully grafted when we return to Kew. We continue collecting into the afternoon. This hilltop has two other gems to yield. *Camellia transnokoensis*, a tall, narrow camellia with small, orbicular leaves is common and has produced masses of crab apple–like fruits; in cultivation it produces small, white, single flowers in great profusion. More striking still and shining like beacons in the gloomy interior of the woods are the sealing wax–red fruits of a skimmia, looking remarkably like the plant collected by Paul Meyer, *Skimmia japonica* subsp. *reevesiana* 'Chilan Choice'. Here it has made a shrub of 2 by 3 m (6.5 by 10 ft) and is plastered with fruits. Unlike other members of the genus, this taxon produces hermaphrodite flowers, rather than only male or female—an important consideration in cultivation, as individual plants can self-pollinate and produce fruit. This Taiwanese genotype of the subspecies *reevesiana*, which is essen-

Skimmia japonica subsp. *reevesiana* in the understorey of the Taiwan beech

tially a mainland Chinese plant, is markedly superior to the two or three other forms known from cultivation, including 'Robert Fortune', a dwarf, spreading cultivar with a weak constitution acquired by Fortune from a Shanghai nursery in 1848.

With the skimmia safely bagged we turn on our heels and head back down. I glance over my shoulder one last time before the brow of the hillside obscures the beech trees. In the deepening mist the trees sit forlornly on the ridge top, like condemned men silently awaiting their fate. By early evening we strike camp and continue down to Dr Pan's waiting car, ready to take us to the warmth and comfort of our Taipei hotel.

The following morning, 4 November 1992, is to be our last foray into the field. Dr Pan arrives early to drive us to the Yangmingshan National Park, which lies just to the north of Taipei. As we disembark we are aware of a strong sulphurous smell; in the distance we can see fumeroles venting foetid gases into the atmosphere. The whole of this area is geologically active, evidence of the great forces being generated as the Philippines plate and Eurasian plate move in opposite directions. The great mountains that

The striking flowers of *Rhododendron nakaharai* in the Savill Garden, Windsor Great Park

have been our home for the last five weeks are another product of these inexorable processes, which will ultimately tear the island in two. Volcanic peaks form an outer circle on the fringe of Yangmingshan and provide a bulwark around the two central cones of Tatun Shan and Chihsing Shan, the latter, at 1120 m (3700 ft), the highest point in the park. Though all these volcanoes are long since extinct, plenty of evidence of geological activity remains; in addition to the fumeroles, hot springs abound in the area.

The day is notable for our collection at 950 m (3100 ft) of the evergreen azalea *Rhododendron nakaharai*—not that we would have discovered it without Pan's help. Knowing this plant and its prostrate habit from cultivation, I imagined it would grow on exposed rock faces. In fact it grows in a community of head-high miscanthus grassland and cannot be found without a very diligent search. This azalea, though only of relatively recent introduction, has found favour with modern breeders not only because it is compact and free-flowering but because it flowers relatively late in the season (June and July) and has flowers of an unusual weathered-brick colour. Numerous excellent hybrids, such as 'Squirrel' and 'Susannah Hill', have been raised

Tony collecting herbarium specimens of *Rhododendron hyperythrum*

from *R. nakaharai*, extending the azalea season into midsummer. What is also remarkable about the plant is its hardiness, given that it occurs at altitudes of under 1000 m (3300 ft).

Yangmingshan also yields another interesting rhododendron, *Rhododendron hyperythrum*. This species, in the subsection *Pontica* of the genus, is very much a connoisseur's plant. It is distinguished amongst other things by the unusual inrolling of the top surface of its leaves, a phenomenon displayed by many rhododendrons in response to freezing or drought conditions, but a permanent feature of this plant. We have already collected this species, a Taiwan endemic, on Chatien Shan, but the two collections are distinct: the Yangmingshan plants have reddish petioles and shoots, whereas the Chatien Shan plant has green petioles and shoots. At first this variable feature seemed to be of academic interest only, that is until they flower in cultivation. The plant from Chatien Shan produces white flowers fairly typical of what is already grown in gardens; by contrast the Yangmingshan collection produces beautiful pink flowers that gradually shade to white, making this a very desirable plant.

The beautiful pink-flowered form of *Rhododendron hyperythrum* flowering in the
National Collection in the Valley Gardens, Windsor Great Park

With these and several other interesting plants gathered, we are well contented. This seemed to be a fitting end to our exertions. Over the next few
days it remains for us to go through the formalities of acquiring export permits, of despatching the herbarium specimens by freight and thanking Dr
Pan and his colleagues for their selfless efforts on our behalf. The latter we
do in some style with a wonderful meal at the Regent Hotel in Taipei. The
food is accompanied, in true Chinese style, with innumerable toasts of rice
wine and much florid language, backslapping and general congratulations.
By the end of the evening we all but fall out into the night air.

We have one last highlight, however, when an old associate from Dr Pan's
institute, Professor Hu, takes us to the National Palace Museum. When first
offered this excursion we are rather lukewarm, feeling that perhaps our time
will be better spent in continued preparations for our departure. On arrival
at the museum, however, this attitude immediately changes. The building is
an imposing traditionally built structure with a sweeping green and yellow
slate roof and tightly mortared biscuit-coloured brickwork. More impressive than the building are its contents. Inside we find the cream of millen-

National Palace Museum in Taipei

nia of Chinese artistry, gallery after gallery of ceramics, paintings, sculptures, tapestries, lacquerwork and calligraphy, the fruits of the patronage of successive Song, Ming and Qing emperors. The collection is breathtaking, and Professor Hu is the perfect guide—knowledgeable, enthusiastic and justly proud, he treats us to what is a memorable day.

Only a tiny fraction of the museum's over 700,000 works of art are on display; the rest, we learn, are contained in huge vaults carved into the hillsides that lie behind the museum. More incredible still is the story of how these riches came to reside in Taiwan. The collection was appropriated from the last of the Qing emperors, Puyi, by the Nationalist Government. When Beijing was threatened by the Japanese after their invasion of Manchuria in 1931, the whole collection was crated up and transported south to Nanjing. When the Japanese menaced Nanjing, the collection moved west to Sichuan Province. When the conflict between the Communists and Chiang Kai-shek's Kuomintang escalated, the collection was re-sorted and its most valuable works were sent to Taiwan. The National Palace Museum was built to house the collection, opening its doors in 1965. The whole collection represents a potent symbol for the nationalists of Taiwan of their Chinese heritage and a black stain of dishonour for mainland communists, who feel its rightful place is in Beijing. We don't get into the politics of it—we just marvel at its beauty.

The following day, with everything packed, we are taken to the airport by Dr Pan and Julie and take our final leave with grateful thanks. On the flight back we have ample time to take stock of our efforts: 201 collections of plant material, ninety-eight percent of which is seed. We have gathered good collections of plants that are barely represented in cultivation (such as the Taiwanese maples), plants that are not growing in Western gardens (*Enkianthus taiwanianus*, for example) and new genotypes of plants that are already established. Taiwan has more than lived up to its promise.

As ever we return with a great sense of expectation. We haven't seen our families for nearly six weeks, our only contact being an occasional snatched telephone conversation. Once customs is cleared we emerge into the arrivals lounge to be greeted by Lesley and Callum with Sally and Jennifer immediately behind. This tearful reunion draws an appropriate line under our Taiwan adventure and provides a springboard to our next challenge.

CHAPTER 5

To Russia with Trepidation

IGOR SMIRNOV WAS A BIG MAN. He filled the doorway, casting a broad shadow into the tiny, cramped office of Peter Wyse-Jackson; Tony and I looked at him with a combination of awe and apprehension. 'Hallo', he boomed, in a voice worthy of his impressive frame. He entered the office and sat down heavily in a chair that was clearly inadequate for him. I'm sure I felt the room shake.

It was the early summer of 1993, and with the expedition to Taiwan well and truly wrapped up we had returned to our ongoing expeditions schedule. Our research had suggested that the extreme far east of the Russian Federation—Ussuriland, the very name had a menacing ring to it—was an area that would provide rich rewards if it were possible to travel and collect there. Fortuitously we had a lead once again. A casual conversation with Peter Wyse-Jackson, who as secretary of Botanic Gardens Conservation International (BGCI) occupied a suite of rooms in Descanso House, an historic building at Kew, had set matters in motion. Peter was developing contacts with botanic gardens in the newly formed Russian Federation and its allied countries. Igor Smirnov of the Main Botanical Garden in Moscow had emerged as a key figure in this rapprochement. Peter had arranged for

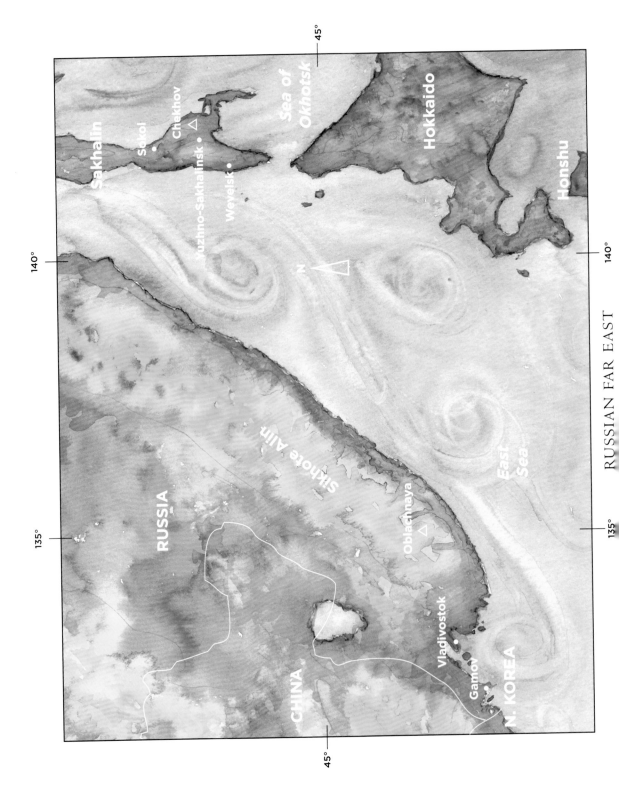

RUSSIAN FAR EAST

us to meet Igor, who was in England on BGCI business, and had kindly loaned us his office for this occasion.

I led the discussions, having rehearsed my intended spiel with Tony beforehand. Igor sat and listened, his face an impassive, emotionless mask. As I rambled on he asked no questions, made no remarks or gestures—he just sat, expressionlessly, and listened. I remember thinking to myself that this wasn't going well and that I needed to finish quickly, if only for the sake of the chair, which was visibly straining under the weight of its burden. With my proposal concluded we waited for Igor to say something. His expression remained fixed and unresponsive. I glanced hesitantly at Tony, who shrugged his shoulders, as if to say 'I don't know what to do either'. Almost grudgingly Igor spoke, his thick Russian accent difficult to follow. 'So you want to go to Ussuriland'. The question was rhetorical. 'Well, you might as well add a visit to Sakhalin Island as well if you are going so far. I know just the person. Peter Gorovoy of the Far East Branch of the Russian Academy of Sciences will take you there'. His voice had risen almost triumphantly as he progressed. We sat back stunned. 'Let us drink to the success of this collaboration'. And with that he produced a bottle of Polish vodka from beneath his voluminous great coat. It was 10.30 in the morning and we were officially at work. Igor would brook no excuses, and so we toasted our hoped-for success with two or three shots of neat vodka. 'Slangibar!'

I ponder this meeting as we sit in the departure lounge at Heathrow Airport. Today is 8 September 1994. The PA system announces the imminent departure of the Korean Air flight to Seoul, and we make our way to the boarding gate. I sense that Tony is as apprehensive as I; this feels very much like a journey into the unknown. Not that we are ill-prepared. Igor has emerged as an organiser par excellence: our itinerary cannot be faulted, our contacts are well briefed and everything seems in good order. Perhaps my apprehension is a result of the rather unusual way that Igor has made the arrangements. Tony received a call in the early summer of 1994; it was Igor. His instructions were precise and clear, like something from a James Bond movie. Elvira Boiko will be attending the International Compositae conference at Kew. We are to give her a fifty-percent advance on the agreed costs for the trip. It is to be in small-denomination notes. She is not to know what is in the bag. Igor will do the rest. To say this is unorthodox is more than understating the case. Never in the history of Kew expeditionary work has such a transfer taken place. The Finance Department are aghast. We seek some assurances and explanations from Igor. No problem, he tells us. Once received, an official receipt will be issued; the money will be fully substantiated in post-expeditionary accounts; it is needed in order that preparatory work can be done—equipment needs to be purchased, accommodation reserved, permits acquired. The Finance Department are somewhat mollified, though they still require a full written and signed explanation before they will release one penny. Sure enough Elvira attends the conference and returns to Moscow with the money. True to his word, Igor issues us with an official-looking receipt.

A second source of apprehension concerns our flight arrangements. During the early 1990s, aeroplanes of the old Soviet airline, Aeroflot, had a rather disconcerting habit of falling out of the sky. This happened with such regularity that, on the advice of the Civil Aviation Authority, the Foreign Office began to insist that UK nationals not use this airline. This presented a problem, as the vast majority of flights to Vladivostok, our destination in the Russian Far East, were by Aeroflot. Fortunately, we were able to book the single alternative, Korean Air through Hong Kong and the South Korean capital, Seoul. Diplomatically Tony and I decided to keep these rather alarming peregrinations from our families. We were now up to two children each following the births of Sophie Flanagan in December 1992 and Robert Kirkham in April 1993.

My thoughts are broken by the urgings of a flight attendant, who ushers me through the gate and onto the 747. The flight to Seoul is interminable but event-free. The transit stop through Hong Kong is speedily accomplished. We enter the arrivals lounge at Seoul, jaded and somewhat disoriented. An obliging porter takes our luggage. We are immediately assailed by an overwhelming smell of garlic, which seems to be expiring from every pore of the man's body. I am reminded of the extensive use of this bulb in eastern cuisine. Tony's aside makes me smile: 'The sooner we eat some garlic the better'.

We seek a hotel for the night and are directed to a bus that takes us to a modest but clean and comfortable establishment. It is 7.30 p.m. and quite dark. We leave the hotel immediately to find somewhere to eat. The city has a familiar feel to it, not surprising given that it is less than five years since we were last here. Though large and cosmopolitan, Seoul offers visitors a safe and secure ambience few capital cities can match. We dine on our favourite Korean dish of bulgogi; as it is fried at the table, Tony notes with satisfaction the large number of garlic cloves in the sauce. We return to our hotel to try and get some sleep before the final leg of

Korean Air flight 9345, our mystery flight to Vladivostok!

our journey to Vladivostok in the morning. Unfortunately, though the local time is nearly midnight my body clock is still reading late afternoon, and it takes me some time to fall to sleep. (I dream that I am an overseas salesman for a garlic grower from the Isle of Wight!)

After a light breakfast we head back to the airport. Our sense of foreboding is heightened when we look at the departures board: our Korean Air flight number, time and gate are listed but the destination is an ominous blank! Even more peculiar: having landed at Vladivostok Airport after a short flight and negotiated the steps to the tarmac, we set off walking toward the terminal building, little more than 60 m (180 ft) away. A burly official bars our way. Nonplussed, we glance around; a wry smile creases the face of one seasoned South Korean traveller. Almost immediately a large, well-armoured coach swings from behind the building and heads towards us. We are gestured on. Once everyone is aboard, the vehicle drives away from the terminal, in the opposite direction, and treats us all to a tour of the airfield, arriving back at the starting point after about five minutes. We never do discover the reason for this bizarre and pointless journey. We walk to the terminal.

Vladivostok Airport presages what we are to see throughout our time in Russia. Lack of ongoing investment has reduced what was clearly a perfectly acceptable building when first constructed into a decaying structure with broken paving stones, nonfunctioning facilities and jerry-built additions. This degree of decay contrasts with the warm welcome we receive from our hosts, Elvira Boiko and Peter Gorovoy, who have come to meet us. The

Peter Gorovoy

Sergei Lobanov

latter is short but solidly built with a shock of greying hair. Both are all smiles and handshakes and rapidly take control of what is rather a chaotic scene. Our baggage is reclaimed, and we are whisked outside and into a waiting van. The driver, Sergei Lobanov, is even more demonstrative, pumping my hand and slapping my back. When he kisses Tony on both cheeks, I detect a mild flushing of the Kirkham countenance.

Our hotel is about 20 km (14 miles) distant, and along the way we familiarise ourselves with the roadside vegetation. It looks extremely promising. We recognise the grey-green leaves of *Maackia amurensis*, clearly just past flowering; the large, imposing compound leaves of the Manchurian walnut, *Juglans mandshurica*; another compound-leaved tree that we take to be *Fraxinus mandshurica*; and the unmistakable silver-striated bark of *Acer tegmentosum*, a choice maple.

The hotel is a huge building, and though it is well presented and our rooms are clean and comfortable, it is cold and impersonal. Few other guests seem to be in residence. The afternoon is well advanced, and Peter and Elvira are anxious to show us around the city, but before this, we have to

Vladivostok's tram system

organise the flight to Sakhalin. Unfortunately, we have no choice but to fly by Aeroflot; as the flight is still some weeks away, I put the darker thoughts to the back of my mind. Peter, who is a native, escorts us through Vladivostok with evident pride, taking us to various vantage points from which we can look out over the port and towards the surrounding hills. My quick impression is that the city developed as an elegant imperial port with broad streets, attractive palladian buildings and good general amenities, to which the communists added substandard buildings with a preponderance of concrete tower blocks and dull, grey administrative buildings. Sadly the city is pervaded by an air of neglect, though some positive developments are to be seen. The stylish and ornate railway station, the terminus of the famous Trans-Siberian railway, is being restored by an Italian consortium who are clearly doing an excellent job, and the tram system, responsible for the city's sobriquet 'The San Francisco of Asia', is clean and efficient.

The view over the port is especially impressive. It provides an excellent, sheltered, deep-water anchorage and easy access to the Pacific Ocean. The remnants of the once mighty Soviet Pacific Fleet lie at anchor. Most of the

The remnants of the Soviet Pacific Fleet

warships appear to be dilapidated hulks and a thought flashes through my mind—'Surely this isn't the Red threat that has kept the West on edge for fifty years?' We enjoy a pleasant snack of bread, cheese, salami and sprats washed down by lashings of hot, sweet tea. We have an enviable position on a knoll above the port, and in the warm, bright sunshine we engage in some small talk with Peter and Elvira.

Peter returns us to the hotel, where he sets out his plans for the forthcoming weeks. He is clearly enthusiastic about the trip, and we are amazed to learn that he has already visited the various sites that will make up our itinerary, including a visit to Sakhalin, in order to ensure that everything goes smoothly. The plan is to collect in close proximity to Vladivostok for a week or so before travelling north and east to the Sikhote Alin Mountains, the range that flanks the East Sea. This part of the trip will culminate in an ascent of Oblachnaya (Cloudy Mountain), the highest point in the southern part of the range. We will then return to Vladivostok, whence we'll take the short flight to Sakhalin. We are to spend ten days on the island.

The menace of the mosquito

The following morning we are on our way. Peter arrives with two vehicles, one a large ex–Soviet army truck complete with canvas-covered back, and the other a Japanese utility van. He introduces us to our team: Sergei, whom we have already met; Oleg Dmitrov, a small, balding man in his mid thirties who is generally called Alec; and Anatoly Zshdanov, who is tall and lean with a taciturn nature and glowering expression. We travel east on a solid metalled road. The traffic is light and we make good progress, stopping occasionally for provisions. By early afternoon we arrive at our first collecting site by a shallow river 2 km (1¼ miles) west of the small town of Steklyanukha. Whilst Sergei and Alec set up the site and prepare for our evening meal, Tony and I disappear into the woods with Peter.

It is still and warm, and the air hangs heavy with moisture. Immediately I hear the all-too-familiar buzzing of mosquitoes, and we are soon assailed by swarms of the creatures. Peter seems unconcerned and merely swats at them lazily. I'm less fortunate, and their sharp, painful bites produce angry lesions on all the exposed parts of my body—hands, face and neck. An application of repellent cools their ardour and allows me to carry on with a modicum of comfort. The woods are rich and varied. Tall trees of *Juglans mandshurica* arch above us, huge bunches of big, round fruits hang from their canopies. The Mongolian oak jostles for position with *Betula davurica*, whose peeling bark makes for an impressive sight. Occasional specimens of the tall, graceful silver lime, *Tilia mandshurica*, add to the diversity. We come across huge, old trees of *Phellodendron amurense*, the Amur cork tree, which must be 25 m (75 ft) tall, their deeply furrowed bark distinguishing them from all the trees around them.

As we press deeper into the woods I become aware of the amazing wealth of the ground flora. It is clear that a fire swept through these woods some years ago, creating large gaps in the canopy. In well-lit clearings a whole host of choice and interesting herbaceous plants have flourished. Though our research suggested that Ussuriland was likely to be rich in hardy perennials, I hadn't imagined they would grow together in such profusion. An exquisite oak fern (*Gymnocarpium* sp.) grows cheek by jowl with the slipper orchid, *Cypripedium macranthos*; the peculiar non-climbing sweet pea *Lathyrus davidii* scrambles over *Convallaria keiskei*, a far-eastern relative of the well-known lily of the valley. The last few magenta flowers of *Lychnis fulgens* are fading whilst, rising above, the airy white wands of *Cimicifuga dahurica* are only just opening. Tallest of all are the flat heads of *Angelica gigas*, a wonderful biennial with plum-coloured flowers, though here now ripening its copious seed. The choicest plant is the dainty *Jeffersonia dubia*, which in the West is generally grown in the peat garden, where its rather exacting requirements can be met. It seems to like a cool root run and dappled shade with a high degree of humidity. Interestingly its nearest relative is the twinleaf, *J. diphylla*, a native of the faraway Great Smoky Mountains of Tennessee and the adjacent Appalachians. Being first collected in North America, the genus commemorates Thomas Jefferson, president of the United States and a principal author of the Declaration of Independence. This is the first, though not the last, time we are to see a genus with closely related species in both eastern North America and the Russian Far East.

The time flies by, but the distant shouts of Alec and Sergei bring us back to reality, and I realise that I'm more than ready for some food. Rain is falling intermittently, though the temperature remains high, and the mos-

Dinner at Steklyanukha

quitoes are numerous: they must enjoy ideal conditions for breeding and development. The only consolation is that this is not a malarial area, though the earlier bites I suffered continue to swell, particularly on my hands. Tony complains that he has been bitten through his shirt, and when he pulls it up the whole of his back is covered in angry red wheals.

Back at the base Alec, Sergei and Anatoly have been busy. Above a roaring fire they have made a delicious stew, full of big chunky potatoes. We eat hungrily and finish the meal off with big mugs of hot tea. Sadly the mosquitoes do not abate, and I am not sorry when we break camp and climb into the vehicles. Twilight is gathering as we follow the riverside track back onto the road. We journey on for two hours, eventually arriving at the town of Lozovoy, where we put up at a dilapidated 'hotel' that Peter says is used by Olympic athletes. We have no reason to doubt his word but wonder at the ability of the athletes, given the primitive conditions they must train and live in.

We begin our evening routine, developed over the last two trips, of herbarium pressing and seed processing. Though at times onerous, this is a vital part of expeditionary work and a useful way to continue to familiarise

Recording field notes with the GPS
and Dictaphone

oneself with the local flora. This year, for the first time, we have brought a Global Positioning System. This device locates orbiting satellites and, by a triangulation process, establishes a position to within a few metres, making the determination of latitude and longitude, a key part of the field notes, easy. After a couple of hours of steady work, we enjoy a nightcap of whisky and end what has been an interesting and productive first day.

A dull but rising pain in my hands wakes me at first light. They are badly swollen and tender to the touch, so I reapply the proprietary insect-bite cream I used last night and catch a hurried breakfast with the others before driving to our collecting site for the day. We emerge from a densely wooded area onto a broad sandy beach. The sun has risen high into the sky, and it is pleasantly warm. The mountains are behind us and the azure sea, spangled with perhaps a dozen verdant islands, glistens before us—the scene is very beautiful. It is striking how few people there are around, which is a theme repeated throughout our time in the Russian Far East: this is a huge area with a small population. A lugubrious oil tanker intrudes on our idyll, slowly crossing the bay in front of us; Peter tells us that the industrial port of Nadhodka is just around the promontory to our right.

The mountain behind us is called Sestra Mountain, which Sergei tells us means 'sister mountain'. Tony jokingly wonders what happened to brother mountain. Peter points nonchalantly to what appears to be a quarry. 'Oh, they blew it up and took it all away for road making'. Tony and I look at each other in utter disbelief: a 300-m (1000-ft) eminence has simply vanished off the map. We begin the climb up the sibling-less Sestra. Once again we are struck by the richness of the herbaceous ground flora, with many plants familiar from our gardens. The inflated blue flowers of *Platycodon grandiflorus* are prominent, along with two turkscap lilies, now carrying their fruiting heads. Narrow leaves in dense whorls mark one out as *Lilium tenuifolium*, whilst we also identify *L. callosum*, a plant with a huge natural distribution and here close to its northern limit. *Allium senescens* is also common as is the unusual *Clematis hexapetala*, its tough leathery leaves and non-climbing habit making it very distinct from the more familiar climbing clematis of cultivation. The white flowers with seven petals account for its specific epithet.

Platycodon grandiflorus in flower on Sestra Mountain

Woody plants are by no means neglected, and once again we are fortunate to secure a good seed harvest. The canopy is formed by a somewhat stunted association of *Fraxinus chinensis* subsp. *rhyncophylla*, *Tilia amurensis* and *Quercus mongolica*, with occasional trees of the Korean white pine, *Pinus koraiensis*, particularly in the higher reaches. None of the trees are more than 10 m (30 ft) in height, and we put this down to the exposed position of the mountain, based on the assumption that its southeastern aspect is likely to make it prone to storms coming off the sea—not that this is a problem today, which has remained warm and sunny. The peak lies at just above 300 m (1000 ft) and affords us a wonderful panoramic view out to sea and back inland. A river is lazily discharging into the sea, its muddy waters gradually blending into the deep blue of the bay. Remarkably we can see thousands of Pacific salmon running up the river to their spawning grounds upstream. Tony, a dedicated fisherman, is very excited and enquires about the possibility of a spot of salmon fishing. 'Not today', says Peter, apparently an equally keen angler, 'but certainly in the next few days'. We spend about an hour on the top and on several of the radiating, narrow spurs, which run in all directions. Our last collection is a hummocky conifer with an occasional arching shoot that we decide is *Juniperus rigida*.

A rapid descent sees us back at the beach by early evening, and we enjoy a fish (locally caught!) and potato soup as the sun sinks behind one of the offshore islands. All around us are masses of *Rosa rugosa*, some with oversize fruits, and this becomes our last collection of the day. We marvel at the ability of this shrub to thrive in almost pure sand and in the salt air.

That night is spent at the Hotel Sport, as we have nicknamed it. I am still suffering from swollen hands, and the temporary relief I gained from the insect cream has disappeared. Sergei appears with some Russian 'baby cream' and, rather sceptically, I apply it. Remarkably, I gain almost instant relief, and by morning my hands have more or less returned to normal. Breakfast is cheese and salami with bread, and then we are off for the nearby Chandolas range, a group of limestone hills that Peter promises have a distinctive and interesting flora. We are not disappointed, and by the end of the day have made over thirty collections.

The walk into these hills is a pleasant and, at first, easy stroll. Along the track tall trees of the Dahurian birch, *Betula davurica*, are common, their mainly black trunks peeling to reveal the younger creamy bark underneath. This tree often proves difficult in cultivation, frequently exhibiting a twiggy canopy full of dead wood. This seems to be a consequence of early bud break: in mild spells in England it can be in leaf in February; unfortunately, later frosty conditions kill back this early growth, producing the dead-wood canopy. More continental climates, such as the northeastern United States, suit it better, and it can make a striking specimen when well grown. It has a near relative in the woody flora of eastern North America—the river birch, *B. nigra*—and the two can be difficult to tell apart. The larger, more triangular leaves with prominent toothing of the latter generally prove to be diagnostic. Indeed, one of our hopes for this trip is that the material we collect may prove more amenable in the British Isles. The unpredictable seasons of a maritime climate can trick plants that are used to more fixed climatic patterns at both ends of the season, encouraging both early bud break and early leaf fall. Perhaps these coastal collections will have a greater degree of adaptability.

The daimio oak, *Quercus dentata*

Another birch, the white-barked *Betula platyphylla* var. *mandshurica*, is also common and mixes with cork trees, ash and *Acer pictum*, an attractive maple with cleanly fashioned five-, or occasionally seven-, lobed leaves. Great swags of the Amur grape, *Vitis amurensis*, drape the trees, and their heavy clusters of ripe fruits are eaten with relish by Sergei, who is up ahead. Tony and I follow up quickly to ensure that some are left for us to collect. Another interesting tree is also common; indeed, in parts it forms almost pure stands. The daimio oak, *Quercus dentata*, grows on Japan, in Korea (where we gathered it on Namhae Island in 1989) and in China; Peter tells us that this is the most northerly occurrence of this species and that the nearest trees to this point are 200 km (120 miles) to the south. In gardens, where it is valued for its large, attractive leaves, it forms a broad spreading tree often wider than it is tall; our previous collection in South Korea has this typical habit. These Russian trees, by contrast, are much taller and shapelier, with several individuals above 18 m (60 ft) in height.

The track so far has been relatively even, but it soon begins to climb, and off to the right a much steeper hillside rises up. Almost immediately Peter leaves the track, and we push up this incline through dense waist-high vegetation. Peter turns to us and says, with real gravitas, 'Be careful, there are snakes'. Tony glances over his shoulder at me. Straightaway I see a small dark brown snake sliding away from me in the undergrowth. At regular intervals on the way up we see sloughed-off brown skins, some over 1 m (3 ft 3 in) in length. Seeking some reassurance, I ask for confirmation that they are not poisonous. 'They are *very* poisonous', says Peter. The Chandolas range is rapidly losing its appeal.

There is little to collect as we climb, and it is a hard slog to the summit, which we are relieved to reach. Basking in the hot sun, on top of the low scrubby vegetation, is an evil-looking yellow and black snake, which has to be strongly encouraged to move on. 'Very, *very* poisonous', declares Peter. Sergei matter-of-factly spreads out a piece of canvas and serves our lunch. My appetite has rather diminished, and Tony also seems less than enthusiastic. Thankfully Peter doesn't dwell too long, and we're soon on the move again, walking in a westerly direction along the ridgeline. Our collecting continues unabated. Amongst the more interesting plants is a species of Solomon's seal that Peter insists is endemic to these limestone hills; he knows it as *Polygonatum dessoulavyi*. Further along, the prominent red, open fruits of *Paeonia lactiflora* are found, with two more lilies, *Lilium distichum* and *L. dauricum*.

A suckering maple is easily identified as the bearded maple, *Acer barbinerve*, whilst nearby is a majestic 18-m (60-ft) specimen of the snake-bark maple, *A. tegmentosum*. The day ends with a collection of yet another familiar maple, the Amur maple, *A. ginnala* (regarded by some authorities as a form of the near-eastern maple, *A. tataricum*). It makes a multi-stemmed specimen, more shrub than tree, and is notable for its outstanding flame-red autumn colour; indeed, a superior clone has been selected in cultivation and named 'Flame'. It is also extremely hardy, and I well remember good specimens of *A. ginnala* (labelled *A. tataricum* subsp. *ginnala*) in the demanding climate of Calgary Zoo, where few other nonnative plants were flourishing.

Back along the forest track we are greeted with a smile by Alec, who hands us bowls of a somewhat evil-smelling barley and fish mash. Its taste is improved by the addition of a fierce chilli sauce. By now it is past eight o'clock, and we jump into Alec's truck for the short journey back to the Hotel Sport. We have reasonable time to complete our end-of-day tasks before turning in. Peter pops his head around our door to inform us that tomorrow we will leave for our next destination and we should pack our bags.

The following morning we breakfast quickly and are on the road by 9.00 a.m. The further we travel from Vladivostok, the worse the quality of the roads. This particular stretch is full of huge potholes, which Anatoly does well to avoid. The constant bouncing around is tiresome and

Acer tegmentosum in the Valley Gardens, Windsor Great Park

does little for our vehicle's suspension, and Anatoly has to stop twice to replace punctured tyres before we reach our destination. We are approaching the southern end of the Sikhote Alin Mountains and are climbing at a modest but steady rate. Remarkably, the warm, dry conditions still prevail, allowing us to see a good way into the distance. The mountains form a low, continuous range somewhat reminiscent of the Pennines in the north of England; certainly there are no dramatic peaks visible. One key difference, however, is the heavily forested nature of the Sikhote Alin: as far as we are able to see, the trees stretch unbroken into the distance, with subtle changes in texture and colour as the deciduous trees on the lower slopes give way to the conifers higher up.

The road follows the course of the Partisansk River, which at first is broad and lazy; as we climb, it becomes more agitated until, at our point of disembarkation, it is a tumbling brook, sparkling in the sunshine. Sergei points to our destination, a peculiar rock formation atop one of the low ridges—Click Mountain. He tells us that this translates as 'tooth mountain',

Taking a breather on Click Mountain

and it is easy to see by its shape how the name was inspired. Once off the road the going becomes very tough very quickly; the vegetation quickly envelops us and the track is barely discernible. We climb steadily, and soon I'm puffing and blowing like an old man; it is some consolation that Tony is equally out of shape.

Once again I'm surprised and delighted by the vegetation. Not only is it almost pristine, but the diversity of woody and herbaceous species is outstanding. Running along the ground is a plant I do not expect to see. The mountain cornel, *Cornus suecica*, is a rare British native plant that inhabits the high moors in the north of England and, more extensively, the Scottish Highlands. Though I knew that it also extended onto mainland Europe, I hadn't imagined its distribution took it across the great Eurasian landmass to the very edge of Asia. But here in the Russian Far East it is native and quite at home, forming extensive carpets and topped with its characteristic strawberry-like fruits. As if to confuse me still further, another link with North America presents itself: we encounter spiny thickets of *Oplopanax elatus*, which seems to like the wetter spots, where it forms formidable colonies. So densely set with spines are the stems that it is impossible to touch them without experiencing pain. The North American species *O. horridus*, equally fearsome, is given the common name of devil's club. I have seen this plant in the forests of British Columbia in very similar situations, and the two species must be closely related.

Young trees of *Betula costata* are common and very striking with their pinkish, peeling bark. In my experience, this is a difficult tree in cultivation; our previous collection from South Korea germinated freely and grew well in its early stages, before exhibiting a complete loss of vigour and attendant die-back. I suspect that old, healthy trees so named in

Young specimens of *Betula costata*

gardens are, in fact, of hybrid origin, presumably with either *B. pendula* or *B. pubescens* as the paternal parent. We are thrilled to see another tree noted for its attractive bark, the Manchurian cherry, *Prunus maackii*. More subtle than the better known *P. serrula*, a native of the Himalaya and western China, the Manchurian cherry has a paler trunk with less prominent lenticels. A clone known as 'Amber Beauty' is occasionally seen in collections and is a choice tree of the first rank. Amongst these cherry trees on Click Mountain are individual genotypes which are as good as or better than anything we know from cultivation, many exhibiting a notably darker bark. With no seed to be seen anywhere, we break with our normal expedition practise and collect scion wood from one of the better forms.

Perhaps the tree of the day is a maple, *Acer caudatum* subsp. *ukurunduense*. It occurs as an understorey plant, never more than 6 or 7 m (20 to 25 ft) tall, and is developing the most wonderful autumn shades of apricot and salmon, much more subtle than the usual flaming yellows, oranges and reds that many maples exhibit. This species further reinforces the link with North America as it has a counterpart in the Appalachian mountains of the

The wonderful autumn tints of *Acer caudatum* subsp. *ukurunduense*

eastern United States, *A. spicatum*, the specific epithet of which alludes to its spicate or upright flower clusters. This feature is common to both species and distinguishes them from most others in the genus which have hanging flowers.

Unfortunately, it is impossible to climb the 'tooth' as the faces of this slab of rock are almost vertical; however, our vantage point is sufficiently high to afford us wonderful views across the whole of the southern Sikhote Alin, including the considerable bulk of Oblachnaya, which, Sergei informs us, is to be our next destination. In the fading light we make our way back to our support vehicles, where Alec and Anatoly have been busy with yet another improvised soup. Unusual but delicious, this potato, sausage and chilli-sauce soup is no product of haute cuisine, but right now it is just what is needed and we eat voraciously.

Once finished we are on the road again. Peter tells us that we are to stay at Field Station Cloudy, which lies close to the foot of Oblachnaya. Unfortunately, he has underestimated the journey time, and we don't arrive until well past midnight. Field Station Cloudy is a collection of timber shooting lodges in a clearing in the all-pervading forest. The cabins themselves are well constructed and reasonably clean. We are given a large cabin that we share with Peter and Sergei; Alec and Anatoly stay with their vehicles.

Peter informs us that the 'station chief' would like to meet us, and we are ushered through the inky night into an adjacent cabin. Inside it is warm and well lit—and it is immediately obvious that most of the occupants are blind drunk. The chief is a bear of a man, not tall but with a great bulk, huge bushy beard and arms like tree trunks. He staggers towards us, standing finally on a seemingly lifeless figure on the ground (who gives out a muffled grunt) before enveloping Tony in a crushing embrace. I'm next and endure a similar greeting; at his final approach (the second kiss), I notice the grease and bits of meat which are stuck to his beard and am almost overwhelmed by the alcoholic fumes on his breath. He gestures to some seats next to a pot-bellied stove, which is giving off a tremendous heat. Glancing around, I take in the rest of the company, men of similar stamp and appearance. All are smiling, that smile which fixes the features just before stupefaction takes over; indeed, one poor soul hits the floor almost at that instant. Nobody turns a hair.

Peter is talking the whole time in Russian; he explains that he has been telling the chief about us and our activities. The chief offers us vodka and long skewers of barbecued venison. It is clear he is not going to take no for an answer. The vodka, a drink I am not partial to, burns all the way to my stomach; the kebabs, by contrast, are delicious, and we are offered a second skewer. Peter tells us that the men are hunters, and I can see the many rifles leaning against the walls of the cabin. The situation is not entirely comfortable, though Peter seems perfectly at ease and Sergei is laughing and joking with anyone sober enough to understand him. I gesture to Tony, indicating that we ought to take our leave, and through Peter we make our apologies, taking the short walk in the cool of the early hours to our cabin. It is after 2.00 a.m. and I'm exhausted. Tony seems to be dead on his feet, and we are grateful to turn in. I am vaguely aware of Peter and Sergei staggering in later, after what seems like hours.

Not surprisingly, there is no movement from our cabin until 9.30 a.m. Sergei is the first to rise and busies himself whilst quietly singing some melancholy Russian dirge. I follow him out into the warm sunshine to be joined by Tony almost immediately. The events of the night before seem almost surreal; there are no signs of the hunters, remarkably they have all already left, though in what sort of state I can only imagine. A tributary of the Ussuri River wends its way through the forest behind the camp, and Tony and I wander down. It is a lovely picture, the sunshine punching holes through the canopy of trees and sparkling on the water. One immense tree on the opposite bank catches our eye; it is clearly a poplar, but it is only when we examine it closely that we realise it is *Populus maximowiczii*. We have already encountered several poplars on our travels over the last week, but this tree is rather special. E. H. Wilson knew this species to be one of the biggest deciduous trees in the Pacific areas of temperate Asia, and the tree we are looking at would certainly hold its own with any other. Not only is it tall, perhaps in excess of 40 m (130 ft), it also has a huge girth; obviously its position on the river bank provides it with ample moisture.

The tree is named for a remarkable Russian botanist of German extraction, who, unlike the frequently eulogised Wilson, is barely known in Britain or the United States. Carl Johan Maximowicz became conservator of the celebrated St Petersburg Botanical Garden in 1852 at the age of twenty-five.

With the encouragement of C. A. Meyer, the institute's director, he joined the frigate *Diana* on its journey to reinforce the Russian naval presence in the seas off the coast of the far-eastern edge of Asia. This in itself required a virtual circumnavigation of the earth. He spent three years botanising in the Amur and Ussuri river basins at a time when this area was absolutely undeveloped wilderness and still technically a part of the Chinese Empire. He returned by the overland 'post road' to St Petersburg. In 1859 he set off on a second great journey east to Manchuria and Japan. Unusually for the time, when botanists concentrated on collecting herbarium specimens, he sent a good deal of seed back to his botanic garden, and many far-eastern plants were introduced to Europe in this way. In his middle and later years he provided botanical support to a new generation of field botanists, whose names are commemorated in the plants he described—Tschonoski (*Malus tschonoskii*), Przewalski (*Ligularia przewalskii*) and Potanin (*Rhus potaninii*), the latter of whom travelled everywhere with his equally intrepid wife, Alexandra Victorovna. Tony and I pay due reverence to the poplar, not just for its majestic proportions but to honour the great man whom it commemorates.

Over breakfast Peter tells us that we will be climbing Oblachnaya tomorrow but that he is not confident he can lead us to the top and back himself and therefore must engage the services of a local guide. He intends to ask for help in a local village, which gives us the rest of the day free. The warm conditions are perfect for enabling us to air our clothes and sleeping bags and to change the papers on the herbarium specimens. We spend a productive morning and early afternoon sorting everything out. It is gratifying to know that everything is in good order. Peter returns by 2 o'clock, having found a suitable guide who will join us for the evening meal. After lunch we take a walk along the river and spend a few leisurely hours browsing through the forest. *Prunus maackii* is abundant, but again we can find no seed, concluding that it must ripen its fruits much earlier and that these are quickly taken by the birds. There is evidence of the activity of wild pigs; in clearings in the forest we can see where they have made huge gouges in the soil, no doubt digging up roots. Once Tony thinks he sees a huge boar skulking in the trees, its hairy snout sniffing the air periodically; I look carefully but see nothing.

Back at the camp our guide arrives at 6.00 p.m. His name is Fedor, and he comes complete with a Kalashnikov rifle. He looks suitably mean and moody; Peter tells us that he is from Poland and a hunter by profession. He is accompanied by his Russian wife, Natalia, who also looks mean and moody, with one of those 'lived-in' faces that is full of character. Fedor's main quarry is deer, and he has a government licence to shoot a certain number each year. We clamber into Alec's truck and set off up the rough track that leads out of Field Station Cloudy: Peter wants to assess the first part of tomorrow's trip and look at the lie of the land, and Fedor intends to shoot a stag. At the end of the track we disembark and walk on foot. Peter is talking intently with Fedor, who is gesturing at the mountain and waving his arm with dramatic sweeping movements. He then produces what looks like a primitive horn; we are told it recreates the noise of a rutting stag and will attract other stags, come to investigate the 'intruder'. Fedor puffs himself up and gives the horn a mighty blast. A weird strangulated noise emanates into the evening sky, echoing off the hills around; then all is quiet. Tony and I look at each other. He blows again. Nothing. Again and again Fedor blows his horn; each time it is greeted by complete silence. We can now hardly contain our laughter but just manage to maintain the necessary degree of seriousness. Fedor looks menacingly at his horn before shrugging and heading back to the truck. By now it is almost dark, and we hurry back to the light and warmth of the camp. Natalia has made a deliciously thick borsch, with wild mushrooms, potatoes and other vegetables mixed in with the beetroot. Peter produces some homemade cognac, and we begin a long series of toasts full of flowery tributes, fine language and ridiculous boasts about what we will accomplish on Oblachnaya the following day. By midnight I'm rather the worse for wear, and with a long day to follow I am happy to turn in.

Peter wakes us just as it is coming light; I have slept well and feel refreshed if a little hungover. It is Saturday, 16 September, and we are about to undertake one of the key elements of this trip, the ascent of Oblachnaya. Tony seems a little disoriented and disappears to find a toilet spot in the woods. I find him stumbling along in the wrong direction; it is obviously too early for him to be fully functioning. We have a quick breakfast, and in the gathering light we board the vehicles and roar out of Field Station

Fedor, Alec and Natalia at the base of Oblachnaya

Cloudy in the direction of the mountain over the track we reconnoitred the previous evening. Tony and I sit in the back of Alec's truck with Peter, the canvas cover flapping violently as we bounce along the track. Fedor and Natalia are in the cab with Alec. The morning is fine, but it is not as bright and warm as the previous days have been, and Peter points to a bank of dark clouds gathering in the east. 'Typhoon', he says.

Soon we arrive at the end of the track and disembark; a solid wall of forest presents a seemingly impenetrable barrier. Tony and I are in full field kit, the best the Western world can offer—Goretex jackets, duck-down body warmers, needle cord trousers and Cordura boots. Fedor is wearing an old double-breasted jacket, white turtleneck sweater, cotton trousers and plimsolls—we feel somewhat overequipped. Our group, Peter, Tony, myself, Fedor, Sergei and Natalia, head up a small woodland path and are immediately swallowed up by the forest. Fedor leads, the Kalashnikov rifle slung over his shoulder ('in case of bears', Peter explains) and an axe in his hand. He moves with sure-footed confidence, stopping occasionally to chop a

Tony searching for a way through the Siberian pine

great chunk out of the trunk of a tree. By this means he will find the way back.

We collect steadily, everyone waiting patiently as we go through our well-practised routine—herbarium specimen, field notes, seeds. *Acer caudatum* subsp. *ukurunduense* is once again startling in its salmon-coloured autumn garb. Below is the Amur barberry, *Berberis amurensis*, loaded with masses of glossy red fruit. At first we are in almost pure deciduous woodland, but soon conifers begin to appear, their numbers increasing as we gain elevation. *Abies nephrolepis*, the Khinghan fir, is the dominant tree with Yezo spruce, *Picea jezoensis*. Occasional trees of *Sorbus amurensis*, with distinctive pointed purple-black buds, yield a generous supply of fruits. As we approach the 1700 m (5500 ft) contour, the high canopy starts to give way and a wonderful association of dwarf shrubs takes over.

The Siberian pine, *Pinus pumila*, forms a dense, almost impenetrable thicket, making the going very demanding. Waist-high bushes of rock birch, *Betula ermanii*, are resplendent with soft butter-yellow autumn leaves; the

Arctous alpinus

dwarf alder, *Alnus viridis* subsp. *fruticosa*, is also common. This attractive plant has a graceful arching habit, each branch carrying clusters of cone-like fruits. I do not know this species from cultivation and am struck by the thought that it would make a marvellous addition to the heather garden in particular.

With no trees overhead we have wonderful views to the south, west and east. We can trace the treeline along the nearby peaks and see the splashes of yellow rock birches set off against the black-green of the Siberian pine. The sun has long since been swallowed up, and the low cloud above is beginning to release an intermittent drizzle; the wind has picked up and is blowing across us as we labour on. We enjoy a brief respite for lunch, snuggling down amongst the protective bulk of the pines. I lift a branch and am amazed to see a small self-contained ecosystem underneath: prostrate bushes of *Rhododendron aureum*, the spoon-shaped leaves of *Bergenia crassifolia* var. *pacifica* and the striking red foliage of *Arctous alpinus*.

The weather is deteriorating rapidly, with low-scudding cloud racing above us. Sleet begins to fall and, with the strong wind, stings our faces; we tuck our heads down and press on. Tony and I keep expecting to see the top of Oblachnaya appear at any moment, but several false summits sap our strength. At 1800 m (6000 ft) prostrate shrubs of *Rhododendron lapponicum* appear. As its name suggests this species was originally described from collections made in Scandinavia by the great Linnaeus (in the genus *Azalea!*). Now, however, it is recognised as a circumboreal species, being found around the globe at high latitudes and on mountaintops in the Northern Hemisphere. This extensive distribution has resulted in its receiving several different names; the plant from the Sikhote Alin was first called *R. parvifolium* before a wider consideration recognised it as conspecific with the Scandinavian plant. Though botanists now make no distinction between these plants the gardener certainly does. The arctic form is almost impossible to cultivate in a temperate climate like that of England. Plants from Ussuriland and Japan, now correctly referred to as *R. lapponicum* Parvifolium Group, are more amenable and are interesting early blooming shrubs, often producing their flowers in January and February. Here on this desolate hillside the plants are completely dormant. Their growing season must be incredibly short; the dirty-brown leaves show not a trace of green—indeed, if the colonies were not so extensive the plant would be easy to miss.

We notice areas where the vegetation has been turned over. Peter tells us this indicates that the brown bear has been present; apparently it feasts on the roots of a species of *Hedysarum* and any fruits it can find as it lays down layers of fat that will sustain it through its long winter hibernation. Though we see plenty of evidence of their activities, thankfully we see no sign of living bears.

By now it is late afternoon, and we are walking into the teeth of a gale, which drives the sleet into a frenzy. Still there is no sign of the summit. I glance over my shoulder to see Tony trudging forlornly behind me. Eventually Fedor stops and gestures ahead. 'The top', Peter says. In front of us is a great pile of boulders, perhaps 80 m (260 ft) in height. No plant clings to its unforgiving face. I have hardly noticed, but the vegetation has all but petered out; a last few bushes of rock birch, here reduced to a height of no more than 1 m (3 ft 3 in), hang on tenaciously, the last vestiges of ochre-coloured leaves hanging limply on its dormant branches—clearly winter is not very far away. Tony and I clamber up the chaos of boulders towards the top; Fedor and Sergei accompany us, the former looking like he is out

The summit of Oblachnaya

for an afternoon stroll in the local park. Peter and Natalia remain at the base of the rock pile. After nearly eight hours of climbing it is a struggle to ascend this last hurdle. The wind is blowing ferociously, but fortunately the sleet has abated. The top is something of a disappointment, a small circular cairn and several plaques with Russian text; the swirling clouds obscure any views and we don't dwell. Sergei tells us that we are the first Englishmen to climb to the top. Strangely, I don't feel any sense of achievement and am pleased that we begin a rapid descent.

Fedor picks up his trail easily, and we work steadily downwards. Reentering the trees, we gain some shelter from the wind, and we are conscious of the rising temperature. My knees and ankles ache with the effort,

Picking up the trail

but with few stops we reach our starting point by 7.00 p.m. Without ceremony we board Alec's truck and head back to Field Station Cloudy. We are pleased with our day's work: Oblachnaya has yielded over twenty collections of a wide range of woody and herbaceous plants, and once again we have gathered good quantities of what appears to be plump viable seed.

After a brief evening meal we are invited to the banya, a Russian bathhouse, and we are not prepared for the complex, near ritualistic procedure that unfolds, the recollection of which never fails to bring a smile. After stripping off we enter a timber-clad building and are joined by Sergei, who gets the room temperature and humidity up to an almost unbearable degree. In the steamy atmosphere Tony turns the colour of lobster thermidor; I'm just the right side of freshly boiled beetroot. Just as it is becoming unendurable we are invited outside onto the cool, dark veranda, where Sergei takes an almost sadistic delight in drenching us with bucket after bucket of cold water. I lose my breath with the shock of the temperature change. This process is repeated several times before the fun really starts.

Back in the sauna Sergei tells us that the next stage involves being thrashed with a besom of branches. I look at Tony incredulously; Sergei notices our expressions but assures us it is good for the skin and muscles. Tony bravely volunteers to go first, selects a cluster of knobbly *Quercus mongolica* twigs, and lays on a slatted bench to receive his treatment. Incredibly the back *and* front are similarly dealt with. I have the choice of Manchurian cherry or birch, both of which look equally nasty. As I lie down I'm conscious of the absurdity of my situation, stark naked, in a steamy room in a remote area of Siberia being flogged by a man I've known for only a few days. Nobody told me this was in the job description. Back at the cabin I expect to fall soundly asleep, as I feel exhausted from the day's exertions and the effects of the sauna. Unfortunately, I toss and turn, beset by strange dreams that are best not related.

We are allowed something of a lie-in the next day, and neither Tony nor I see the light of day until after 9.00 a.m. We have a fairly leisurely morning, as we have to pack and make ready for our departure from Field Station Cloudy for Anisimovka, a settlement close to a known location of the endemic conifer *Microbiota decussata*, an important plant on our target list. This monotypic species was discovered in 1921 and named by the celebrated Russian botanist Vladimir Leontjevich Komarov. Like certain of the junipers it produces single-seeded fruits, though in the case of *Microbiota* the cones are woody (rather than fleshy, as they are in junipers). One interesting school of thought suggests this plant might be merely an abnormal form of *Juniperus pseudosabina*. It is by no means a common plant and remains little known, having not been established in Western gardens until 1957; it was only after it was exhibited at the 1973 Chelsea Flower Show that it became more widely known. It forms a low-growing, spreading specimen; in the winter its sprays of fresh green foliage turn purplish-brown, which hue is regarded as one of its chief ornamental features.

Before we begin our journey Peter calls into the local village of Yasnoya to have his papers stamped as proof that he was in the area—a requirement of his institute. Tony and I take time to walk around, taking photographs as we do. Many of the houses appear jerry-built though most are probably quite cosy; closer inspection reveals they are all constructed almost entirely from recycled materials—old bricks, sheets of corrugated iron, reclaimed timber beams. Each has a well-kept vegetable garden and extensive firewood stacks. We are reminded again of how hard life is in the far-flung corner of

The village houses at Yasnoya

the Russian Federation and how self-sufficient people need to be to endure the long winters.

Inevitably our activities attract the attentions of the village children who appear, cautiously at first, from various directions. Once we have handed out sticks of chewing gum, all is well, and, squirming and giggling, they are happy to smile whilst we take pictures of them. With his business finished Peter beckons us back to the vehicles, and we give the children several chocolate bars to share. Our last glimpse of them, as we mount into the cab of Alec's truck, reveals them squabbling over who should have the next bite.

The journey to Anisimovka is a long and tedious one over atrocious, poorly surfaced roads. The chief highlight is when, just at twilight, we spot a grove of mature woodland by the roadside which is manifestly full of desirable things. We can see the hanging keys of fruits on the Manchurian ash, *Fraxinus mandshurica*; trees of *Malus baccata*, Siberian crab apple, are covered in their small, shiny red fruits; and there are *Acer ginnala*, *Betula costata*, *Populus koreana*, *Maackia amurensis* and the Japanese elm, *Ulmus japonica*, besides. This is an opportune place to stop and collect, and we charge enthusiasti-

The local children

cally into the copse. Straightaway we realise this is a mistake. Stagnant pools of water lie within the wood, and great clouds of mosquitoes rise in unison into the air with one thought in mind. Like the other mosquitoes we have encountered on this trip, they have a vicious bite and are extremely persistent and aggressive. We manage to collect the crab apple, the ash, and a hawthorn, *Crataegus maximowiczii*, before we are driven back to the sanctuary of the vehicles.

It is another five hours before we reach our destination at 11.30 p.m. The building complex appears to be deserted; certainly it is dark and eerily quiet. A light drizzle starts to fall. Peter and Sergei attempt to discover signs of habitation, and their persistence is eventually rewarded when a wizened old man emerges from the far end of the compound in a pair of washed-out pyjamas, he is muttering Russian oaths under his breath and is clearly less than pleased. The buildings around have a neglected air about them, and I imagine they are some kind of research station. We are shown into a comfortable room with two double beds and an adjacent bathroom. Sergei and Alec start to prepare our evening meal on an aged cooking range, whilst

Peter heads off to formally register our arrival. Soon the delicious smell of some sort of stew fills the air, and we compliment the chefs on their wizardry in turning out excellent food from such primitive equipment. Peter returns with the 'station chief' in tow. Apparently we are at a holiday camp for submarine workers! After dining together, we begin a series of toasts with Peter's lethal cognac. I am happy to escape to bed, where I enjoy a sound sleep.

I wake refreshed and raring to go. It has been raining throughout the night, and everything outside is saturated. The holiday centre looks no more appealing in the daylight than it did the night before, and it seems that the holiday season is over, as the majority of buildings are unoccupied. A sad, broken-down play park is all that is on offer for children. The rain relents briefly as we are driven by Anatoly along a muddy track into the woods. When we reach the end we continue on foot.

Light rain is falling again, but this gets progressively heavier as we advance until it is absolutely torrential, so heavy that it is difficult to see very far ahead. Our footpath turns into a stream, and soon we are ankle deep in water. Despite the conditions we are once again rewarded with a plethora of trees; the seemingly pristine woods are full of choice and interesting things. The attractive alder *Alnus maximowiczii* is common and easily identified by its large, very dark buds and its glossy, well-fashioned, crisply toothed leaves. Large clusters of cone-like fruits make easy pickings. *Acer caudatum* subsp. *ukurunduense* makes another appearance, its flaky bark contrasting with the smooth green stems of *A. barbinerve*. Large trees of the ever impressive silver lime, *Tilia mandshurica*, and its near relative *T. amurensis* form a tall overstorey. The climbing *Actinidia kolomikta* clambers into the canopy. This much prized species has leaves that are blotched pink and white in the spring, and it is always the subject of interested comment when grown in gardens; it is a close relative of the kiwi fruit (*A. deliciosa*) but has smaller, glabrous fruits that look not unlike large gooseberries.

As we gain altitude the now familiar Khinghan fir, *Abies nephrolepis*, and Yezo spruce, *Picea jezoensis*, appear along with huge specimens of the Korean white pine, *Pinus koraiensis*, most attractive with long, slender needles in bunches of five. Peter tells us these forests are home to the rare Siberian tiger and jokingly shouts into the trees, 'Stay away, Mr Tiger!' There seems little

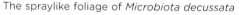

The spraylike foliage of *Microbiota decussata*

Bergenia crassifolia var. *pacifica*
flowering at Kew from seed collected
on Litovka Mountain

danger of us being molested, as this beautiful creature has been pushed to
the verge of extinction. Also, horticulturists are not noted for their stealth;
any sensitive animal will have heard us coming the moment we disembarked
from the vehicle.

We emerge from the woodland to be confronted by a fast-flowing stream
that, with difficulty, we manage to ford by hopping from one large boulder
to the next. On the other side we continue climbing up a slippery track.
Through breaks in the canopy we can just make out the rising bulk of
Litovka Mountain, our destination. Huge unstable screes, composed of
masses of boulders, begin to spill from the mountainsides, causing great
gashes in the woodland. And still it rains. We almost walk on the microbiota, so sudden is its appearance. It occurs at the edge of the woodland,
just where the screes are beginning to stabilise, growing with the attractive
Bergenia crassifolia var. *pacifica* and scattered bushes of the early flowering
Rhododendron mucronulatum.

Once again our luck is in as the bushes are carrying masses of small, one-seeded fruits, but collecting them in the pouring rain is a tedious and unpleasant job. After nearly an hour we feel we have enough; still, we take the precaution of gathering some cutting material as an insurance policy should the seed fail to germinate. We stop for a miserable lunch. Though we are surrounded by trees, there is no shelter from the incessant rain. Pushing on up the mountain we see little that is new, and Peter, sensing our drooping spirits, indicates that we should turn back.

All around us are innumerable channels of water; they start as innocuous rivulets, gaining in volume and power as they combine. In the distance I can hear a muted roar, and I glance at Tony. 'I don't remember that when we came up'. Tony looks concerned. Worse, Peter looks concerned. 'We should hurry', he says. If anything, the rain is heavier, and the downhill track is very treacherous. Sergei slips badly and crashes into the trunk of a tree; he rises rather gingerly, rubbing his shoulder. At the point where we crossed the stream, just a few hours before, the scene has changed dramatically. We are now confronted by a broad, swift river. The rainwater has swelled it enormously; there are no boulders in sight and no way to ford it other than by wading through. The current looks powerful, and we are none too confident about being able to cross safely. Peter tells Sergei to cut some stout poles from the forest; almost absently I note they are the flaky branches of *Acer caudatum* subsp. *ukurunduense*. Peter and Sergei lock their arms across Tony's shoulders and push out into the swirling water. Their progress is ponderous, Peter slips and is briefly submerged before he is hauled upright by Sergei, who braces himself against the current by leaning on his staff. At the midpoint the water is almost chest-high, and the group of figures seems to falter. Peter barks at Sergei, and they press on. Gradually they emerge from the water and flop, exhausted, onto the opposite bank, 18 m (60 ft) away.

Within a few minutes Peter and Sergei are in the water again, returning to help me across. In the short time that has passed I imagine the river has risen still higher. I am anxious, to say the least, as we enter the water. Despite already being soaked I gasp at its frigidity. Immediately I am aware of the force of the water but worse is the bouldery nature of the riverbed, which makes every footstep a potential stumble into the torrent. Tony shouts

Sergei, Mark and Peter fording the swollen river

encouragement from the other side—something about keeping the Kew end up! Suitably apposite. Our progress seems snail-like, but the sturdy support of Sergei, who is taking the full weight of the current, never wavers, and, aided by Tony, we scramble up the bank. My relief is immense, and I sit quietly for several moments, composing myself. We continue through the forest. Everywhere paths are awash, and we cross several more, mercifully much smaller, streams. At last we arrive at our departure point to be greeted by Anatoly's sardonic smile. I look at my companions; we are quite a sight—wet, muddy and dishevelled. 'Why do we do this?' is Tony's heartfelt question. The van, finally, gives us relief from the rain, which has not let up, and we are happy to sit back and let Anatoly drive us back to the camp.

A change of clothes, a delicious meal of mashed potatoes and what looks and tastes like ratatouille, and my spirits are quite lifted. It is important to dry our herbarium specimens and air our seeds as much as possible, and despite being greatly fatigued, we ensure that everything is in order before turning in for the night. And still it is raining.

The following morning I poke my head tentatively out of the door—rain, and heavy rain at that. Peter sees my forlorn expression; he explains that all the rain is a consequence of the landfall of a decaying Pacific typhoon. Apparently it is not uncommon at this time of year, though he concedes that he has not known so much rainfall for many, many years. The old cooking range has done a sterling job in drying our clothes out, which were left hanging above. Even my boots, admittedly still very wet on the outside, are reasonably dry on the inside.

Today we are to move to our next collecting station. This is a long way south, the other side of Vladivostok, and Peter confides that he is worried about the condition of the roads and intends to ring his institute to see if they have more detailed information. This gives Tony and me time to pack all our seeds, herbarium specimens and equipment. Though we get an okay to leave, we do so with some trepidation. Peter's concern is well founded: the whole of the countryside is awash, and the roads are in a terrible condition. Our journey takes us back to Vladivostok, whence we intend to take a shortcut by ferry to our destination. Unfortunately, the rough seas, strong winds and continuing rain mean that no ships are sailing, and we have to complete the whole trip by road. It is not until 2.00 a.m. that we reach our harrowing journey's end, a comfortable field station of Peter's institute next to the sea at the village of Andreyevka.

The tribulations of the trip are fully compensated for next day by a tremendous collecting session. The weather has improved, and we head still further south to the Gamov Peninsula, a finger of land projecting into the East Sea between Vladivostok and the North Korean border. We emerge over a hilltop to a panorama of sweeping, sandy bays. Sunlight shafts through holes in the remaining cloud cover. Several small, rocky islands topped by Japanese red pine, *Pinus densiflora*, stud the Telyakovsky Inlet immediately below us. The whole scene is quite magical and very Oriental.

We begin collecting immediately. Several species of roses are growing in the dunes within a few metres of the sea. *Rosa maximowicziana* forms a low-growing mound with arching stems covered in densely set thorns. Nearby is

R. acicularis, more upright and with bristly stems. As we progress inland, the mix of species is bewildering. Given our proximity to the sea and the salt-laden air, it is surprising to enter broadleaved woodland composed of *Betula davurica*, *Tilia mandshurica* and *Quercus mongolica*. The black-barked *B. schmidtii* also makes its appearance, its bark showing a very different pattern to flaky *B. davurica*: stiff curling plates are peeling from the trunk and nowhere is there any hint of the white pigments we associate with birches. The ecology of this tree is also very different from that of other birches, as it is long-lived, shade tolerant and happy to compete as part of the climax association in these woods; most birches, by contrast, are regarded as quick-growing pioneer species. Another interesting tree, *Kalopanax septemlobus*, becomes increasingly common. Often called the prickly castor-oil tree in cultivation because of a supposed resemblance between its leaves and those of the castor oil plant, *Ricinus communis*, it is a member of the ivy family (Araliaceae). This family is highly developed in eastern Asia with many different genera. As if to illustrate this point we come upon *Aralia continentalis*, a herbaceous plant which annually produces stems up to 1.8 m (6 ft) topped, towards the end of summer, with ball-shaped inflorescences. Though not showy in flower, it is one of those plants, often called architectural plants by garden designers, that have a strong garden presence by dint of their stature and striking leaves.

Other constituents of the ground flora are equally interesting, and I am delighted to see *Lysimachia clethroides*, a familiar species from cultivation, its curling inflorescences, recalling a shrew's nose, giving it away immediately. Nearby is a fine form of *Astilbe chinensis*, with tall slender racemes composed of masses of small fruits now rapidly ripening and ready to discharge their tiny seeds. Strangely, in gardens this species is most often represented by its dwarf selection, var. *pumila*, which, though a striking plant, has none of the grace and charm of the type.

The weather deteriorates again, and soon the rain is falling torrentially, literally putting a damper on what has so far been a pleasant and productive day. We end up taking a loop over the hills behind the bay before returning along the beach to where Alec is waiting. Our last collection is the delightful *Lilium cernuum*, a lily characterised by its numerous, closely set narrow leaves. This is a popular and amenable species in cultivation, where its nodding lilac-pink scented flowers, with darker spots, are a feature of woodland and peat gardens in July.

We return to Andreyevka for the night before moving on to what is likely to be amongst the more interesting parts of the journey. Our destination is the village of Khasan, a settlement right on the border with North Korea at the southernmost point of Russian territory in the Far East. On the way we pass within 8 km (5 miles) of the Chinese border and are reminded of the sensitive nature of this part of the world, where volatile nations share long borders. It is a warm sunny day, and where the road surface is well made, we make rapid progress. Unfortunately, these stretches do not last, and the road becomes rough. A tall barbed-wire and electric fence marking the border with North Korea tells us our destination is at hand. Along its length are numerous tall watch towers, though they seem deserted. We enjoy an elevated view into North Korea; I can see roads in the distance snaking their way over grassy, denuded hills and the occasional cyclist, wearing a broad bamboo coolies' hat. Time almost seems to have stood still, and I imagine the view would have been much the same a century ago.

It takes all Alec's driving skills to negotiate safely the pot-holed and slippery track. Eventually we emerge onto a broad, sandy beach. At its far end is a huddle of buildings, looking very much like converted cargo holders. Peter tells us it is a marine experimental station, and we are to spend the night here. We disembark from Alec's vehicle and continue on foot. The view is dominated by Golubiny Utyos, a huge granite outcrop, flat-topped and sheer-sided, which is to be our collecting location for the rest of the afternoon. Though at first rather uninspiring, the area turns out to be very rich. At the foot of the rock is a water meadow full of wonderful things, including the ripening fruits of *Iris ensata* standing obligingly on tall stems. Mixed in are the now fading feathery heads of *Poterium tenuifolium*, a choice herbaceous member of the rose family and too infrequently cultivated. Where the meadow peters out and dune slacks take over, we find masses of *Rosa rugosa* carrying its clusters of bright, glossy, shining hips. Underneath, the dainty *Gypsophila pacifica* is common and still covered in airy pink flowers. Most interesting is a climbing monkshood that weaves its way through the roses, its sinister, blue hooded flowers still in evidence; this is later identified as *Aconitum volubile*.

We move across to Golubiny Utyos itself and find a completely different range of plants. Two woody climbers, well known to us from gardens, make a home on the rock face. The scandent, scrambling *Celastrus orbiculatus* has difficulty in gaining a hold, unlike *Parthenocissus tricuspidata*, whose finger-like tendrils allow it to ascend the rock face with ease. As a novice horticulturist in the 1970s, I had assumed that the common name of this plant—Boston ivy—marked it out as a native of North America. George Bradshaw, a kindly old gardener who took me under his wing, disabused me of my error by telling me the common name was merely a reflection of its widespread use in the city of Boston as a climber for building façades, and that it was really a plant from eastern Asia. I think of George, now long gone, whilst admiring the plant on Golubiny Utyos, its leaves turning their characteristic fiery red as it prepares for the coming winter. A rare and unusual ash, *Fraxinus densata*, forms rather stunted, unhappy specimens in pockets of pink, granite spoil on ledges. It looks like a downy version of the widespread *F. chinensis* subsp. *rhyncophylla*, and I'm not surprised to discover later that it is listed as a form of this taxon in *Flora of Korea* (Lee 1996). We never encounter this variant again.

By early evening our work is finished, and we take a leisurely walk across the sands back to Alec's truck. At the marine station, which is, in fact, a series of converted cargo containers, Sergei is left behind to prepare our evening meal whilst Tony and I tag along with Peter and Alec, who are intent on shooting duck in the salty lagoons inland from the shore. We put on waders and in the gathering twilight make our way out to one of the low sand bars and squat down, waiting for something to happen. There are other hunters in the area, the discharges from their guns sending pulses of light into the darkness. After half an hour, nothing whatsoever has happened; after an hour, we haven't seen a duck, let alone shot one. Peter reluctantly calls the shoot off, and we head back to base, where we enjoy Sergei's rice and sausage meal.

Tony asks where we are to sleep for the night and is told that, as we don't have keys to the marine station, we will have to sleep in the banya. Perhaps Tony's earlier experience at Field Station Cloudy haunts him, as he is not at all happy with this arrangement. I leave him arguing the toss with Peter and walk across to the bathhouse. With my torch I can see that there are two benches, one considerably wider than the other. I quickly grab my sleeping bag and set myself up on the wide bench. Soon after Tony joins me and is less than enamoured about his 'bed'; it cannot be more than 45 cm (18 in) wide, and once in place he dare not move for fear of falling off. He is very disgruntled, still cursing to himself as I fall to sleep. A little later Sergei arrives with his bedding and, without complaint, makes himself comfortable on the cold, stone floor. (That night, I dream that Tony has mastered the art of levitation and spends the entire time gently hovering over the bench with a broad, contented smile on his face.)

Next morning, I am roughly woken by Tony and open my eyes to find it is barely light. He's had an awful night and is determined no one else should enjoy their sleep. I can hear him outside banging on the canvas sides of Alec's truck, 'Peter, it's time to go'. Sergei looks at me wearily from the banya floor. After breakfast we begin the long, uncomfortable journey back; on the way out, Peter stops the vehicle again and again to shoot several scrawny sandpipers. He seems triumphant with his prizes, and it is as much as we can do to make him get on with the trip. We have even greater difficulty renegotiating the track that skirts the North Korean border, and we get stuck several times. The rain is once again falling in torrents, which only adds to our difficulties. Each time we get stuck, Tony and I jump out to see what's around. We collect *Lilium dauricum* and an interesting asparagus, *Asparagus schoberioides*. Emerging onto better roads, we make rapid progress and are back at our comfortable lodgings at Andreyevka by 5.00 p.m. The weather has improved temporarily, again, and with it our spirits.

Peter informs us that he has finalised our programme for Sakhalin and in order to catch the flight from Vladivostok we have to leave at 5.00 a.m. He advises us to split our bags: anything we don't need in Sakhalin is to be left at his institute. He also requests that, before leaving, we speak to the local school children about our work and the purpose of our visit, which we are very happy to do. We walk across to the school building and are introduced to the class. All the children are very attentive and well behaved, ranging in age from perhaps seven to fourteen. We spend a pleasant hour or so talking to them, with Peter and a local girl acting as translators. They bombard us with questions afterwards, being mainly interested in our gadgetry and clothing. Before leaving we judge their arts and crafts competition and are delighted by the skill and ingenuity of several of their pieces.

We return to the lodge at 9.30 p.m. and are served potato and sandpiper stew, which is surprisingly tasty! Conscious of our early start, we retire soon after eating in order to complete our preparations. Before too long the heating comes on; our room is stifling, and after a very uncomfortable night, I'm glad to be up and away. Almost inevitably it has been raining, and Peter looks worried and tired. Tony is concerned that the strain of organising and conducting the fieldwork is beginning to take its toll on him. The added complications brought on by the awful weather do not help. Peter has taken the precaution of sending Anatoly ahead in the van to give him time to carefully negotiate the worst sections of the road. We all, therefore, board Alec's truck, and in the gathering light of dawn, we head north back to Vladivostok. It is relatively mild, but the rain falls unceasingly. The road conditions are execrable, and I marvel that Anatoly has been able to get through at all; his little Nissan Vanette seems barely capable of the journey. Nevertheless, 20 km (12 miles) up the road he is waiting for us. From this point the roads are better, and we make good progress. Peter's intention is that we should go straight to the airport to catch our flight, which departs for Sakhalin at 11.00 a.m. We arrive in good time and unload our field bags. Alec and Anatoly bid us farewell, as only Peter and Sergei will accompany us. Peter conducts us into the VIP lounge, and we wait for our flight to be called. Clearly, the Russian concept of a 'very important person' is different from the Western notion of the phrase, but we are comfortable and our needs are modest. We even enjoy an Australian lager, so we don't grumble.

Our bags receive a cursory check before we are invited to carry them to the Aeroflot propeller plane that is waiting on the tarmac nearby. Our luggage is stowed, and we climb aboard. Rumour has it that a famous Russian pop star is on the flight, and we note that the cabin is full of long-haired musicians. Take-off proceeds smoothly, and the reservations we have been harbouring about the professionalism and competence of Aeroflot seem to have been misplaced. That is, until the in-flight catering arrangements unfold. Like the ice-cream girl in an old-fashioned movie theatre, our flight attendant walks down the aisle with a shallow tray, complete with strip light, from which she offers cigarettes—yes, cigarettes—stale crisps and out-of-date chocolate bars. Her uniform is stained, and her lips are painted bright, sealing-wax red; her peroxide-blond hair adds a comic air to the whole proceeding. Not surprisingly, almost everyone ignores her, and we hear the rustling of silver foil and the opening of sealed boxes as homemade fare is produced. Peter offers us some cold, cooked potatoes, bread and cheese and ham paste.

The rest of the flight is entirely eventless, fortunately, and we are soon descending through the low, grey cloud cover to Sakhalin Island, which lies between the 45th and 55th parallels and covers 96,400 km² (29,498 sq miles), about the size of Scotland. Sakhalin is not only strategically important but has rich natural resources—oil, gas, iron ore and gold deposits as well as extensive forests; these provide the island with its main industries of mining, oil extraction and forestry, though visibility being what it is, we can see very little of this as we make our descent. We land with a thump on the tarmac and taxi to a squat, rather mean airport terminal. Once again we are obliged to collect and carry our own bags. We are immediately aware of a drop in temperature, a consequence of the several degrees of latitude we have gained. After passing a perfunctory inspection, we are met by Georges, a representative of the local branch of the Russian Academy of Sciences. He drives us to their headquarters through the island's capital, Yuzhno-Sakhalinsk, which seems to be bustling.

The architecture is typically Soviet Communist, concrete tower blocks and featureless civic buildings; it is difficult to tell residences from shops, as all structures have the same bland exterior. I had naively expected to see some remnants of the Japanese occupation of the island, but I am sadly mistaken; anything relating to that era has long since been obliterated. Following the Treaty of Portsmouth in 1905, which concluded Japan's shattering military defeat of Tsarist Russia, the southern part of Sakhalin, below 50°N, was ceded to the Japanese and became the colony of Karafuto, with a capital at Toyohama. By the time of the Second World War, the population of Japanese people in Karafuto had risen to 400,000. Their world was about to be turned upside down. On 8 August 1945 Stalin broke his four-year neutrality pact and declared war on Japan. The following day Soviet forces launched an attack on Karafuto. By 25 August the invasion was complete, and the whole

Yuzhno-Sakhalinsk

island became part of the Soviet Union. Between 1946 and 1950 almost the entire civilian population was repatriated back to Japan.

Nevertheless, I see lots of Asian faces amongst the people going about their business in Yuzhno-Sakhalinsk. I learn from Peter that these people are, in fact, Korean, and my subsequent researches reveal the sad tale of these forgotten people. During the final years of the Japanese colony of Karafuto, over forty thousand Koreans were forcibly sent to Sakhalin to work as labourers. They existed under appalling conditions and were treated with great brutality. When the Soviet authorities took control, these Koreans were not repatriated; they and their children and grandchildren have existed in a kind of political limbo ever since. Even at the time, without knowing their history, my impression of these unfortunate individuals was of a mournful, melancholy group of people at odds with their surroundings.

The institute buildings are semi-derelict and squalid. The first set of lodgings we are offered are roundly dismissed by Peter, who, it is clear, is not best pleased by our treatment. The ones we finally settle on are little better, and this puts an immediate dampener on our enthusiasm for this strange new island. Whilst Peter and Sergei are unpacking, Tony and I have a wander outside. Tony is feeling decidedly low, and I don't feel particularly lively either. We have been away from home for nearly three weeks under trying circumstances; our living conditions have been primitive and the fieldwork demanding. As if to emphasise our feelings of vulnerability and despondency, Peter mentions almost casually, upon our return, 'Be careful not to drink the water—there is a hepatitis epidemic on the island'. Home feels a long, long way away, and Sakhalin like a very foreign place.

At 8.30 p.m. Sergei takes us for a shower at the local energy plant. The hot water is refreshing, and it is nice to be clean again after several grubby days, but the surroundings are grim. I half imagine that the plant is powered by nuclear energy and that I will emerge from the shower glowing with radioactive isotopes, like Homer Simpson after an accident at the Springfield Nuclear Power Plant. As we leave, Sergei points to a photograph on the wall of the tea room. 'Russian woman', he says with lascivious pride. Tony looks at me ironically; it is, in fact, Maria Whittaker, the English pin-up model. We decide to say nothing, though I am intrigued as to how her image came to adorn the wall of Russian power plant over 10,000 km (6000 miles) from her home in Kingston-on-Thames.

Our first full day on Sakhalin dawns grey and wet. It would seem that the poor weather has followed us from the mainland. A driver from the institute turns up soon after breakfast in a battered old jeep, and we head out of the city to the nearby peak of Mount Chekhov. Peter tells us that it has recently been given back its original name, having lived under the moniker of Mount Bolshevik during the Communist era. There is some confusion as to the start point, but we disembark by a muddy track and in the pours of rain make our way up, with Peter in the lead and Sergei taking up the rear. The going is relatively easy as the ascent is not steep, and we collect steadily along the route. At first we gather plants that are familiar to us from the mainland—*Acer caudatum* subsp. *ukurunduense*, *Betula ermanii* and *Pinus pumila*—but soon new and interesting taxa begin to assert themselves.

The Japanese rowan, *Sorbus commixta*, appears in quantity. This tree has long intrigued me, as trees bearing this name in cultivation are very diverse. One genotype is tall and narrow and colours magnificently in the autumn; another has a more vase-shaped canopy and is not so vigorous. Few of these

Birches and rowans on the flanks of Mount Chekhov

plants can be traced to wild collections. There are two possible explanations for this situation: either some element of hybridity exists in the cultivated populations; or there is a great deal of diversity in the wild, and the plants introduced into gardens represent narrow genotypes from a much wider gene pool. This latter explanation is supported to some degree by the presence of a third 'commixta' first collected by Thor Nitzelius on the South Korean island of Ullung-Do. This is the same as the plant we collected on our visit to Ullung-Do in October 1989 and mentioned by Tony in chapter 3 (see also photograph on page 278). This tree is very distinctive with thick twigs, large lustrous leaves and huge flat inflorescences, which eventually produce masses of red fruits so heavy that the branches are weighed down by them. Several authorities, recognising the singular nature of this taxon, have said it deserves a clonal name in order to distinguish it— *S. commixta* 'Ullung' has been proposed. I would go further and suggest it is so distinct that it should be described as a new species, unless intermediaries can be found to link it with the very different trees we are now seeing on Mount Chekhov. These have slender twigs, with rather small corymbs of

Sorbus sambucifolia

fruits, and form small trees; the Ullung-Do species almost always wants to form a strong-growing multi-stemmed tree or large shrub.

Another rowan is soon evident but cannot be confused with its relative. *Sorbus sambucifolia* is a suckering shrub, no more than 1.2 m (4 ft) high; it has large fruits, almost the size of rose hips, borne in small numbers. This shrub is not well established in cultivation, and I know of only one specimen that grows by the streamside in the Savill Garden in Windsor Great Park. Though the Savill Garden plant flowers and fruits, it never looks really thrifty and loses its leaves to become dormant by September. Herein lies the familiar problem discussed earlier: plants that are strongly adapted to a demanding continental climate such as exists in Ussuriland and on Sakhalin find the more effete conditions of the maritime parts of the temperate world uncongenial and fail to prosper.

Other specialities of the island begin to yield themselves. *Euonymus sachalinensis* emerges, developing into an arching deciduous shrub up to 6 m (20 ft) tall with hanging fruits, which split to reveal an attractive orange interior and red seeds. *Viburnum furcatum* is also common and distinctive as it carries fruits of two different colours—black and red—though my assumption is that the latter is merely a stage of maturation to the former colour. The proximity of the Japanese archipelago—the northernmost island of Hokkaido is 75 km (45 miles) from Sakhalin—becomes increasingly apparent in the flora. Typically Japanese species are everywhere. *Hydrangea paniculata* sports its cone-shaped flowers; lower down *Weigela middendorffiana* is common, and occasional trees of *Betula platyphylla* var. *japonica* present themselves.

Unfortunately, the conditions do not improve, and as we approach the treeline the rain is driven on by a fierce wind. At 1.30 p.m. we stop for a cheerless lunch; the wind is so strong that several times I'm nearly blown over and have to seek shelter amongst the Siberian pines. It is clear that Peter, whose canvas clothing is wet through, hasn't the appetite to go on any farther. There are at least 3 km (2 miles) and about 250 m (800 ft) of elevation to be gained before we reach the top. Nobody protests when Peter decides we should turn around.

The descent is treacherous; the rain has made the track extremely slippery, and we have to take great care. If anything the rain comes down in even heavier torrents, though thankfully, now that we are back amongst the trees, the wind has abated. Our pick-up is not scheduled until 6.00 p.m. so that by the time we reach the road we have several hours of walking ahead of us. Despite our fatigue and discomfort, we collect several plants of interest, including the red-fruited herbaceous perennial *Actaea erythrocarpa*. This genus has an interesting distribution, with the British native species *A. spicata*, herb Christopher, representing a European outlier; I have seen this plant growing in the beautiful upland ashwoods of Ingleborough in North Yorkshire. *Actaea rubra* and *A. pachypoda* are found in North America; the latter is often called doll's eyes, as the white fruits retain the shrivelled black calyx, giving a superficial resemblance to the ceramic eyes of Victorian dolls. Asia also provides a black-fruited species, *A. asiatica*. They make interesting additions to the woodland garden and are at their showiest in autumn when carrying their fleshy fruits, though some caution needs to be exercised as another common name, baneberry, gives a hint of the poisonous nature of these fruits.

Interestingly and not uncontroversially, English botanist James Compton has sunk the genus *Cimicifuga* into *Actaea*, thus enlarging it considerably. Gardeners in particular are unconvinced, believing that the tall, wand-like flower heads and dry fruits of *Cimicifuga* have little in common with the shorter, more rounded or pyramidal flower heads and fleshy fruits of *Actaea*. Compton's case is based on detailed molecular research, and he maintains that the form of the fruit—dry or fleshy—is unimportant as a diagnostic character. In Compton's revised circumscription the genus *Actaea* now contains twenty-eight species. (Incidentally, this collection of *A. erythrocarpa* was used in Compton's study and found to be conspecific with *A. rubra*.) The nice plump pods of *Lilium hansonii* bring a conclusion to the day's collecting, and we return to our base cold, wet and exhausted.

Having had a rather monotonous series of breakfasts, Tony and I offer to cook on the following morning. We make a concerted effort to produce an appetising meal; Tony prepares gypsy toast, and I make a nice ham and tomato omelette. Peter and Sergei eat without comment; if anything, they seem rather unimpressed, leaving Tony and me somewhat miffed. The day that follows is spent in a small area of local woodland, and we are obliged to catch a bus in order to get there. This turns out to be quite an experience. Somewhat melodramatically, Peter warns us about talking to each other— 'This is dangerous', he says. When we board the bus it is already full, and we are obliged to stand. At the next stop more people climb aboard, and again at the next stop. By now there is quite a crush, but at each stop more people are waiting, and all are quite unabashed about forcibly entering the bus. The driver seems completely unconcerned, as do the rest of the passengers; this is obviously normal behaviour. Tony seems more discomforted than any one, and it is only after we have reached our destination and fought our way off the bus that he reveals that the man breathing right down his neck had extreme halitosis!

We continue on foot, gradually leaving behind the crumbling tower blocks of Yuzhno-Sakhalinsk. The trees begin to thicken until we are in quite diverse woodland, principally made up of *Sorbus commixta*, *Betula platyphylla* var. *japonica* and *Alnus hirsuta*, with infrequent trees of the two local

The eye-catching fruits of *Actaea erythrocarpa*

conifers, Sakhalin fir (*Abies sachalinensis*) and Yezo spruce (*Picea jezoensis*). Occasional areas have been cleared for ski runs. The day is spent at a leisurely pace; we collect a wide range of things, perhaps the gem being the little woodland herbaceous plant *Trillium camschatcense*. By late afternoon we have exhausted the potential of the area, and a light drizzle is falling. We make our way back, stopping for bread and cheese before boarding the bus for the return journey; as it is evening, things are a lot quieter and we actually get seats. That night I take a shower at the power plant again, only to discover that I have picked up athlete's foot—great! Back at our lodgings, Peter outlines our next few days' itinerary; we are to move to the north and base ourselves at a field station at Sokol run by the marine biology section of the Russian Academy of Sciences.

The following morning Peter is up early to organise transport and provisions and to visit the herbarium at the institute in order to check on the occurrence of plants of interest. Tony and I organise our bags and equipment. By mid morning we are waiting by the roadside for our transport. I am expecting some sort of Land Rover or jeep, as there are only four of us

Sergei, Tony and Peter outside the accommodation at Sokol

and we are relatively lightly burdened. Not a bit of it—a forty-seater single-decker bus swings into view and powers up the road towards us, trailing a cloud of oily black smoke. I half expect it to have 'No. 26—Sokol' on the front. We have the luxury of a great deal of room and relative comfort for what turns out to be a journey of not much more than twenty minutes on a well-made and well-maintained macadam road.

The field station appears to be the usual collection of poor-quality buildings, but we have a pleasant surprise when we are taken to our lodgings, which are well-constructed timber-clad chalets. Inside they are clean and bright with comfortable beds and easy chairs. An attractive woman, in her early thirties, is putting fresh sheets on the bed. She is introduced to us as Yelena, the wife of the head of the station; with her is her daughter, Olga, a charming six-year-old with a strawberry-blond bob. Outside I can hear Peter talking animatedly with another man; great roars of laughter and the sounds of energetic backslapping rise from them. Sergei tells us it is the head of the base and an old friend of Peter's, whom he hasn't seen for some time. Peter introduces us to this impressive man, Alexander Maximovich

Peter Gorovoy 'fishing' for salmon

(the same surname as the great botanist). An archetypal Russian with a confusion of greying hair and a great bushy beard, he greets us with tremendous bear hugs and a thunderous 'Welcome, welcome'. He is joined by his wife and daughter; the three of them make a handsome, if somewhat incongruous family, given the age difference between husband and wife.

It is warm and sunny, and straightaway Peter takes us into some nearby woodland, promising Tony that he will see some salmon running in the local streams. The base is sited in this area because of its proximity to the spawning grounds of Pacific salmon, one of its key research subjects. Given Tony's passion for fishing, this is quite a prospect. We don't have to wait long; there is a tremendous smell of rotting fish and, sure enough, the first stream we come upon is full of pink salmon trying to make their way against the current, so thick in the water that there is barely a gap between them. The stream is shallow, and Peter steps in and picks up several large fish by hand. On the banks are the rotting remains of salmon whose journey is complete.

I leave Tony and Peter to marvel at this amazing sight and start exploring the woodland in earnest. Its composition is not dissimilar to what we have already become familiar with on Sakhalin, with a canopy of mainly Japanese rowan and Japanese white birch and the odd single tree or small group of Sakhalin fir. However, the understorey and woodland floor is filled with new plants. I am thrilled to see the spikes and big green fruiting capsules of the giant lily, *Cardiocrinum cordatum* var. *glehnii*. This genus, best known in cultivation by its Himalayan representative *C. giganteum*, ranges eastwards through Yunnan and Sichuan in western China (where a very similar plant to the Himalayan species is distinguished merely as a variety of it, var. *yunnanense*), to central and eastern China with *C. cathayanum* and on into eastern Russia to Japan, where two varieties—*C. cordatum* var. *cordatum* and *C. cordatum* var. *glehnii*—are native. These latter three do not attain the heights of the Sino-Himalayan plants, which can push flowering spikes up to nearly 4 m (12 ft) tall.

In well-lit clearings in the forest a fine rose occurs. It has large ripe bunches of red hips, and we later tentatively identify it as *Rosa amblyotis*. Rejoined by Peter and Tony, I push on towards an open, level site. Though relatively dry underfoot at present, the lack of any trees (apart from scattered individuals of *Alnus maximowiczii*) suggests that periodic inundation with floodwater characterises the area. The floral composition is also very different from the immediate surroundings, and many new and interesting plants present themselves. The tall spikes of *Veratrum lobelianum* are numerous, as are clumps of the day-lily *Hemerocallis dumortieri*, still carrying its orangey-yellow flowers. Tiny rivulets snake their way across the site, and we are amazed to see salmon still pushing their way along in water that is barely deep enough to cover their bodies. How these fish manage to find their way back to their place of birth is remarkable. Along these small water courses we find *Symplocarpus foetidus*, an interesting member of the arum family. This plant is familiar to me from cultivation, where it produces dark shield-like flowers in the early spring. They are very striking and not easily mistaken for anything else, and, as its botanical name suggests, they give off an unpleasant, though barely discernible, odour, which further distinguishes the plant. I assume the malodorous flowers attract pollinating insects, presumably flies.

The dusk is gathering as we leave the floodplain and make the short journey back to the field station. Sergei has been preparing the evening meal, which is—inevitably—salmon lightly floured and gently sautéed in butter.

It is delicious, and we enjoy several chunky steaks. Less appetising are the salmon eggs that the Russians eat with relish, particularly Alexander, who with Yelena and Olga has joined us. After dinner Yelena brings out an acoustic guitar, and by candlelight the Russians sing folk songs. All are slow and mournful and, though beautifully sung, I find them overly melancholy. I needn't worry, as when Tony is asked to join in, he rouses us all with his signature rendition of 'The Ballad of Jed Clampett', which draws from our Russian hosts, as if on cue, the incredulous looks we've come to expect. I'm then put on the spot for a 'traditional' English folk song; at short notice, the best I can do is a rather limp version of 'Once I Caught a Fish Alive', though this does seem appropriate given the day's activities. With the entertainment finished, Tony and I retire to our cabin, and I sink into a clean, soft bed and a deep sleep. (I dream I'm the English representative at an international singing competition which is being judged by Nikita Khrushchev, John F. Kennedy and Harold Macmillan—I cannot remember the outcome, only my anxiety to choose the right song and give a good account of myself.)

Our next collecting area is further north still. Alexander accompanies us to a river estuary at Starodubskoe, about 40 km (25 miles) from Sokol. The river is discharging into a large bay of the Sea of Okhotsk, with woodland growing to within 200 m (650 ft) of the shoreline. We make our way towards the woods, leaving Peter with Alexander and several colleagues from the field station to undertake some 'research'. We see them setting up a gill net in the estuary, and within a few minutes, they are landing an endless succession of large chum salmon.

We are soon immersed in our own activities, for an interesting littoral flora is colonising the sand dunes; present are various marram grasses and the attractive *Glehnia littoralis*, a member of the carrot family with large umbels of white flowers and shiny, much-divided leaves. Soon woody plants begin to appear, including great banks of *Rosa rugosa*, interspersed with clumps of *Iris setosa*. The woodland edge is composed of Sakhalin fir and Yezo spruce with Japanese yew (*Taxus cuspidata*) and *Ilex rugosa* in the understorey. This holly forms a prostrate shrub no more than 25 cm (10 in) high; its bluish foliage reminds me that it is a parent of the important garden hybrid *Ilex* ×*meserveae*, the result of a cross with English holly, *I. aquifolium*, made in the United States in the early 1950s. Selections from this hybrid

Alexander Maximovich and colleagues with Peter and Mark,
eating a hearty meal on the beach

have given us *I.* 'Blue Prince' and *I.* 'Blue Princess' amongst others. Further inland on exposed low ridges, curious pygmy woodland composed almost entirely of a local form of the Mongolian oak, *Quercus mongolica* var. *grosseserrata*, is to be found. The gnarled, wind-moulded specimens are no more than 6 m (20 ft) tall; only an occasional tree of *Sorbus commixta* breaks up their hegemony. Interestingly, it is from this variety that the Mongolian oak is chiefly known in cultivation, certainly in the British Isles, simply because the typical form performs so poorly.

Making our way back to the estuary, we can see Sergei preparing food over an open fire made from driftwood collected on the beach. He has made a delicious salmon and potato soup, which we all enjoy in bright sunshine, despite the attentions of literally thousands of flies. After lunch, Alexander and his team turn to filleting the dozens of salmon they have by now beached. Out of the corner of my eye I catch sight of swift movement. Two large black saloon cars are racing across the sand towards us. They come to a halt mere metres from Alexander and Peter, and three menacing figures jump out—a scene from a Hollywood spy movie. The men are dressed in long, black leather coats, one with a broad-brimmed hat; they move with the false confidence that official sanction confers. Alexander continues with his work on the fish.

Peter gestures for us to fade into the background, but we don't go too far as we are fascinated by what unfolds. Very quickly a shouting match develops, with elaborate gesturing and much posturing; Alexander stands tall and firm in the face of obvious threats and abusive language from the three dark figures. It doesn't take a genius to work out that they are not happy with his activities, but he is unmoved and produces a sheaf of official-looking papers. 'He has a licence', Sergei quietly confides. Eventually things calm down, and the three retire to their vehicles, rather licking their wounds it seems to me. Nonetheless the fishing stops, and Peter tells us it is time to leave. He is very reticent about the incident and doesn't respond to our questions; he gives Sergei a sideways glance, as if to say 'Keep quiet'. We decide it is better to let the matter rest.

We pack and leave the beach. Back at Sokol we unwind and sort out the day's collections; Sergei helps Alexander finish cleaning and filleting the salmon, and it is not until after 10.30 p.m. that we are on the road back to Yuzhno-Sakhalinsk. Alexander drives us back to the institute; the gates are locked, and we are obliged to carry our bags along the drive until we find a hole in the fence. Our lodgings look as unwelcoming as ever. We turn in straightaway, and though Tony falls immediately to sleep it takes me some time. I'm still awake when the familiar whining of the mosquitoes starts up, leading to a miserable night.

The twenty-eighth of September dawns bright and warm, and Peter is off to the main buildings again, talking to the director and making arrangements for the next two days. We have a quick breakfast and are waiting outside by 9.00 a.m. An hour later we are still waiting. Eventually a large truck with a spacious cab on the back puts into the yard. Peter introduces us to Mica, the driver (who can be no more than sixteen), and to Andrei, a local botanist who will guide us during the next two days. The delay is explained: there was difficulty acquiring petrol for the journey. We load up and are off. Our journey will take us to the southeast of the island, close to the village of Prigarodnoe, and we have a bumpy 75 km (45 miles) of potholed road

The transport to Prigarodnoe

to endure. Tony is somewhat dubious about the trip, as we are heading back towards the coast and the flat cultivated fields look decidedly uninteresting.

On arrival Andrei takes the lead, and our concerns are immediately allayed. He leads us into a forest clearing, where a rich meadow with an impressive array of plants has developed. The pink feathery flowers of *Poterium tenuifolium*, previously seen in the water meadow at Golubiny Utyos, immediately catch the eye, as do the now skeletal remains of *Angelica gigas*. Colonies of the attractive fern *Osmunda cinnamomea* are turning a beautiful russet colour; occasional white wands of flowers identify *Cimicifuga simplex*, and another white-flowered plant, *Aruncus asiaticus*, the far-eastern relative of European goatsbeard, vies for attention.

Amongst the dense herbage we can see the fruiting heads of *Lilium hansonii* and lower down still the striking, dark blue fruits of *Clintonia udensis*, a refined member of the Liliaceae whose nearest relative is *C. alpina* from the Himalaya and western China. More species occur in North America, including queens cup, *C. uniflora*, from the Pacific Northwest, which reminds

Osmunda cinnamomea in the meadow at Prigarodnoe

us once again of the important floristic links between the two continents. Occasional plants of the herbaceous *Aralia cordata* var. *sachalinensis* add a stately air to the plant associations. Tony comments that it is a pity we were not able to see the meadow in full flower in the early summer, when it certainly must be a beautiful spectacle, a kaleidoscope of colours. The ground becomes increasingly wet, and eventually a dense colony of reeds begins to dominate; even so, one or two choice plants can be found. The small, strap-like leaves of *Hosta lancifolia* provide us with another collection, as does the unusual *Lobelia sessilifolia*, which rises to nearly 1 m (3 ft 3 in) in height and is holding on to the last of its bluish flowers.

Our walk has been circular, and we eventually reemerge from the woods close to the vehicle, where Mica and Sergei have been waiting patiently. By now it has become overcast, and a light rain is falling. We retire to a small dilapidated hut, where Sergei makes some hot, sweet tea. We gaze out of the door into the rain; in the distance we can see the coast. In the darkening conditions, the sea is the colour of gun-metal, and it is difficult to distinguish the horizon as the low cloud blends seamlessly with the water. We can reflect on another successful day: our collections have now risen to above 200. We thank Andrei for his invaluable help before we all rejoin Mica for an uneventful journey back to Yuzhno-Sakhalinsk.

On the return journey Peter outlines our movements for the few days we have left on Sakhalin. Tomorrow he has another site for us to visit close to the southwest tip of the island, where the influence of Japanese plants is most highly developed and where several of the important plants on our hit list are to be located. This will leave us with a day for organising ourselves and collecting the permits we need to take the seeds back with us to the mainland. He then wants to make a second attempt to climb Mount Chekhov where, his researches have confirmed, we will find *Rhododendron camtschaticum*, a key target plant for the island. This all sounds very satisfactory, and we are reminded once again just what a competent botanist and logistician Peter is. His performance in leading the trip has been nigh on flawless, and we owe him a great debt for the care and consideration he has shown us under frequently difficult and trying circumstances.

On the following morning Mica and Andrei arrive bright and early, and we climb into the big cab for the journey to the southwestern town of Wevelsk. The journey is nearly 100 km (60 miles) in length, and the road is variable; there is little we can do other than to sit tight and endure things. Tony and I while away the time chatting about home, family, plans, aspirations—all the usual things that go through one's mind when time is available to reflect. Journeys to faraway places tend to bring out the contemplative elements in a person's character. It is after midday when we finally arrive at our destination; after a light snack Peter and Andrei accompany us into the woods. As Peter predicted, things get very interesting very quickly. The low-growing evergreen shrub *Skimmia japonica* var. *intermedia* f. *repens* straightaway confirms Peter's assertion about the intrusion of typically Japanese plants in this part of the island.

The canopy rapidly develops a range of species. Tall majestic specimens of the cork tree, *Phellodendron amurense* var. *sachalinense*, appear first, though intriguingly these trees are far less corky than those we have seen on the mainland, making the common name something of a misnomer. The Japanese umbrella tree, *Magnolia obovata*, follows along, with *Kalopanax septem-*

Skimmia japonica var. *intermedia* f. *repens* in the woods at Wevelsk

lobus. Maddeningly, none are in fruit. Whilst it is not unusual to find the occasional species taking a year out, to find three climax species sterile is most odd and suggests poor weather conditions at flowering time.

Happily, other plants are more obliging, and we gather another collection of *Sorbus commixta* in the slender-twigged, smaller-leaved form we have seen across the southern parts of the island. Clambering into the trees is the climbing hydrangea, *Hydrangea anomala* subsp. *petiolaris*, as is *Vitis amurensis*, which is carrying masses of its delicious bluish-black fruits (having already collected this species, we are relaxed about Peter's 'one for you, two for me' approach). *Acer pictum* is also common and carrying abundant amounts of seed, contrasting with our earlier collections of this species on the mainland, which were rather poor. Once again it is satisfying to acquire Sakhalin material of this widely distributed tree. The afternoon is warm and sunny— in fact, in the dense woodland it is quite oppressive, and we are pleased when the sun starts to sink towards the horizon and the temperature cools noticeably. Still the collecting goes on; extensive, low-growing colonies of *Taxus cuspidata*, Japanese yew, are heavily fruiting and make for easy collecting. It grows to no more than I.2 m (4 ft) and conspicuously prefers the shady northeast-facing slopes. We don't leave the area until it is dark and with a long return journey don't arrive back at the institute lodgings until nearly midnight; a busy day sees both collectors falling into their beds with little appetite for conversation.

The following day is spent navigating the labyrinthine bureaucracy of the Russian customs service, a task that occupies all Peter's negotiating skills for several hours. The interrogation is conducted by a fearsome lady with fluorescent orange hair, bright red lips and arms that Arnold Schwarzenegger would be proud of. She insists on going through every seed packet and each herbarium specimen in turn and at great length. At the end of the process, however, we are issued with our export permit, which is the most important thing. By the time we are all back at the institute it is raining, and the day is cold, grey and uninviting. We decide to spend the time preparing for our imminent departure and saving our strength for the climb to the top of Mount Chekhov. This is the first day in nearly three weeks that we haven't been collecting or travelling, and we are beginning to feel a growing sense of that deep, enervating fatigue that sleep alone cannot dispel.

A bright dawn greets us on I October, and Peter is encouraged to try and complete our unfinished business on Mount Chekhov. Sergei sends us off with a hearty breakfast of fried potatoes and ham. As there is no vehicular support, we are obliged to journey to the peak by public transport and on foot. This takes a considerable time, and we begin the actual ascent just after noon. The weather is quite pleasant, overcast but warm—in fact, if anything the humidity is, once again, slightly stifling. With the warmth and steepness of the slope, we are all soon sweating and panting. Peter calls a brief halt at about 700 m (2400 ft) but is clearly not anxious to dwell too long. Given that we have already taken this route before, our collecting is limited; we are keen to get to the point where we finished on our last visit. Already we can feel a chill creeping in, and the sky now seems more threatening; we can clearly see that the topmost part of the mountain is shrouded in a gently swirling mist. No sooner have we set off again than we are enveloped by this miasma. The air is still but saturated, and we are soon wringing wet.

Almost as soon as the 1000 m (3300 ft) contour line is gained, the flora seems to change dramatically, and we give a collective cheer as we spot the

Rhododendron camtschaticum and *R. aureum* near the summit of Mount Chekhov

first of the low-growing plants of *Rhododendron camtschaticum*. Our voices are muffled by the heavy air, and the sodden silence reasserts itself. We have long since left behind the shelter of the subalpine woodland and are now in a habitat of low, scrubby birches and alder with a rich assemblage of other dwarf woody plants dominated by members of the Ericaceae, all of which form a mosaic at ground level. A second rhododendron, *R. aureum*, jockeys for position with its sibling and is joined by *Vaccinium vitis-idaea*, the cowberry, a plant familiar to me from the Lancashire fells. Indeed, at this high elevation I note a number of familiar plants, including another member of the heather family, *Empetrum nigrum*, which is also a British native and confusingly called crowberry; its shiny black fruits are hard to see in the low light levels. These plants form the second element of Sakhalin's vegetation and are part of what is known as the circumboreal flora, in that they occupy a great swath of the earth's surface in the high northern latitudes and occur almost unchanged across Europe, Asia and on into North America. On Sakhalin they migrate down from the north to meet the dominant Japanese

A triumphant pose for the camera

plants in the southern third of the island, where the laws of natural selection confine them to the highest ground.

Rhododendron camtschaticum has obviously flowered prolifically, as evidenced by the masses of seed capsules on the plants; unfortunately, many of these have already opened and much of the seed has been discharged. Nonetheless we make a good collection, working briskly across the flat top of the peak. Having stopped climbing, I am suddenly aware of just how cold it has become and how much the mist has closed in on us. I add another sweater and continue with the collecting work. Peter draws our activities to a close by 6.00 p.m., knowing we have a long return journey and that the twilight is gathering. It is with a sense of relief and sadness that we conclude things.

This is our last day in the field; we leave for the mainland tomorrow and will then use what time remains us for a final processing of all our collections before the departure for England. We pose for a photograph together; it is fitting that Peter should stand with us, given his towering contribution.

Mark with the giant leaf of
Lysichiton camtschatcensis

Without further ado, we descend the track to the base of the mountain. In the near darkness I spot one final plant of great interest, characteristically occupying the wet flushes which run down the sloping flanks. Often called skunk cabbage, *Lysichiton camtschatcensis* is a member of the arum family and produces typical Araceae inflorescences in the early spring: a shield-like spathe protecting the fertile phallus-shaped spadix. The spathe, a beautiful pure white, is very striking; in gardens in April it never fails to elicit fascinated comment. It has a close relative on the other side of the Pacific in the western states and provinces of the United States and Canada, *L. americanus*, which has almost identical spathes of a rich, golden yellow. When brought together in gardens, they form intermediate hybrids with creamy-coloured spathes. Of the two, the Asian plant is far less frequently grown, and so it is of considerable interest to see it here in its native haunts. Its flowers, and indeed its fruits, are now long past and the large paddle-shaped leaves are turning yellow as the plants prepare for the onset of winter.

By the time we make Yuzhno-Sakhalinsk it is quite dark, and the dim streetlights reflect back off the slick pavements. We sit on a bench, waiting for the bus (which is a long time in coming), grateful for the opportunity to rest after a strenuous day. When we finally arrive at the institute, at 9.30 p.m., we are met by Sergei, who quickly ladles out steaming bowls of potato and onion soup. This is followed by a shower at the power plant, and then we all stumble into bed.

The following morning Peter wakes us rather vigorously at 7.00 a.m.; we breakfast and then spend the morning sorting through the previous day's small number of collections. All is in order—we are in good shape. It now begins to feel as if our work is almost complete, except for the final organisation of our affairs in Vladivostok. We can now look forward to a cleaner, more comfortable and more leisurely environment! Inevitably my thoughts are all about the family, and I imagine Tony is similarly occupied. I hope everyone is well and that Lesley has not had too difficult a time of it with two small children and a limited amount of help. It is over three weeks since we even had a snatch of conversation.

We are collected at 3.30 p.m. and driven to the airport. We wait outside the small terminal building whilst Peter and Sergei go inside to sort out any formalities. They emerge looking very concerned—problem—we are way over our baggage allowance. There follows some protracted and intense discussion. Sergei does a very good job at flattering and flirting with the check-in girls, and after several duty managers are called and engaged in heated negotiations, we get the go-ahead to proceed. There is a long wait before we board, and it is not until 8.30 p.m. that we carry our bags to the waiting aeroplane. With few formalities, the plane lifts off half an hour later; the flight is brief and uneventful, save for the reappearance of the singular stewardess we met on the outbound flight. Vladivostok is an hour behind Sakhalin, and we land at 9.00 p.m. local time. Arrival procedures are relaxed to say the least; we don't even go through the airport terminal but exit through a side gate to the outside. Anatoly is waiting for us and greets us warmly. We are pleased to be met, as in the darkness the airport is a brooding and threatening place with groups of men milling around with purpose. After collecting the remainder of our bags we depart for the hotel. Given our recent accommodation, the hotel—the one we occupied when first in Vladivostok—seems classy and palatial, and when everyone has left us, Tony and I enjoy a quiet beer and a muted conversation at the bar before turning in.

Our last two full days in Russia are spent at Peter's institute preparing all our collections—seeds, herbarium specimens and field notes. We have an excellent haul, 224 collections weighing in at nearly 20 kg (45 lb), and are

The team outside the Russian Academy of Sciences, Vladivostok

delighted with the outcome. There are two more highlights before we say our farewells; both Peter and Sergei invite us to dine at their homes with their delightful families. The food is excellent, and the company more so; it is wonderful to feel that we have forged real friendships with these people from the other side of the world and that, though our real purpose has been to conduct fieldwork on behalf of the Royal Botanic Gardens, Kew, Tony and I have grown as individuals as a result of our experiences.

The protracted return flights via Seoul and Hong Kong merely raise our anticipation, and we finally hit the runway at Heathrow Airport on 7 October 1994. As soon as we enter the arrivals lounge, we are swamped by a writhing mass of children—how they've grown! Lesley and Sally stand back for a moment and then join in the reunion.

In due time, we assess our success. We have been able to collect seventy percent of the species from our target list from the mainland and nearly sixty percent from Sakhalin. Many interesting plants have been gathered, notably the endemic conifer *Microbiota decussata*, perhaps the first new germplasm since its original introduction. Further collections of *Sorbus com-*

mixta will add to the representation of this confused taxon in cultivation. A full set of mainland rose species have been gathered. All the main species of alders and birches have been collected, as have other important tree genera, *Juglans, Quercus* and *Tilia* amongst them. A surprise is the richness of our herbaceous collections from an area that has perhaps been underestimated for its herbaceous flora.

This expedition to eastern Asia has neatly dove-tailed with the past visits to South Korea and Taiwan and those of other Kew personnel to the main Japanese island of Honshu. All that remains to be done is to undertake a trip to Japan's northernmost island, Hokkaido, to close a temperate loop all the way from Sakhalin to Taiwan.

CHAPTER 6

Hokkaido, Alone?

AS THE ANA BOEING 747 LEAVES the runway and circles back over Heathrow, I look out the window in economy class to see the trees below; they are beginning to look tired, preparing for winter with early signs of autumn colour and some premature leaf fall. The undercarriage comes up with a whirring and clanking noise, locking into place, and we are truly bound for Japan.

It is 16 September 1997. A few days before I left, Mark invited me over to his home, Verderers, in Windsor Great Park, for a traditional Sunday dinner of roast beef with the first of the homegrown parsnips from his prized vegetable garden—an invitation not to be turned down. That night, he gave me a sealed envelope, which I am now clutching in my hand. On the outside it reads, 'Mr Anthony Kirkham (Not to be opened before you are airborne)'. I open it now and find a postcard from the Hokkaido University Press; a print of *Sorbus commixta* is on the front, and the back reads as follows:

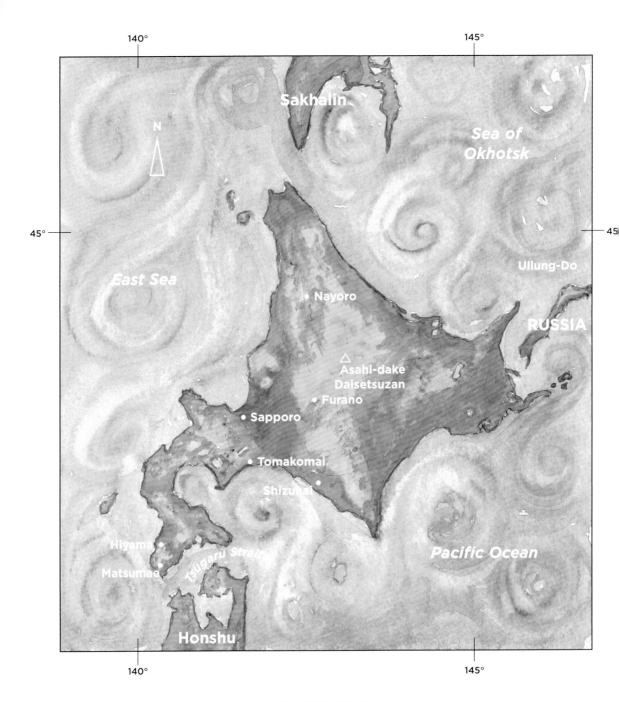

HOKKAIDO

Dear Tony,

Just a short note to wish you the very best for the EHOK trip. Sorry
I can't be with you, but I know that you will be as successful as ever.
Keep the KIFL end up and enjoy yourself. Best wishes to Giles,
Charles and Bill.

Regards, Mark

PS Make sure you bag the plant on the front of the card!!

EHOK (Expedition to Hokkaido), the acronym for this collecting trip, will
follow every plant, both on the label and the plant records, wherever it is
planted; KIFL is the acronym for our donor code on the Kew database—
Kirkham and Flanagan. True, three good friends from England and the
United States will be with me on this trip, but my long-standing field part-
ner, with whom I have experienced so much in such demanding conditions
in the past, will not. I suddenly realise that it may seem as if I am alone in
Hokkaido.

This expedition, the culmination of two years' preparatory work by Mark,
will complete the temperate loop we began together in 1989. Mark began
the planning process with the help of Dr Hideki Takahashi, a lecturer in
botany at Hokkaido University and the curator of the Sapporo Botanic
Garden, which is linked to the botany faculty at the university. Unfortunately,
Mark left his position at Wakehurst Place to take up the post of Keeper of
the Gardens at Windsor and so was unable to participate in this final trip. It
was left to me to pick up where Mark left off and reorganise the schedules.
Mark had left everything in good order, and Takahashi was still keen for the
trip to go ahead, despite the change in expedition personnel.

I will lead our team of four on this trip; the three new members are Lord
Howick (whom I will henceforth refer to as Charles) from the Howick
Arboretum in Northumberland, William (Bill) McNamara, director of
Quarry Hill Botanical Gardens in California, and Giles Coode-Adams,
recently retired chief-executive of the Kew Foundation. In the autumn of
1996, between our trip to the Russian Far East and this trip to Hokkaido,
Mark and I spent four weeks in the Micang Shan mountain range of north-
ern Sichuan, China, collecting with Charles and Bill, both regular travellers

Tony and Mark collecting in the Micang Shan, western China

and collectors in China and the United States; this was to conclude a series of seed collecting expeditions hosted by the Institute of Biology at the Academia Sinica, Chengdu, so I am familiar with their fieldcraft. Giles has helped fund, through the foundation, most of our previous trips to the Far East and was keen to participate in one himself, having heard so many of our tales. He knew Mark would be a tough act to follow, but this was his opportunity.

I am now sat in the rear of the shuttle bus with Charles taking us from Narita Airport to Haneda Airport in Tokyo for our connection to Hokkaido; Giles will join us a few days later in Sapporo. Bill, coincidentally, has already arrived from San Francisco and is waiting at the bus stop, about

Hideki Takahashi collecting *Sorbus*

to board the same shuttle as ours. Its great to catch up with him and swap stories and information about how plants collected from previous trips to the Far East are faring in our gardens. All the flights are on time, and we finally arrive at Chitose Airport around 8.30 p.m., where Takahashi, smartly dressed in a jacket and tie, meets us. With his thick, dark beard and spectacles, he looks like he will be at home with us botanising in the forests of the island. He looks pleased to see us but is very serious in his welcome, electing to carry some of the bags to the mini people carrier in the car park that he has hired for the duration of our trip. The drive into Sapporo is very busy with lots of traffic; we are tired after a long flight, and there is very little exchange of words on the way in.

Once at the University of Hokkaido, we are shown our rooms at the Poplar Kaikan, an extremely comfortable campus residence for visiting professors. Takahashi leaves us once we are settled in, as he is also tired from a long day lecturing to his students, and we all retire to our rooms to catch up on some badly needed sleep.

In the morning I experience my first traditional Japanese breakfast in the communal dining room downstairs: cooked salmon, rice, eggs and pickled plums. I make the first mistake; I assume the egg is hardboiled and crack it on the table. It is raw, and I watch as the yolk and white spread across the bare tabletop and then slip onto the floor. Bill and Charles, who are both well versed in the cuisine of Japan, find this highly amusing and offer their culinary expertise, which I gladly accept. After cleaning up I am given another egg; I break it into the rice and salmon, whisk it all together, making a very glutinous concoction, and proceed to eat it with chopsticks. Unfortunately, I can't get on with the pickled plums, which are unusually bitter and salty; my taste buds seem unable to cope with them.

At 9.00 a.m. Takahashi arrives, and we go through the detailed itinerary that he has planned around our target list of plants. He suggests that we first drive to the very north of the island and then work our way south, as he is concerned that the weather may break for the worst early and make it difficult for us to collect in the northern forests later in the expedition. It all looks good—lots of time working in a variety of locations with different habitats and plants. All the forests we are to visit are under the control of the university, and the university's director, Dr Yasuo Kikuta, has given us carte blanche to collect seed and herbarium specimens in any of them, with the help of his staff. We will also spend one or two days in a national park, and permits and permission to collect have been given. Takahashi looks pleased with our approval of his plans and eagerness to get to the forests and begin collecting. He suggests that, whilst we settle down and adjust to the time difference over the next day or two, we visit the Sapporo Botanic Garden to have a look round and meet the staff. We gladly take up his offer.

The 13-ha (33-acre) garden, located in the centre of Sapporo, not far from the university, is the second oldest botanical garden in Japan, next to Koishikawa in Tokyo, dating back to 1877, the beginning of the Meiji Era. It was planned and laid out by Dr Kingo Miyabe, the first director, and contains a mix of over four thousand native plants of Hokkaido's flora, with some exotics set amongst the original forest trees of *Ulmus davidiana*, *Acer pictum* and *Populus maximowiczii*. A magnificent specimen of *Acer miyabei*, named after the director and first introduced into the West by Charles Sargent from the Arnold Arboretum in 1892, stands at the front of the Batchelor

Memorial Museum, on the garden's grounds. This museum houses one of the largest collections of Ainu artefacts, left behind by an Englishman, Rev. John Batchelor, who spent decades researching the indigenous people of Hokkaido and Siberia in the nineteenth century, of whom the Ainu are amongst the most important.

Before leaving, we collect a telescopic longarm pruner and a box of newspapers for drying the herbarium specimens from the tool shed. The pruner is the Japanese ARS model, complete with a grip adjacent to the blade to hold the specimen once cut; it will prove to be an essential piece of the plant collector's armoury over the ensuing weeks. The rest of the day is spent exchanging sterling into yen at the bank and shopping for maps and local floras in a departmental bookstore, followed by a whistle-stop tour of downtown Sapporo. We return to the Poplar Kaikan, where Takahashi leaves us to attend what will be 'a long meeting' before leaving town for several days with us. Before dark we take a walk around the campus, which is an arboretum in itself, with every Hokkaido native tree planted and well labelled. In the evening we meet Giles at the airport and convey him back to the university, where we bring him up to date with the proposals from Takahashi. He only has tonight to rest up before we travel north to begin the expedition, and despite flying out business class, he still looks a little tired and in need of some sleep.

This morning we have the same breakfast as yesterday, only I am more versed in the preparation of the rice and egg dish and look like a skilled operative at the table. I warn Giles before we enter the dining room, so that he will not make the same mistake as I did. He doesn't let us down.

Once our personal bags and field kit are packed and ready, we load the van to the gunnels, make ourselves comfortable in the rear and are soon on the expressway heading north, with Takahashi behind the wheel. Notwithstanding our 80-km (50-mile) roundtrip drive to the airport last night, in the dark, without him, he is not comfortable with one of us driving, and it looks like we are set to spend the rest of the trip in the vehicles as passengers. No matter, it gives us the opportunity to take in some of the beautiful scenery and botanise through the windows, despite the heavy rain that is now starting to fall.

We are making for Nayoro City, where we are to stay in rustic lodgings on a forestry nursery belonging to the Nayoro Forest Station. When we arrive we find them extremely comfortable, with tatami (straw mats) and futons—exuding traditional atmosphere in the ryokan style. Once inside we have to remove our day clothes and wear the yukata (lightweight robes) provided, and I soon enter into the mood of Japanese lifestyle, which I will easily get used to. At 5.00 p.m. I have a meeting with the director of the Uryu Forest Experimental Station, Dr Kuramo, who couldn't be more helpful. He marks on maps what he thinks will be the best collecting stations and gives us the keys for all the gates in his zone, which will allow us to drive right into the forests. After the meeting, we dine locally on tempura and toasts of sake, all excited at the prospect of making our first collections tomorrow.

I am awakened to the sound of an electronically engineered cockerel crow, followed by another computerised electronic female voice informing us of the time—'Good morning, it's 6 o' clock a.m.' This is Giles's alarm clock—quite disturbing, especially to Bill and Charles in the room next door. However, it manages to rouse everyone from their tatami and gets us ready in good time for the day ahead. We procure breakfast from a local shop in the form of a takeaway consisting of glutinous rice, a piece of chicken or pork and various pickles, and consume it in Kuramo's office whilst discussing the next few days of the trip. We thank him again for all his help and hospitality, and by 9.00 a.m. we are driving along a good forest track in the Uryu forest, due northeast of Shumarinai Lake.

This is mixed deciduous and coniferous forest, the main elements being large trees of *Quercus mongolica* var. *grosseserrata*, *Magnolia obovata* and *Abies sachalinensis*. The oaks make large, wide-spreading trees similar in appearance to our English oak, *Quercus robur*, compared to the same species found growing further north on Sakhalin, which are generally more stunted. From where we are now, Sakhalin is the next island of this archipelago, lying across the Sea of Okhotsk, and it seems like a long time ago since Mark and I were collecting there in 1994. There is certainly a close resemblance between the flora here and that of Sakhalin, which Mark and I witnessed three years ago. We look hard into the crowns of many of the oaks but struggle to find any acorns; it has been a lean fruiting year, and we fail to make a good collection. The magnolias (or honoki, as the Japanese refer to them), however,

Mixed woodlands in Uryu forest

make trees larger than the oaks, up to 25 m (80 ft) tall with substantial boles, and, despite the close onset of winter, still have their large obovate leaves intact. It's difficult to see (until we get our eyes in) the scarlet-coloured cone-like fruits, and there turns out to be an abundance of them. Most are very high and prove difficult to collect; however, after a vigilant search, we are able to find some within easy reach.

One of the first collections of the day will please Mark. It's *Sorbus commixta*, the Japanese rowan, making a large multi-stemmed understorey tree, with large clusters of red berries hanging from the branch tips; the structure of its canopy and the stoutness in the stems varies considerably from the collection we made on Ullung-Do. The telescopic pruners really come into their own now, making collecting so easy.

We soon get into a pattern, with Bill and I collecting and bagging the seed, Giles taking the herbarium specimens and Charles writing the field notes. Considering Charles is a technophobe, he isn't doing too badly; with the GPS (Global Positioning System) and Dictaphone around his neck,

Sorbus commixta

among other things, he looks quite at home. During the trip to Sichuan in China last year, Mark and I introduced him to new technology that has revolutionised his means of making field notes.

The weather is dry, and the temperature is perfect for this type of work. The biggest problem is the thick chest-high sasa bamboo on the forest floor—it's extremely difficult to push through it in order to get to the trees. What will it be like when it's wet? The thin canes wrap around your legs, pulling you down to the ground, and prevent any steady progress, especially on the steeper slopes. In some areas it's totally impenetrable, and we have to negotiate alternative routes through to individual trees we can see from the tracks.

Charles Howick showing the full array
of his field equipment

Takahashi preparing his herbarium
specimens

Growing up the trunk of a large *Acer pictum*, pushing well into the high canopy, we find a climbing hydrangea, *Hydrangea anomala* subsp. *petiolaris*, reaching 12 m (39 ft) in height. It clings to the trunks with its aerial roots and is covered in old flowers that are turning into seed heads—still a little unripe for collection, though. In the canopies of several trees adjacent to the maple, a *Vitis coignetiae* has swamped several large rock birches, *Betula ermanii*, its plate-sized leaves turning a deep plum red at the very top and ripe bunches of purple fruits with a grey bloom hanging along the vine.

'What time do you want to finish?' asks Takahashi.

'How about you?' I reply.

'We should work till dark and make the most of the dry weather', he says. This is great for us, a dream come true. Wherever we look there is something new to collect, and the day goes very quickly. Whilst we are busy, Takahashi is happy making the most of his time in the field, collecting specimens for the Sapporo Botanic Garden by the dozen.

We leave the forest exhausted at around 5.30 p.m. and arrive back in Nayoro City in the dark. Tonight is the beginning of our evening work, adding the new field notes to a laptop computer holding Q Collector, a software programme written specifically for the purpose. We then cross-check the seed and herbarium collections against the collector's numbers.

Charles lets us have a wee dram of a wonderful Highland malt whisky he has brought with him, which helps us to work into the night before a soak in the hot tub downstairs. Bill is the expert here and briefs us all on the etiquette of using this modern type of Japanese bath. It is a deep stainless steel tub, about a metre square, full of scalding hot water, with a lid on it to keep the heat in. In order to keep the water clean for the next user, you soap yourself down outside the bath, rinsing off all the soap before entering the hot water. No soap must enter the water! It takes some time to submerse yourself, given the heat of the water, but eventually you get used to it—and then it's difficult to get out. Just right to get rid of the aches and pains from the first day in the field. As I lie there turning my usual deep lobster red, I think of the banyas in Russia and the significant differences between the two styles of bathing.

The next morning, breakfast consists of strong coffee and bread and jam in our rooms and then straight off to the forest—a different type of woodland compared to yesterday, with slightly different vegetation. It's very wet on either side of the track, with lots of water lying on the forest floor; many of the trees are inaccessible without a boat—or one of us wading up to our waist in icy cold water. No one volunteers, so we wait to see if the trees are more accessible further into the forest.

Picea glehnii, the predominant conifer in these wet areas, grows amongst shapely deciduous broadleaf trees, *Fraxinus mandshurica* var. *japonica* and *Alnus hirsuta*. We find an oak with lots of acorns and make a good collection, compensating for yesterday's poor one. Most have fallen from the tree, and we have to hunt through the sasa to find dormant ones, as they have already begun to germinate, ready for a good start next spring. A perfect conical specimen of the Yezo spruce, *Picea jezoensis*, reaches into the sky, framing the forest track, and after I climb it to collect some cones, we take our lunch at the base of it. The specific epithet is apt: it references the old name for Hokkaido, Jezo Island. There are lots of goodies on the forest floor, including *Skimmia japonica* var. *intermedia* f. *repens*, *Menziesia pentandra*, two *Ilex* species and several *Euonymus* species. Giles is very excited; he has an affinity for these deciduous euonymus, and I must say they look terrific, with the spindle fruits hanging in abundance from the branches. He later confides that he intends to plant a large collection back at Feeringbury Manor, his home in Essex.

This is a good stop, and it is well into the afternoon when we complete our work and head back to the base, where plenty of work remains to be done. Takahashi needs to make some telephone calls to the director of the forest on tomorrow's itinerary, to check one or two important locations in Nakagawa forest.

Next day, as we drive along the excellent roads with hardly a car in sight, I can only wonder at how they'll be in a short time: there are red and white marker poles all along the sides, at even intervals, which Takahashi informs us are to identify the whereabouts of the roads when they are deep in snow. It is also ironic to be driving on the left-hand side of the road so far from home. At the entrance to the forest, in the administration offices, the director produces several detailed maps with potential collecting sites clearly marked with the names of several of the plants on our list—extremely exciting. We arrange to come back to the office at 3.00 p.m. if we fail to find any specimens of the important *Magnolia kobus* on our own, in which case the director will help us.

Our first challenge is the monarch birch, *Betula maximowicziana*. This is a rare, beautifully majestic tree in the northern forests of Hokkaido, growing tall, with a definite straight silver trunk, well lenticelled, and the largest leaves of all birches. Unfortunately, there are no lower lateral branches that might hold the fruiting catkins, and we struggle to find a means of climbing it to get seed. We even contemplate climbing a neighbouring spruce and, once high enough, jumping across into the crown of the birch. We deliberate for nearly an hour, as we are told we may not see any more after today and this is one tree worth growing in any arboretum. With great disappointment, we climb into the van and drive off, leaving the specimen still with copious amounts of seed in the upper crown. If only we had brought the throw line! This is a small bag, usually weighted with sand, attached to a long, fine cord; an experienced arborist can easily throw it to a great height

A majestic specimen of the monarch birch, *Betula maximowicziana*, showing the typical tall straight trunk

into the crown of a tree, enabling a much thicker climbing rope to be pulled up over a strong anchor branch.

We drive around a bend in the forest track, barely 100 m (330 ft) from the last stop. We cannot believe what we see immediately in front of us. Another monarch birch, about 20 m (65 ft) tall, completely covered in scaffolding, set up by a PhD student from the forestry school carrying out a project on why this species is quickly disappearing from the forests of Hokkaido. We engage the student in conversation, and she allows us to gather seed from the tree, providing we mark each branch where we pick the seed with a red ribbon and number it. I am soon up on the structure, pick-

Monarch birch with a difference!

Hanging fruits of *Schisandra chinensis*,
a prominent feature of the forest
canopy

ing seed and tying ribbons around the branches, and despite the safety of
the scaffold, with the light breeze high up in the canopy, I would feel much
more comfortable and relaxed tied into the tree with my climbing rope and
harness.

We leave the birch and drive for a mile or two into primary forest along
a very rough track and soon find ourselves amongst stands of large ash,
Fraxinus mandshurica var. *japonica*, with butter-yellow leaves, and *Cornus contro-
versa*. A strong climber is growing through the lower branches of the dog-
wood, making it difficult to get anywhere near the base of it. I can see some
red fruits hanging in bunches; it turns out to be *Schisandra chinensis*.

Whilst we are collecting the schisandra fruits, the scent of candyfloss or
burnt jam lingers in the air, and occasionally we get stronger smells on the
light breeze. I recognise it immediately as the dried-up leaves of the katsura
tree that I have smelt in the arboretum at Kew in the autumn months. We
search along a narrow stream and are soon confronted by several magnifi-

Tony amongst the trunks of a giant
katsura tree, *Cercidiphyllum japonicum*

cent specimens of *Cercidiphyllum japonicum* towering in the sky above us. They are just starting to don their pinky-yellow autumn colour, but some are still very green and making the most of the late autumn sunshine before retiring for the long, cold winter. I have never seen the fruits of this tree before, and we soon find a female tree covered in small green banana-shaped pods about 2.5 cm (1 in) long in the leaf axils all along the slender twigs. Many of these trees are secondary regrowth from old rotted-out tree stumps that must have been felled many years ago, some stumps easily reaching over 5 m (16 ft) in diameter. These must have been some of the largest deciduous trees in these forests and will once have dominated the forest canopy.

On the ground in the moist soil, several 2-m (6.5-ft) fruiting spikes of *Cardiocrinum cordatum* var. *glehnii* are competing for light, and Charles is eager to photograph them. Bill is also eager—to collect the seedpods, and begins to break them off into a bag before Charles has found his camera. We have to rebuild a spike in order that Charles can pose for a photograph, much to his annoyance.

This is an exciting location, and we never know what we will find around the corner. Our next thrill: we come across a large specimen of *Magnolia kobus* var. *borealis*, to 20 m (65 ft) high, loaded with red fruits right down to the ground. As we fill a muslin bag with the ripe fruits, Takahashi informs us that this is possibly the most northern site of any magnolia species (with *M. obovata* sharing honours). Three gems found in the same location on the same day—this calls for a celebratory bathe in a real hot spring. Takahashi knows

The unusual plum-like fruits of *Cephalotaxus harringtoniana* var. *nana*, the Japanese plum yew

a perfect one on the route home and is as eager as we are to soak in the naturally piping-hot sulphur pool.

We check in at the hot springs reception desk, where we are issued with soap, towels and a bathrobe. Sitting on small plastic stools, we wash ourselves down and rinse off the suds; then, armed with only a flannel to cover our modesty, we plunge into the overcrowded water. It soon empties of the local people, and we have the whole pool to ourselves (it must be the flannels!). This is the most relaxing way of winding down after a long day in the office or field, but instead of waking you up, it makes you drowsy. It's not until venturing out into the cold evening air, just above freezing, that you are stirred to do some important evening work.

We spend the better part of the next day in this area but, with a lot of repetition in the plants, we decide it is time to move on to another location on the itinerary. We follow the River Uryu along the east bank and find a precipitous slope running up into the dense forest. Whilst we are examining the green plum-like fruits of the many plants of *Cephalotaxus harringtoniana* var. *nana* at the foot of the slope, Giles brings me a piece of plant bearing red foliage and asks its identity. There is a trace of panic on Takahashi's face when he sees it, and he asks Giles where he found it. He shows us the spot, and on closer scrutiny we find it running all over along the ground under the other plants. It turns out to be *Rhus ambigua*, the poison ivy of Japan, and Takahashi is worried that Giles has come into contact with sap from the broken stem.

'Is it toxic?' asks Giles.

Takahashi peels back his sleeve and shows us old scars along his arm, the reminders to him of the last time he came across this plant under similar circumstances. He didn't need to say anything in reply to Giles. This plant is the cousin of the North American poison ivy, *Rhus radicans*, and the sap can be a serious skin irritant to some people, leaving sore blisters for lengthy periods and finally resulting in lifelong scars. We decide to use antihistamine cream as a precaution and to keep an eye on Giles's affected skin parts for blistering through the day. Takahashi asks us all to be extremely cautious about handling any pinnate-leaved plants, especially when using them as a climbing aid to access the vegetation on the steep slopes.

Another *Rhus* species that we find in abundance in this same area today is *Rhus trichocarpa*, a plant with high horticultural merit and a kinder demeanour! It's easy to spot amongst the surrounding vegetation: its bright scarlet autumn foliage lights up the forests and singles itself out.

We decide to finish the day early, as the plants have dried up and it is a holiday in Japan to celebrate the equinox. As we have had the vehicle with us all day, Giles has put the herbarium specimens straight into the press in the field, which has reduced the amount of pressing that we have to do in the evening. This gives us plenty of time to check the previous few days' specimens and change papers whilst Charles and I bring the field notes up to date on Q Collector. We have a quiet evening with a walk into Nayoro City for a meal and a call home to England. The latter should be a simple task, but it turns out to be impossible, as it appears an international fraud scam has meant an embargo on the use of phone cards to make long-distance calls. Takahashi suggests that if we are to call home, we must find someone who will allow us to use his or her personal telephone. Easier said than done!

The vibrant autumn colour of *Rhus trichocarpa* hints at the coming winter

The following morning we pack all the seed bags that have been airing in boxes and load the car in preparation for the drive south to our next collecting site in Daisetsuzan National Park. This is Japan's largest national park, covering 230,900 ha (578,000 acres) right in the centre of Hokkaido. It is home to Asahi-dake (among other volcanic peaks), which at 2290 m (7513 ft) is the highest mountain in Hokkaido, and the source of the great Ishihari River that has gouged out the many spectacular ravines and gorges in the park on its way to the Sea of Okhotsk. It is also home to many interesting woody plants, which we hope will be freely bearing seed for us to collect.

Yukomambetsu Spa, a lodge belonging to the national park, is where we will spend three nights. It's a superb wooden structure with three floors and all the luxuries you would not expect on a plant collecting trip. We are shown our rooms, two large dorms separated by removable screens, Japanese in one and Westerners in the other. It is extremely comfortable with fresh linen for our futons and crisply pressed yukata gowns. From the windows upstairs the views of Asahi-dake are spectacular, with plumes of smoke exiting the many vents just below the summit and tantalising scenes of real

Yukomambetsu Spa

autumn colour against a flawless blue sky. Tomorrow can't come soon enough, and if the weather stays the same for us as it is today, we should have great day.

In the early evening, three staff and a student from the Sapporo Botanic Garden arrive to join us to take advantage of the opportunity to collect plants and herbarium specimens for their garden. They are a very friendly bunch and have brought many supplies from the city for us to share, including several bottles of Japanese and German wines. This should help with the seed cleaning. Before we retire for an early night ahead of a long day on the mountain, we take a bath in the outdoor spa attached to the lodge—an incredible experience. Imagine you are lying outside, submerged in very hot steaming water coming naturally from the ground, in a large pool constructed from rough boulders; it's pitch dark, with no moon, and you are

Plumes of sulphur venting from Asahi-dake

staring at the stars in a cloudless sky with air temperatures below freezing; the only sounds are from the river making its way down the mountain. What a perfect way to end one day or start another!

We are all awakened by Giles's cockerel clock at 5.00 a.m., which must have been a real shock for our Japanese friends from Sapporo as no one thought to warn them. We have a light breakfast of bread and jam and coffee before heading for the cable car station, where we will catch the first one out to start our planned day's fieldwork. As we climb the lower flanks of the mountain in the cable car, above the canopies of mixed deciduous and coniferous trees, we are treated to a dramatic landscape of autumn colour. Mainly yellows of *Betula ermanii* and *Acer tschonoskii* and pinky-orange hues of *Acer caudatum* subsp. *ukurunduense*, with a distinct lack of reds. Towering above this layer is the grand *Abies sachalinensis*, with its symmetrical well-structured,

The full team assembled outside the lodge

tiered upper canopy and dark upright cones on the tips, and *Picea jezoensis*, with its more graceful and delicate branching and clusters of pendulous lightly coloured cones. This is certainly the best way to view these trees— looking down on them.

As we ride, Giles strokes the left-hand side of his face and announces to us all that he has shaved only one side, forgetting the other. Bill, very concerned, asks, 'How can anyone forget to shave one side of their face?' No one can give Bill an answer, including Giles.

We disembark from the car and set off, away from the tourist sections, along a clearly marked route around the north slopes of Asahi-dake. We are given green armbands by Takahashi which indicate to other Japanese hikers that we are scientists working with the national park and have permits to make collections of plant material. Most people tend to stay around the well-fenced zones with clearly defined paths, where wild plants are labelled and interpreted by educational panels, rather than hiking further onto the mountain along the rugged, often muddy and wet trails. One of the first collections is from a dwarf *Rhododendron aureum*, to 20 cm (8 in), and as we stop to collect seed we feel a drop in the temperature and notice ice on the paths from several nights before. The average winter temperatures here are

A sea of *Betula ermanii* punctured by the dark spires of fir and spruce

-30°C (-22°F) with 4 to 5 m (12 to 16 ft) of snow, and Takahashi suggests that this is only one or two weeks away.

As we clear the first ridge we have to stand and stare and take in the awesome colourful view of the vegetation and terrain that confronts us. The dominant plants as far as the eye can see are Siberian pines, *Pinus pumila*, and a rowan, *Sorbus matsumurana*, the blue-green foliage of the pine providing a wonderful backdrop for the rowan's purple-red foliage and buds and bright red berries. The pines are no higher than 3 to 4 m (10 to 12 ft), but wide-spreading along the ground, laying with the wind and obviously well designed to take the weight from heavy snowfalls. As usual, there are no cones visible despite a frantic search through the growth of many plants, and it soon becomes apparent that the ground squirrel common in these parts has been busy and beaten us to them, filling its larder in preparation for winter. Instead of searching the branches for the cones, we change tack and begin a search of the ground underneath the canopies for the squirrel's larder, and it isn't long before we find one full of the large pine nuts. We

The leafless branches of *Sorbus matsumurana* amongst *Pinus pumila*

take enough for our needs and leave plenty for the animal's winter feast, which begins in a few weeks' time.

There is no shortage of fruit on the *Sorbus matsumurana*, and we take several collections from different plants along with copious shots of this photogenic plant. As we climb higher up the flanks of the mountain, the deciduous sorbus is totally dormant but continues to stand out with the many long-pointed glaucous purple buds and large clusters of red fruits.

We continue collecting like combine harvesters from the many low, ericaceous shrubs represented here. *Vaccinium vitis-idaea*, *Gaultheria miqueliana*, *Phyllodoce caerulea* and *Empetrum nigrum* form carpets between the pines and rowans. For lunch we find a small alpine meadow and pull out the sandwiches we prepared earlier this morning, watching a couple of ground squirrels totally ignore us and hurry about their business. It gets cold whilst we sit eating, so lunch is cut short and we decide to make a push towards a high pass between two peaks. A very small population of *Weigela middendorffiana* is growing in an exposed situation beneath the pass. This is one of my favourite weigelas, and I am reminded of its sulphur-yellow bell-shaped flowers seen in early May by the many plumes of sulphur emitting from the blow holes in the rocks around us. It often needs some protection in the garden, which is surprising considering where we have found it today.

We climb into the pass, where several young female hikers are standing about or sitting on the rocks with their bare feet dangling in the hot water from the thermal springs, and we rest, deliberating whether or not to join them as they encourage us to do so. We decline the invitation in the end, as a young man appears from behind us, taking little encouragement, and joins the girls. Within a few minutes he has stripped off to nothing and, armed

A fruiting branch of *Sorbus matsumurana* showing the conspicuous purple buds

with only a flannel to cover his private parts, is totally submerged in the cloudy, steaming water, all bar his head. The girls find this highly amusing, judging by their giggles, and they ask us to take some photographs for them with their cameras, which we kindly do.

After a brief rest and drink Takahashi advises us that we must make our way back to the cable car station, which is about a three-hour hike, if we are to make the trip off the mountain tonight. We bid our farewells to the hikers in the pool, and I can only wonder how the young lad is going to dry himself off with only a small, wet flannel in these cold air temperatures before getting dressed again. The thought sends shivers through me—I have got quite cold whilst resting fully clothed, and I need a steady-paced trot to warm me up again. We make one last collection of the rowan from a very well-fruited specimen before pushing on to the cable car station, where we catch the last car off the mountain. On the way down, Giles closes his eyes and goes to sleep whilst standing, only the press of the other people in the

Hikers soothing their aching feet in the natural hot springs

crowded car preventing him from falling over. Bill, shaking his head, looks perplexed once again.

The following morning is to be spent in the lower valleys around Yukomambetsu Spa, and we have agreed to meet in the car park at 6.00 a.m. As the day dawns and the sun begins to rise, we are all waiting for Giles, who is taking his time despite having risen and gotten ready with us all. He suddenly appears on the balcony of the lodge, urgently shouting my name and summoning me back with a hand gesture. I worryingly oblige and return to the entrance, remove my boots once again before entering the building, and am met by Giles, who seems to be quite distressed.

'There's a problem downstairs', he explains on our way there. 'I was on the squat [toilet], gripping the down pipe, when I lost my balance, let go of the pipe and fell backwards . . . ' I have difficulty containing myself as I inspect the damage, a large hole, the shape of Giles's backside, in the paper-thin wall between the two squats. Luckily, there was no one in the squat next door.

The team descending the higher reaches of Asahi-dake

I leave the building and Giles—keeping a serious face, trying not to laugh—and join Takahashi and the others, still waiting in the car park, to break the news. After I embarrassedly explain the episode, Takahashi turns and speaks to the botanic garden's staff in Japanese, looking very serious indeed. I am slightly worried at how it will be taken—you could cut the atmosphere with a knife—and await their response with trepidation, when suddenly there is uncontrollable laughter from our friends. I take Takahashi away to show him the wall, and the caretaker joins us. We of course offer to pay for the repairs and inconvenience.

At last we are ready to leave for the forest, albeit an hour late. We head along a narrow track north of the Yukomambetsu River, the main forest trees being spruce and fir with an understorey of birch and rowan. Both the maples we have previously seen, glowing through the vegetation, are present and bearing seeds in abundance. *Acer tschonoskii* makes a shrubby tree to 3 m (10 ft) high and wide and lights up the dark forest with its small, bright

The bright golden leaves of
Acer tschonoskii

yellow leaves. *Acer caudatum* subsp. *ukurunduense* makes a tree a little taller with upright racemes of pale green samaras and pinky-orange autumnal leaves.

Bill is in his element, as there is a wealth of herbaceous material along the track, albeit a shortage of woody plants. Fortunately for me, Bill is looking down at the ground in search of said material and so sees a snake, coiled and ready to strike, in front of me on the track. He pulls me out of its range, and I turn round just in time to see quite a large bright green snake, about 90 cm (36 in) long, slithering off into the undergrowth. Another step, and it probably would have bitten me!

We continue along the track, but before venturing into the forest, we make lots of noise to scare off any other potential snakes making the best of the late warm seasonal sunshine. *Maianthemum dilatatum, Trollius* species and *Aconitum* species grow with *Euonymus macropterus* and *Rhododendron albrechtii* in the partial shade of the forest edges. Lower down in the valley in damp open clearings, *Filipendula camtschatica* grows with *Lysichiton camtschatcensis* and *Senecio cannabifolius*.

We've been very lucky with the weather up to now, but it is beginning to look dark and the temperature is dropping again. We have a quick sandwich for lunch, and it starts to rain, as forecast, so we head back to base. No wonder Takahashi was reluctant to climb Asahi-dake again today.

Since tonight is our last night here in Yukomambetsu Spa, we are to have a feast—a combined effort to celebrate our larger and very successful joint venture—but not before a hot bath in the outdoor spa. I prepare a salad using all the leftovers and make noodles, and, to the accompaniment of wine, we chat and laugh about our exploits over the past few days, including Giles's squat incident. We're all loosened up and in friendly mode when

Takahashi decides it is time for an international game of cards, preferably three-card brag, which he has been quick to learn and master. After several hands, only a Japanese student and Bill remain, two opponents with one life left each. Takahashi makes an announcement before the final hand: 'Japan versus America. World War Three'. Bill lets us down, and the student wins easily. The Japanese go wild, but it does not matter, as this has been a great few days with our new friends in Daisetsuzan.

We have to pack, clean the rooms, and be out of the lodgings by 9.00 a.m., so it's another early rise. This is a good opportunity to go through all the seed as we pack them in the transport box and check for any anomalies in the sequence of collection numbers against the herbarium specimens. Whilst we are doing this and packing, the student—who, following his dramatic defeat of Bill in the card game last night, is now low with a severe headache—is given squat-cleaning duties, which further adds to his suffering. Once packed and ready, we bid farewell to our friends from the botanic garden, and we each go our separate ways. Ahead of us is a three-hour drive to our next stop, Furano.

It pours with torrential rain the entire way, so on arrival at our bed and breakfast, we commit the day to seed cleaning. None of us are eager, but we know that this is an opportunity too good to miss and some of the seed is more than ready. Wet seed first, followed by the dry seed. Sunday's weather is no better, so we carry on where we left off yesterday, not feeling as though the day is wasted, with the bad weather outside. I spend over three hours cleaning the fruits of the Amur cork tree, *Phellodendron amurense*, removing the dark, oily fleshy fruit to reveal the small seeds, after which my fingers are stained a blue-black with the dye. No one wants to clean the *Euonymus* seed, of which we now have about five collections in the bag, including *E. macropterus*, *E. hamiltonianus* subsp. *sieboldianus* and *E. oxyphyllus*. This is a painstaking job: removing the seeds from the capsules, then removing the greasy, orange skin attached to each individual seed with a pair of tweezers before laying them on newspaper to dry. *Euonymus* seed never really dries, as it has an oily coating, as does berberis and you have to continue checking the cleaned seed once packaged, as it can go mouldy in the seed packets and deteriorate. Giles has decided that he will clean them because the genus is growing on him after seeing them in fruit in their natural habitat. We are now beginning to make an impression on the cleaning, with the clean seed

The hanging fruits of
Euonymus oxyphyllus

box getting larger than the dirty seed box.

On Monday morning we report to the forestry offices of Tokyo University Experimental Forest in Furano, where we meet Dr Kisanuki, an assistant professor in the forest ecology department. He has a serious logistical problem that he is trying to sort out at distance: two plant collectors on Honshu, an American and a Hungarian, both under his jurisdiction, have been involved in a car accident that has left one with a broken leg and the other with a fractured skull; both are in hospital, and he is trying to get them home. Whilst Dr Kisanuki makes a few more telephone calls, the landlady shows us our accommodation for the next two nights. The wooden building is set in a plantation of large Korean white pines, *Pinus koraiensis*, and it has plenty of warm, dry space for seed cleaning. We even have a cook!

Within the hour, we are climbing through the typical mixed coniferous and broadleaved forest. Whilst we are busy making collections of *Acer palmatum* and *A. japonicum*—which are both hanging with fruit, their leaves starting to show the plum-red colours of autumn—a worried Dr Kisanuki is keeping a watchful eye out for signs of bears. Forestry workers in this neck of the woods have recently spotted bears looking for food to bulk up their winter reserves before hibernation, but the only wildlife we see are the occasional deer we disturb on our way through the forest. The ground is covered with *Pachysandra terminalis*, and this is the first time I have seen the silver-white fleshy fruits of this plant, which take some finding, as they are few and far between and well hidden in the foliage. It takes a good hour to find enough to make a collection.

The autumn foliage of *Acer japonicum* amongst white-stemmed birches

On the steep slope above us is a large individual ash tree, *Fraxinus lanuginosa*, standing out from the rest of the vegetation by virtue of the brilliant red autumn colours of its leaves and keys. There are no other specimens in sight. The light is starting to fade now, and Takahashi is eager to begin our return to base before it gets dark, as the tracks we are following are in bad shape, overgrown with the surrounding vegetation, and the occasional fallen tree blocks the route. As the sky gets darker we turn a bend in the road and complete the day with a sighting of a large *Kalopanax septemlobus* growing by the roadside. I am reminded of my climbing exploits in South Korea with Mark, on this same species, and the nasty puncture wounds I received from its heavy-duty spines. We also saw this tree in the southeast of Sakhalin in 1994, and, unlike then, I am somewhat relieved when Bill, after a lengthy search of the canopy with the binoculars, informs me there is no ripe seed to be had.

It is dark by the time we arrive back at our evening's accommodation, and the temperature has dropped noticeably. Giles attempts to light the gas

Heading into the mist on Tairoku-dake

burner in our room, muddling his way through the controls, which he does-n't understand as they are all in Japanese characters. I begin to get nervous when I hear the clicking of an ignition; this is followed by the sudden whoosh of a flame igniting and a loud roar. Bill, who has just entered the room with a procedural question about the day's cache, quickly leaves, with his fingers in his ears, a grimace on his face and me right on his tail. Bill has experienced faulty gas heaters blowing up in China whilst on an expedition and doesn't want to be around when this one goes in Japan.

We are on tatami mats again, but they are very comfortable and warm, which is a good job, as there is frost on the window when we get up in the morning. The cook decides to spoil us and presents us with an English breakfast; unfortunately, it had been prepared the night before, so the fried egg is cold on a piece of ham, and the chopsticks make hard work of it, but we show our appreciation for her efforts to make us feel at home by dis-pensing another Kew calendar.

The ghostly white stems of *Betula ermanii*

This, our last day in this part of Hokkaido, is to be spent collecting on the summit of Tairoku-dake, a mountain that dominates the skyline in Furano. We drive up a forest road from about 235 m (770 ft) elevation until at 1035 m (3400 ft) we can go no further, stopped by deep potholes in the road and the overhanging herbage; we then head off on foot, along a narrow mountain track towards the summit.

The mountain is clothed in a thick shroud of mist, and I can see no further than about 20 m (65 ft). The mist is so thick that my waterproofs are covered in a film of water, as if it were raining; collecting is very difficult, as it's hard to see anything apart from plants right on the path and everything is soaking wet. As we climb higher in elevation, through the layer of spruce and fir, the forest around us becomes elfin, with very old dwarf specimens of *Betula ermanii*. They are no higher than 3 m (10 ft), gnarled and stunted in appearance with pinky-white bark, resembling something from an eerie scene in *The Lord of the Rings*.

The dense undergrowth of bamboo, *Sasa senanensis*, and the steep inclines that fall away below us make it impossible to get to any plant off the path. Bill tries to get into the lower crown of a fine old birch, loaded with seed, but slips and disappears into the bamboo below. Giles lowers his shepherd's crook for him to grip, and it takes three of us to pull him back to the path. He is absolutely soaked, and his waterproof jacket is covered in mud, but this is not enough to deter him from another attempt; he again leaps and lunges forward, grasping at the lowest branch and pulling himself up into the stunted, slippery crown. He sends down two herbarium specimens and spends the next ten minutes collecting seed. Whilst making the field notes with Charles, we notice that growing amongst dwarf *Pinus pumila* there are three species of rowan in this locality, *Sorbus commixta*, *S. matsumurana* and *S. sambucifolia*, the latter being the scarcest of the three. I am once again reminded of the close proximity of Sakhalin Island, as this species occurred in some quantity on the ascent that Mark and I made of Mount Chekhov with Peter Gorovoy.

We finally make the summit, marked by a cairn of local stone, but can see no further than a mere few meters, when suddenly a break reveals tremendous views down into the valley below. It doesn't last long and soon closes in again, and we begin to get cold standing around waiting for a further opportunity to photograph. We decide to make our descent to the car (several of us disappearing into the undergrowth off the treacherous path on the way), where we lunch before continuing on. As we drive down, Bill has a bout of déjà vu and begins to recognise parts of the track. Suddenly he shouts to stop, and Takahashi slides to a halt. Bill turns to Charles. 'This is where you lost my binoculars in 1988! I lent them to you to take a specimen under that large spruce just below the road!'

Bill and Charles indeed had been fleetingly to Hokkaido in 1988, plant collecting; Charles denies the present matter, but Bill insists we take a look to see if we can find the binoculars, despite the condition they are likely to be in by now. We all clamber out of the vehicle and spend the next twenty minutes looking for Bill's binoculars on the forest floor, sifting through the fallen biomass of needles and cones, but to no avail. Bill is still convinced that this is where he lost them, and he and Charles argue the question like squabbling children for an hour or so, until the next stop.

The number of different types of plants seems to have dried up in this area; we aren't coming across anything new to us, so I recommend that we go nearer to where we were yesterday. I am sure we missed things in the fading light—I thought I saw a Japanese yew in fruit as we drove back to base at the end of the day. I was right, and sure enough the red fruits of *Taxus cuspidata* can easily be seen against the dark evergreen foliage in the dense shade of the mixed coniferous and broadleaved forest. We make a collection and come across *Ostrya japonica*, the Japanese hop hornbeam, bearing in abundance the hop-like fruits that give it its common name. As we return to the forest lodge, the rain is falling heavily, and we are told it is here to stay—which makes us thankful we are leaving for a new site tomorrow, Shizunai Farm, a livestock farm further south.

The drive from Furano to the livestock farm, which belongs to the University of Hokkaido, takes about four hours, and Takahashi tells us that the vegetation here is very different to what we have been used to in the mountains. As a teaching station, Shizunai Farm is geared up for boarding students, with plenty of rooms packed with large built-in wooden bunks, ten in a room, but really comfortable; the students aren't on campus, so we can have a room each, giving us all plenty of space. We quickly unload the gear and place seed and herbariums out in the afternoon sun to dry before taking a walk in the neighbouring woods. We don't have long, as the sun is already falling behind the horizon, but we have enough time to find and collect seed from Miyabe's maple. *Acer miyabei* is a close relative of our European field maple, *Acer campestre*, and does looks familiar with its corky bark and lobed leaves. Growing with it on the edge of a marshy piece of broadleaf woodland is an alder, *Alnus japonica*, and an oak, *Quercus serrata*, also introduced to the West by Charles Sargent, with Miyabe's maple.

We take a shortcut back to the campus, walking across a grass meadow with *Sanguisorba tenuifolia* var. *grandiflora* growing through the sward to just under 1 m (3 ft 3 in) high. Suddenly Giles points excitedly to a large tree poking out of the woodland canopy in the near distance. It is distinguished from everything else growing around it by its pale green-yellow foliage. I crawl on my stomach, flat to the ground, through a thicket of *Viburnum dilatatum*, lilac and young ash seedlings on the perimeter of the woodland into denser undergrowth. Once in, I can't see a thing above this vegetation

Acer cissifolium in its solitary outpost on Hokkaido

layer, and I rely on Giles and Charles to direct me. We shout back and forth, and eventually I find the tree and discover that the pale green colours we saw from a distance are the leaves and samaras of *Acer cissifolium*, a medium-sized tree with trifoliate leaves and long racemes of seeds.

In cultivation, this tree is often confused with *Acer henryi* from China, the leaves of which are greener and have entire margins. I am able to scramble to the lowest branch, pull myself up and climb to the very top of the crown, where I can see the others gathered in the meadow. We have found that, with maples, the higher in the tree you are able to collect seed, the better the fertility, especially in a woodland situation. Most maples are insect pollinated, producing relatively small amounts of pollen per flower compared to wind-pollinated trees, and often the flowers on the lower branches in a woodland are missed by the pollinating insects.

Bill joins me, and together we make collections and get them out to Charles and Giles, waiting in the meadow. This is a collection that is high on our target list and certainly the plant of the day; Giles is still very excited, as he was the first to see it, and in the evening we celebrate with a ten-year-old malt whisky and a toast to Giles whilst recollecting the day, a short but interesting one in the field, before leaving for Sapporo.

Back in Sapporo we do laundry and spend as much time as possible cleaning seed, whilst Giles tends the herbarium specimens. That he trained with Susyn Andrews before we came out to Japan is clear, and the specimens are looking excellent after all the hard work and effort he has put into them. We also confirm our return flights home in the ANA (All Nippon Airways) offices, where Charles is renamed 'Clord' by the ticket clerk. We are all sitting waiting when she calls for a Clord to step up and retrieve his tickets—his initial came before his title ('C. Lord Howick') on the travel document. He tries explaining her mistake to her, but she doesn't understand. After several minutes' exchange of words and frustration, he, along with the rest of us, decides to adopt his new title.

Takahashi has some work to do, so for the day we are to go to Toma-komai, an experimental forest 50 km (30 miles) from the university campus, before we head further south for the final few days collecting. The forest is on a flat plain of thick volcanic ash, deposited from the Shikotsu-Tarumae volcanoes, the peaks of which are showing the first dustings of winter snow. Broadleaved trees such as *Quercus mongolica* var. *grosseserrata* and *Ulmus davidiana* var. *japonica* dominate the forest with the occasional, now familiar conifers, *Abies sachalinensis* and *Picea jezoensis*. Fortunately, we are to spend the day on the lower plains and not at high elevation, where the temperatures and conditions would not be to our liking. But less fortunate, this site has poor seed set. It is difficult to find good seed on any tree; in fact, it is difficult to find any seed at all. The highlight of the day is a look round the amazing wood museum in the field station's arboretum.

I decide to drive the car back to Sapporo, and it's not long before everyone in the back is asleep, judging by the snores bellowing out. Dr Funakoshi, our guide for the day, appears to be getting rather nervous; he keeps reminding me of the speed limit and directs me with relief off the expressway and round the houses back to the campus. This was not a successful day, but that is what plant hunting is all about, and you have to hope that the next day's collecting goes better.

Our final destination for four days is to be Kaminokuni, a small town on the coast of the East Sea in the very south of the island on the Matsumae Peninsula, where our base is Hiyama, another forestry office. Before we leave Sapporo we have to call at the Poplar Kaikan to pick up Charles's slippers, which he left behind on the first night; he's been lost without them!

On the six-hour journey south we drive through some spectacular scenery and past a flat-topped mountain locally known as Jezo-Fuji for its close resemblance to the near perfectly symmetrical cone of Mt. Fuji, which at 3776 m (12,400 ft) is the highest mountain in Japan. This finale in the field in Hokkaido is the most exciting part of the trip for me, as we are hoping to find two of the most interesting native trees on the island, the Japanese horse chestnut, *Aesculus turbinata*, and the Japanese beech, *Fagus crenata*. They are the most important for me because I have never seen horse chestnuts growing in their native habitat; I wonder what they must look like, being used to seeing them as exotic avenue or street trees, or as individual specimens in a park or arboretum. As for the beech, both Mark and I have been so unlucky with seed collections of this genus on our previous expeditions, I would desperately like to collect one. I keep asking Takahashi if it has been a good seed year in the south of the island, but he does not know, he never knows, and I can see my pestering is beginning to tire him. I am merely trying to convince myself that there *will* be seed on both trees—or preparing myself for the worst. In twenty-four hours, the question will be answered either way!

Takahashi suggests we stop off for a hot bath before we reach Kaminokuni town; he knows a special place en route that we will enjoy, or, more to the point, that he will enjoy. We pull off the road into the gravel car park of a low traditional building set into a gorge in the middle of nowhere, with steep lower mountain slopes towering up on either side and the roar of white water in the air. We enter the stone building, are given robes and a towel by a female attendant and, after changing, go down several steps and through a door into an outdoor pool by the river, with hot water bubbling up through the floor followed by plumes of steam. Perfect! I relax physically once in the water, but the beech still weighs heavily on my mind and I am eager to get to Hiyama forest.

Another hour sees our arrival at the forestry offices, where we are greeted by Dr Natsumae, the director of the experimental forest. I waste no time asking him about the beech and horse chestnut, but he shakes his head, he does not know. I will have to wait until tomorrow.

We have a good evening settling in to our rooms, with Takahashi sharing stories of our exploits with Dr Natsumae (in particular Giles and the squat incident in Yukomambetsu Spa, which he finds hilarious), but there is bad news on the television. Severe weather conditions are forecast; winds from the Tsugaru Straits are creeping in, and there will be heavy rain and high winds on the peninsula by early afternoon tomorrow, and snow in the north of Hokkaido. Takahashi was wise to suggest we go north first to collect, but tomorrow is likely to be wet and unpleasant even so far south in the Hiyama forest.

It's an early start, six o' clock, and I wake up with a bad throat and feeling run down with the onset of flu, so on the way to Hiyama, Bill stops off at a Lawson Store for some medicine and lunch for the field before we head into the forest. As we drive along a track through grassy meadows by the banks of the Amanogawa River, I am remarkably revived by the abundance of fruiting irises growing above the tops of the grasses. We stop, wait for the dust we have stirred up to settle behind us, then struggle through thorny banks of *Rosa multiflora* and *Elaeagnus umbellata*, both heavily in fruit, to get to the irises. The field is full of *Iris ensata*, as far as you can see, and must look incredibly blue when in full flower. We make short work of it, filling a muslin bag with the dry fruiting capsules, which are full of the black seeds, followed by hips from the rose and the pale red berries with white blotches from the elaeagnus, before we push on to the beech. We drive through acres and acres of the Japanese cedar, *Cryptomeria japonica*, planted as a major reforestation project, all in regimental rows and well manicured, as it is not native to Hokkaido.

We finally stop the car under the canopy of a large tree, and, once out and looking up into the crown, we can see that it is the horse chestnut, *Aesculus turbinata*. Down on the ground are some leftover conkers, and another collection is in the making. Unfortunately, the foliage is almost brown, withered and ready to drop for the winter; another couple of days

A mosaic of Japanese cedar and beech in Hiyama forest

and it will be bare, so a herbarium specimen is out of the question. We are struggling to find good seeds—most have been taken, probably by animals—but on delving into the undergrowth we find more, hidden. It's a small collection, but they are all good seeds, and each of the twenty will make a tree.

The sky darkens, the wind gets up and it begins to rain—at first the odd spot, then slightly heavier, and before long it has developed into a downpour. Here comes the storm that was predicted last night, almost to the minute, so on go the waterproofs and probably just in time, if we are to remain somewhat dry. We still have something to do before we can go back to our base, and there is now a sense of urgency if we are to be successful before the weather gets too bad to carry on. We pack as little gear as we think we will need and once ready set off at a brisk pace, with our forestry guide, to find the beech. Despite it being early afternoon, the low light levels give the appearance of early evening.

After about an hour I see the first beech tree—a small specimen about thirty years old. Several more follow, and at last we are amongst a pure dom-

The foliage of *Fagus crenata*

inating stand of *Fagus crenata*, easily recognised by the silvery, straight trunks to about 20 m (65 ft) and the typical orange, pointed cigar-shaped buds. These are relatively young secondary-growth beeches with the occasional mature tree, but nothing like I had imagined, as they bear little resemblance in stature to our large, mature, noble beech trees, *F. sylvatica*, at home in southern England. I spend several minutes looking up into the crowns of one, then another, and another, and can see no sign of any seed, even on the larger specimens. I am gutted, dejected and demoralised, beaten again by nature and the beech. I have failed yet again: *Nothofagus* in Chile, *F. japonica* var. *multinervis* in South Korea, *F. hayatae* in Taiwan, *F. engleriana* in China—what do I have to do to find beech seed?

Takahashi suggests that we call it a day and head back, but I need a few minutes to console myself. I try not to let my disappointment show—sitting down on the moss-covered ground, leaning back against a largish trunk—and advise that I will catch up with the team shortly. I stare down at the ground, and after a few minutes I can't believe what I see in the moss: an empty seed capsule—from this season. On my hands and knees I fossick around, finding more seed capsules and eventually a fresh beechnut. In no time I have up to ten nuts in my hand.

I call the others back, and they know from the smile on my face what I have found. I show them the nuts, and they are as happy as I am. Despite the now driving rain, we all comb the ground, every inch of it, on our hands and knees searching for beechnuts, which appear to be everywhere in quantity. If they had remained on the tree, we would probably not have been able to reach them anyway. In a short space of time we fill a good-sized muslin bag. I know that back home all I want to do is to tell Mark of our success, or luck, and I know he will be pleased with this collection.

I am beginning to feel cold now. I can feel water running down the back of my neck as we walk back to the car, left parked under the horse chestnut, but it is worth it for the collections that we have made today. Warm sake with our dinner is the order of the day, and we make a toast to the beech before retiring for an early night.

Before we return to Sapporo we have one more tree to find, *Pterocarya rhoifolia*, the Japanese wingnut. We drive along the coastal road until we reach the tributary of the Ishkizaki River and then follow the river into the mountains. We stop off at a forestry station and trek on foot a short distance into the forest to see hiba, *Thujopsis dolabrata*. The foresters tell us that this is a 16-ha (40-acre) natural stand of hiba, but this is doubtful, as there are only relatively small trees, all of one size, with no big trees apparent. It just doesn't seem natural; however, it's an interesting stand and amazing to witness so many hibas in one area. I am reminded of a very large multi-stemmed, variegated specimen on an estate in Liphook, Hampshire, that I used to visit when I first began my career at Tilhill Forestry Nursery in Tilford at the age of sixteen. I would never have believed in those early years that I would have the opportunity in later life to witness one growing on a mountainside in Japan.

In the lower part of the valley, by the river at the foot of a large escarpment, we find a small stand of tall slender pterocaryas, easily identifiable from a distance by their long pendulous, brown fruit clusters. We are lucky to find a low branch with seed, as most of the trees are devoid of any branches until about 10 m (30 ft) up the trunk and we have no climbing equipment with us.

The ripe fruits of *Pterocarya rhoifolia* hanging like necklaces amongst the foliage

The rich harvest of cleaned seed ready for the nursery

With the fruits of this tree safely in the bag, we leave for Sapporo. It's going to be a long journey back, and we ask Takahashi to take the expressway (we will pay for the tolls). He obliges, and after a good sleep in the back of the car, we are soon at Chitose Airport to drop Giles off for his return flight to England, as he is leaving us a few days early.

Once in Sapporo, all that is left for us to do is to tie up loose ends with the seed and herbaria and permits, and attend a few parties thrown by the arboretum staff in our honour. One features karaoke in a strangely painted booth, with sky and clouds represented on all the walls and ceiling, where I give another stirring version of 'The Ballad of Jed Clampett' and Charles (or Clord, as he is now known) sings 'O Danny Boy'.

> *O Danny boy, the pipes, the pipes are calling*
> *From glen to glen, and down the mountainside.*
> *The summer's gone, and all the roses falling*
> *'Tis you, 'tis you must go and I must bide.*

A rather appropriate song for the occasion, I thought! Bill, not known for his singing capability, joins in at the chorus enthusiastically, his eyes filled with tears.

On our last evening Takahashi, with his wife and three children, takes us to the Sapporo Beer Park, a massive hall where we are served freshly brewed beer and as much Ghengis Khan mutton barbecue as we can eat. Just up my street! The Beer Park is attached to a Beer Museum, established in 1876, where you can learn all about the history of beer brewing in Hokkaido; it is one of the most popular tourist destinations in Sapporo, attracting over one and a half million visitors each year. We are led by a waitress past throngs of people to a table and given a kit bag consisting of plastic aprons and large plastic bags to place any loose jackets or bags in; apparently this is a very greasy operation, and the plastic bags are to protect your belongings from fat splash. Once we are dressed in our new apparel, the barbecue on the table is lit, and trays of fresh marinated meat and various vegetables are brought in, along with large steins of beer. Mrs Takahashi takes charge of the catering arrangements whilst we exchange tales from the last four weeks in the field, shouting to be heard above the noise of the other visitors and the sizzling of cooking food. Not surprisingly, the most amusing topic of conversation is once again Giles and the squat incident, and Takahashi's family is hungry to hear more of our exploits between bouts of laughter.

The following morning, Takahashi drives us to the airport, seeing us safely through passport control before we say our goodbyes. I will miss him over the next few days, his friendliness and professionalism both in and out of the field, but I know that we will keep in touch with our new international botanic garden colleague and friend by e-mail.

Once in Tokyo, Bill and Charles are to travel to the south of Honshu by the bullet train to see an old friend, leaving me to complete the last leg of the trip home alone. Shigeto Tsukie, a close friend of Bill's who, as a student, helped him on his 1988 expedition to Japan, comes to meet us at our hotel; he is joining them on the trip south, but first they are taking me to the airport via the subway to see me off. Shigeto insists he knows the best and cheapest route as he's a local boy, so we trust him and I hand him the leader's baton. The next two hours are the most horrendous imaginable and not an ending (to an otherwise memorable expedition) you would ever want to recall.

It all begins at the entrance to the main railway station in Tokyo, where we alight from two taxis lugging all our bags and gear. There are no trolleys, and we have too many bags to carry between us, so we form a relay chain. Charles stays with the bags back at the taxi stop, whilst the three of us ferry as many bags as possible to another suitable rest station about 500 m (1600 ft) down the subway. Shigeto stays with these bags whilst Bill and I return to Charles, the three of us then ferrying the rest of the bags to the waiting Shigeto. And so on. After about five stints of relay, we arrive at the top of the escalator for the train platform, drained. I can feel beads of sweat running down my back, and my arms feel twice their length from carrying the heavy bags. We all collapse in a heap on the bags, whilst Shigeto disappears off to check platforms. He soon returns to us and his face says it all. 'Wrong platform. We need to go back'.

Bill is not best pleased, nor are Charles and I happy at the prospect of doing this all over again, as time is marching on and we need to make Narita Airport on time to check in. We do the relay journey in reverse, back to where the taxi dropped us off, none of us speaking, apart from the occasional muttering under our breath, and finding the going harder, as we are all physically exhausted. The correct platform turns out to be immediately below the entrance where we were first dropped off, only a short descent in a lift and a 100-m (350-ft) walk away. None of us can believe what we have just been through for nothing—we would far sooner have climbed to the top of Asahi-dake again. We are lucky. The first train in is the Narita express, and once all the baggage is safely stowed away, we settle down for a short journey, resting and recuperating before the fun of the airport.

At the ANA check-in desk, I weigh my luggage, and, as expected, I am faced with an excess baggage charge totalling 110,000 yen, about £580. I pull out the last of the infamous Kew calendars, explain Kew's mission statement and the roles of conservation, and ten minutes later, after lots of pleading, the clerk knocks the fee down to 27,000 yen (about £150) and the Kew calendar. I am very grateful to All Nippon Airways. Bill and Charles are watching pensively from a distance, knowing what is going on, when I turn round and put the thumbs up, to clear signs of relief from them. Before I go through passport control, we congratulate each other on a successful trip and say our goodbyes. Soon I am in the air, settling down for the long flight back home.

It's a real shame that I was in Hokkaido without Mark. It would have been fulfilling to complete together the temperate loop we both began eight years ago in South Korea. I know that he so wanted to get to Japan, but there'll be another time, and I am sure that many of the 179 seed collections made over the past four weeks will find their way into the Savill and Valley Gardens at Windsor as well as the arboreta at Kew and Wakehurst Place.

CHAPTER 7

In an English Garden

ON A WARM AFTERNOON IN JULY 2000 I accepted an invitation from Tony for a walk around the arboretum at Kew. His excited tone had filled me with anticipation: 'Mark, you've got to come over—the Taiwanese roses are in full flower, and our trees of *Betula davurica* from South Korea look stunning near Victoria Gate'. He promised much else besides, as he had been taking stock of the collections from the four trips.

Throughout our time in the field, we had always held firm to the central objective which marks the success of any seed collecting venture—getting living plants into the ground. We were both fortunate in that we could continue to exert a strong influence over the destiny of our plants, given that we both occupied senior positions in important gardens. During my time at Wakehurst Place I oversaw the raising and planting of the material from South Korea, Taiwan and Russia, into the revamped botanical collections there. Not all collectors are so fortunate; Kingdon Ward and other plant hunters from the golden age, being full-time professional collectors, were in the hands of others and had little say in how their plants were grown. Perhaps Wilson, of all the collectors, had the greatest level of control, given that he was assistant director at the Arnold Arboretum in Boston and in direct charge of the living collections there.

When I left Wakehurst Place in March 1997 to become Keeper of the Gardens in the Royal Park at Windsor, I did so with a sense of satisfaction, having achieved much of what I set out to do when I had arrived nearly ten years before. The revised botanical collections at Wakehurst Place, including the Asian collections in Westwood Valley, boasted an impressive array of strong, young saplings grown from the seed gathered on the trips I had participated in as well as that of other collectors at both Kew and other institutions worldwide. Following the carnage of the Great Storm of 1987,

One of the group of *Betula davurica*
by the Victoria Gate at Kew

Wakehurst Place had been transformed into a vibrant new arboretum with high-quality, wild-source material underpinned by accurate and extensive field notes.

And so to Kew, where Tony had been labouring with similar intent. Parking opposite Lion Gate, I experienced the usual expectancy when visiting Kew. For anyone interested in plants, the Royal Botanic Gardens, Kew, with its great history, wonderful collections and trained and dedicated staff, is a mecca. Though I have both worked at Kew and visited on innumerable occasions, I still experience a buzz whenever I arrive.

It was a memorable afternoon. It was during this visit that I realised, perhaps for the first time, just what a contribution our collections had made to this premier garden and gained the first inkling of what we had achieved. Hitherto, we had largely been focussed on the task of bringing plant material back and ensuring that it was properly grown, rather than assessing its importance.

The Pagoda built by Sir William Chambers in 1761

Tony was waiting in the bright sunshine by the famous Pagoda just inside Lion Gate at the southern end of the gardens. This marvellous Georgian landmark, designed by Sir William Chambers, is as much an icon of Kew as the better known Victorian Palm House. In the past I have been fortunate enough to climb its timber stairs and enjoy the view from the top; at 50 m (165 ft) it affords a wonderful panorama over the housetops of prosperous Kew and Richmond. Sadly, it is no longer possible to make the climb as modern health and safety concerns have curtailed such access.

The beautiful weather had encouraged a large number of visitors, and it was wonderful to see people enjoying the plants and landscapes. The arboretum at Kew is principally the work of Sir Joseph Hooker who, working to

A winter view down Pagoda Vista, looking towards the Palm House

a design provided by William Nesfield, laid out the plantings in the middle decades of the nineteenth century. Nesfield's landscape made use of the flat, river terrace on which Kew lies by establishing a series of vistas which radiate out from key buildings, such as the Palm House, or terminate on distant features like the façade of Syon House, the London home of the Dukes of Northumberland, on the other side of the River Thames. Within this framework Hooker established his arboretum. In keeping with the prevailing fashion, he used a taxonomic arrangement, allotting discrete areas for each plant family with the intention that the arboretum should act as a living textbook.

Today the scientific overlay of the arboretum is less obvious, and most visitors are happy to enjoy the majesty of the mature trees. But for the staff, and more knowledgeable visitors, the taxonomic arrangement of the collections is still the key to understanding the arboretum, and it was by follow-

The stunning autumn colour of
Sorbus commixta collected on
Ullung-Do in 1989

ing this composition that Tony and I tracked our collections that day. Almost immediately we came upon one of our star plants, a group of the strong-growing *Sorbus commixta* from Ullung-Do, which we collected on the rocky promontories above the town of Todong in October 1989. Already they were carrying crops of still-green fruits, which they do every year, often so heavily that their branches are weighed down, until greedy birds relieve them of their burden. More striking than the fruits, however, is the autumn colour, which is unfailingly of the most vibrant red.

Nearby, in the section set aside for the Hydrangeaceae, we found a posse of deutzias. These can be the most uninspiring of plants in the wild, often stunted, occasionally browsed and easily overlooked. Once in cultivation, however, their true potential can be realised, and they make wonderful early summer–flowering shrubs of a generally easy disposition. On the Korean trip, three different and little-known deutzias were gathered. For classification purposes, botanists broadly separate the genus into those species in which the petals overlap in the bud (imbricate) and those in which the petals do not overlap (valvate). *Deutzia coreana* is an example of the latter group, and our collection from Sorak-san is one of the very few introductions of this species. Uniquely in the genus, it produces its flowers from axillary buds and, importantly from a gardener's point of view, blooms much earlier than any other species, sometimes being in flower in March and April. The other two Korean species we collected belong to the imbricate group and are very closely related; *D. parviflora* var. *amurensis* has a hairy calyx and *D. glabrata* does not—talk about splitting hairs—but such is botany!

The outstanding deutzia of all our collections was the next one we considered. *Deutzia pulchra* was gathered on the hillsides above the Cross-Island Highway on Taiwan and has proved to be a stunning garden plant. We well knew the potential of this species; Wilson collected it during his visit to Taiwan in 1918, and plants probably derived from this can be seen in several collections, including Wakehurst Place, where a huge arching shrub with wonderful peeling bark grows in the Specimen Beds. Our collection has not disappointed; it carries large inflorescences of pure white flowers in great abundance in early May and is already developing the characteristic flaky bark. The textbooks suggest

Deutzia coreana flowering at Kew in early spring

that the species is far from hardy, but our collection has so far shown that it is well adapted to the climate at Kew.

Moving across to the Woodland Garden, which lies to the south of Kew's lake, we were astounded to see the progress made by *Acer pictum* subsp. *okamotoanum*, the endemic maple we collected on Ullung-Do in 1989. By now it had attained a height of 8 m (25 ft) with a dbh (diameter at breast height) of 100 mm (4 in) and is obviously full of vigour. Already it is the UK champion tree. Though not the most ornamental of trees, as a little-known endemic species it is a valuable addition to cultivation, if only because its presence as a living plant provides some safety against the prospect of its extinction in the wild. Sadly, this fate has befallen too many island endemics, admittedly more so in the tropics and subtropics than in temperate areas. Tony almost pulled me to another maple, this time from the Taiwan trip. It was making a wonderful arching specimen beneath the shelter of high pruned oaks. Its bright green, almost snake-like, trunk and narrow, barely

A flowering shoot of *Deutzia pulchra*,
one of the gems from Taiwan

lobed leaves set it apart as *A. caudati-folium*. With a reputation for being tender, this maple is rare and much prized in collections, but here it seemed to be in rude health and was a delight with its graceful, airy appearance.

As we progressed, more and more plants from our trips presented themselves. In the Oleaceae (olive family) collection, the Manchurian ash (*Fraxinus mandshurica*) from the mosquito-infested copse near Yasnoya in Russia's Sikhote Alin. In the Pinetum, the Japanese red and black pines collected in South Korea and their supposed hybrid (*Pinus densi-thunbergii*). By the Orangery, a veritable Taiwanese banquet with *Cotoneaster rokujodaisanensis*, masses of the magnificent, free-fruiting *Skimmia japonica* subsp. *reevesiana*, the delicate Taiwanese snowdrop tree, *Styrax formosanus*, and the spiny, suckering *Aralia bipinnata*.

We admired the profusion of flowers on the roses that had first prompted Tony to invite me over. Most had proved to be *Rosa transmorrisonensis*, an arching, white-flowered species with ferny leaves. Though part of the same species complex, each individual collection was subtly different. And finally we stood by the five saplings of *Betula davurica*, the Dahurian birch, and remembered the day nearly eleven years before when we collected it on the trek in the Sorak-san National Park, South Korea. Tony was right; they, like the roses, were developing into beautiful specimens. Each was unique, their trunks peeling to reveal a mixture of shades of pink and cream.

At this point in time, the collections from the trip to Hokkaido had yet to make their way into the gardens, and so Tony was anxious to take me to the Temperate Nursery to check on their progress. As we walked along the field rows, he told the stories behind the saplings we examined—the 'scaffolded' monarch birch, the giant katsura trees, *Cercidiphyllum japonicum*, and the finding of the seeds (finally!) of the Japanese beech. His anecdotes made me realise just what I'd missed—how, in the end, I had been unable to complete the temperate loop. The great promise these plants displayed in the nursery that day has continued now that the majority of them have found their way into permanent positions. Indeed, I would contend that the trees and shrubs from Hokkaido have performed better than any of the other collections, with the possible exception of certain of the South Korean plants. Tony and I assume that this is due to their compatibility with the English climate. The plants, almost without exception, come into leaf relatively late, grow strongly and are dormant by early to mid October, an almost ideal development pattern. In all the gardens in which I have seen them, admittedly only in the UK, these northern Japanese plants are dazzling performers.

The visitors were all gone and the gates closing as we retired to a local pub to continue with our reminiscences, but not before we had passed by Tony's office to check on Kew's plant database. This revealed that the four trips had contributed 1223 accessions to the collections at Kew and Wakehurst Place, comprising 426 different species and varieties, a total that any collector could be proud of.

Our collections had been introduced primarily by seed; perhaps ninety-eight percent of everything we have brought back was by this means. This was very much the intention, as not only does this method make the least impact on natural environments, but it is the simplest and most efficient way to introduce plants. We realised from the outset that if we were to be successful in introducing plants we had to collect, handle and store the seed carefully; this meant attention to detail. It wasn't going to be good enough merely to gather the seed and leave it at the bottom of the rucksack until we arrived back in England.

From our first days in South Korea, Tony and I developed a routine which we believe played a big part in the success we have achieved in translating our fieldwork into plants growing in the ground in gardens. There are two elements to this routine. The first is the selection of the right seed packet from the point of collection. All seeds continue to respire after collection and need good gaseous exchange. Whenever possible, we used paper packets or muslin bags; dry seeds, such as the samaras of maples or the achenes of clematis, are easily contained in such packages and can continue to 'breathe' in them. But a different approach is needed for the wet drupes of viburnums and the berries of *Arisaema*; whilst it is necessary to hold these in sealable polythene bags, their need for oxygen and carbon dioxide is no less than their dry-seeded counterparts, which requires that they be opened to the atmosphere and agitated to aerate them at every opportunity. Whilst this may all seem very simple, after a hard day in the field it is often the very last job that one feels like doing.

The second element in the care of seeds in the field is to try and clean them as soon as possible. Whenever we had a day or so spare, we would invest it in seed cleaning. This can be a laborious and unpleasant task; many fruits are difficult to clean. I well remember the tiny seeds of *Gaultheria itoana* embedded in a sticky, glutinous pericarp on the Taiwanese trip. Some are downright dangerous—the ends of our fingers were badly burnt in cleaning the alkaloid-rich fruits of arisaemas in South Korea. Despite all this, the job is well worth doing; not only does it greatly reduce the weight of the material brought back, but clean seeds can be happily transferred to small paper packets. We were also of the opinion that it is unfair to leave the job to propagation staff, whose real role is to germinate and grow the plants.

Propagation represents the next stage in the successful transition from seeds collected in the wild to plants flourishing in the garden. Once again, Tony and I developed firm ideas about what does and does not work in practise. We have found that a balance of simple human psychology and good nursery practise achieves the best results. Propagation staff will give their best efforts if they are well-informed and enthusiastic. We tried to enthuse our colleagues by giving them information about the plants, where they were collected, what grew with them, what they looked like and any other anecdotes that we could remember. We also believe that it helps to keep up a dialogue with nursery staff, to visit and encourage them and to give them praise when their efforts are successful. Discussions with Kew specialists like Annette Whickham, Clive Foster and Chris Clennett allowed us to develop simple, low-tech methods to germinate and grow on our seeds. We found that all our woody plants responded to a period of cold weather (vernalisation), during which their embryos would complete their development or chemical inhibitors in the seed coat would be dissipated. This was

Young seedlings ready for pricking out

easily achieved by sowing them in pots, which were then placed in a cold frame for the winter. Germination occurs in response to the warmer temperatures of the occasional sunny day in late February and early March. Once seedlings are seen to be developing, the pots are brought into a heated glasshouse, which stimulates rapid germination of any remaining seeds.

Seedlings are pricked out into pots and grown on for several weeks; as soon as they are large enough, they are planted out into soiled frames, where, with a free root run, they make rapid, often spectacular, progress. We have seen fast-growing trees, such as alders, reach 2 m (6.5 ft) in their maiden year. Often such trees can be planted straight from the frame; most, however, are moved into nursery fields to continue their development. The real purpose of frame- and field-growing is to encourage balanced, extensive root systems, with a good fibrous edge. Experience has taught us that, without special treatment, container-grown trees and shrubs have tight, spiralling root systems and often blow over many years after planting.

Herbaceous plants receive a different treatment, as they seem to have much less requirement for a cold treatment. These are sown in late winter in gentle heat under glass. Germination is often speedy, and the plants make steady growth. By the end of the first summer, it is not unusual to have

Westwood Valley at Wakehurst Place, home to the East Asian Arboretum

plants ready for the garden. Irises and astilbes are good examples of such plants; lilies and arisaemas take longer.

It is always a thrill and a pleasure to see quality stock coming out of the nursery, ready for planting. Much the best job in this whole process is the selection and planting of that material. We have already discussed several times the raison d'etre for our collecting trips, thus the sense of satisfaction gained from actually seeing the material being planted is acute. At Wakehurst Place the South Korean material had two principal destinations, and during the winter of 1991–92, material was finally available to fill the considerable holes the 1987 storm had left behind.

The first destination was the East Asian Arboretum in Westwood Valley—a superb and atmospheric wealden ghyll (a local name for the characteristic steep-sided valleys in this part of England). I can recall vividly setting out the planting positions with David Ross, the horticulturist in charge of the area set aside to represent this important region. With great diligence David planted the stock, the first plant being the *Sorbus amurensis* collected on the ascent of Chiri-san. Planting continued in the following winter, and soon, as the Taiwanese material came on line to be joined by the Russian plants, there was a continuous stream of new stock.

Before I departed for Windsor in March 1997, hundreds of trees and shrubs were added to Westwood Valley, masterminded by Paul Richards, who had joined me at Wakehurst Place in the winter of 1992–93. Paul, more than anyone, is responsible for the successful establishment of these plants. The planting followed a revised collection rationale based on the work of Armen Takhtajan, the great Armenian plant-geographer. Takhtajan classified the world's flora not into units of closely related species within genera and families, as in the traditional taxonomic

Young specimens of *Betula ermanii* from Mount Chekhov growing above Westwood Valley

approach, but into geographic units. He set out floristic regions whereby whole assemblages of plants from many families could be classified into a system that reflected actual wild plant communities. Takhtajan's seminal work, *Floristic Regions of the World*, provided a template for the post-storm plantings at Wakehurst Place that embraced not just Asian plants but all the temperate woodlands of the world. Indeed, as the East Asian Arboretum developed in Westwood Valley, my colleague, Andy Jackson, was, if anything, forging further ahead in the North American collections in the adjacent area, Horsebridge Wood. By the end of the decade the collection boasted a strong representation of material from the Pacific fringe of Asia; our collections were added to collections made by other Kew personnel in China and other temperate areas of the world—a rate of planting unprecedented since the time of Wilson, Forrest and the other collectors from the Golden Age.

A view across the Tony Schilling Asian Heath Garden with our
Taiwanese rhododendrons in the foreground

The second destination for South Korean material at Wakehurst Place was the Tony Schilling Asian Heath Garden, an inspired scheme implemented by Tony Schilling during his last years at Wakehurst and into which he put a huge amount of energy. In an area completely devastated by the Great Storm, Tony envisaged an ecological planting, a style of which he was very much an innovator, displaying the flora of the subalpine regions of eastern Asia. He wanted not just to delight visitors but to educate them as well, to take them on an imaginary journey to the high places of Asia and allow them, in a small way, to experience some of the thrill that we had been fortunate to experience firsthand. I had a great sense of pride as I set out some of the Korean plants with Tony in his new garden scheme prior to his retirement in 1991. Tony had lived and breathed Wakehurst Place for over twenty years, and the devastation caused by the Great Storm had affected him deeply. This new garden replaced a much admired feature at Wakehurst Place—Rhododendron Walk. It was evident that this was Tony's key contribution to the renaissance of the estate after the 1987 storm, and we both

Tony Schilling with *Rhododendron succothii* in Bhutan

took pleasure in placing the strong young plants that had resulted from the trip to South Korea.

Other parts of the garden were the beneficiaries of our efforts as well. The redevelopment of the Water Gardens, another area that had suffered grievously, allowed a whole range of moisture-loving plants to be added. The fine strong form of *Astilbe chinensis* gathered on the Gamov Peninsula in Russia found a home here, as did the unusual autumn-flowering alder *Alnus henryi* from the slopes above Chiayang on the Cross-Island Highway in Taiwan.

As we have seen, a similar picture emerged at Kew, where Tony was instrumental in ensuring that, as they became available, our collections began to occupy their rightful place in Kew's arboretum. For the purposes of management the arboretum has traditionally been organised into three units—North Arboretum, West Arboretum and South Arboretum, with Tony in charge of the former. With the unwavering support of his boss, Charlie Erskine, Tony joined colleagues Mark Pitman and Mark Bridger in integrating the newly acquired material into the arboretum's taxonomic areas.

Spiraea formosana flowering in the Tony Schilling Asian Heath Garden

The excellent nursery at Kew provided first-rate material, and with good aftercare the plants established quickly. Tony also had a strong ally in Tony Hall, the manager of Kew's Alpine Unit. Tony Hall developed a wonderful collection of woodland herbaceous plants in a sheltered copse at the southern end of the Kew's famous Rock Garden. With great enthusiasm Tony Hall raised and planted all the herbaceous material we brought back. Korean irises were joined by Taiwanese astilbes, Russian lilies and Japanese hostas. Tony's woodland garden is an inspiration to anyone who loves these woodland gems, and for the collector, it is satisfying to see their own plants thriving in near perfect conditions.

I believe that all collectors secretly harbour the desire to discover plants new to science. Both collectors and cultivators are captivated by the new and the novel. In the early days this was relatively easy, as collectors were operating in virgin territory. Today, particularly in temperate areas, new species are very much the exception; in some ways, this increases their allure. Amusingly, Tony and I were hugely embarrassed by our first 'new to science'

Iris ensata from the water meadows of Golubiny Utyos, Russia,
growing in the woodland garden at Kew

plant. On Namhae Island, off the southern coast of South Korea, we collected in a rich broadleaved forest. One plant was completely unfamiliar to
either of us; it was a deciduous shrub of about 3 m (10 ft) with leaves composed of seven to nine leaflets and keel-shaped fruits which split to reveal
black seeds. We were told that it was *Sambucus sieboldiana* var. *pendula*, but it
manifestly was not an elder. 'Perhaps it's a new species', said Tony breath-
lessly, and I was only too happy to be drawn into this fools' paradise. When
we returned to Kew, our companion Peter Boyce had strict instructions to
make sure that his very first job was to determine whether or not we had
discovered something new. Within about forty-five seconds Nigel Taylor, at
that time Kew's horticultural taxonomist, had identified it as *Euscaphis japonica*, a rather undistinguished and resoundingly well-known member of the
bladdernut family (Staphyleaceae). To add to our indignity, it didn't prove
remotely hardy at Kew or Wakehurst Place, nor did a second collection
made on Yangmingshan in Taiwan in 1992.

Euscaphis japonica growing wild on Namhae Island, South Korea, 1989

Not surprisingly, Taiwan yielded the two genuine new species from amongst our collections. I say not surprisingly, as of all the places we visited, Taiwan is probably the least thoroughly botanised: the work of the Japanese botanists who did the original inventory work at the turn of the twentieth century has only in recent decades been advanced by the Taiwanese themselves, with the result that the island still has new species to yield. Given the great number of ecological niches that Taiwan supports, from almost tropical at sea level in the south of the island to alpine on the tops of the high mountains, it is to be expected that new plants might emerge.

During our time on Taiwan we relied upon *The Woody Flora of Taiwan*, edited by H. L. Li, as our authority. This work is a widely used, though somewhat dated, account, and one that we found congenial to utilise, not least because it is written in English. It lists two species of *Cotoneaster* as being native, one deciduous and upright (*C. konishii*) and one evergreen and prostrate (*C. rokujodaisanensis*). This seemed to make life easy, and we duly collected a deciduous plant on Hohuan Shan and an evergreen plant close to Tayuling; both appeared to fit the published descriptions. Back at Kew, both seed lots germinated readily and found their way into the collections. Nothing remarkable there, that is until the English cotoneaster specialist Jeanette Fryer and her co-worker Dr Bertil Hylmo of Bjuv in Sweden began looking at herbarium material at Kew and then at living plants. Jeanette is one of those precious, wonderful botanists who actually like to look at living plants in gardens as well as dead ones in the herbarium. She and Dr Hylmo have done an enormous amount of work in unravelling the complexities of the genus *Cotoneaster* and making life simpler for the gardener. In examining the material of *C. konishii* Jeanette decided that she was in fact looking at a new species. As well as being taller growing and having larger leaves, our collection had up to four pyrenes in each fruit, whilst the true *C. konishii* has only two. Jeanette and Bertil named this new species *C. hualiensis*, commenting that it is 'proving to be an extremely desirable and garden worthy shrub of good habit, with numerous pretty flowers much loved by bees, and weighed down by the many rich red fruits which contrast well with the striking autumn leaf colour'. Sadly, this was amongst the last plants to be named by Dr Hylmo, who died in June 2001 (in a long and varied life he was responsible, amongst many other things, for having helped to found the frozen food company Findus).

At more or less the same time, on the other side of the world in Japan, a great friend of Western horticulture and botany, Yuji Kurashige, was puzzling over the evergreen azalea we had gathered on Chilan Shan as *Rhododendron lasiostylum*. At that time Yuji was the curator of the Akagi Nature Park, a garden and natural area developed under the auspices of Seibu, one of Japan's biggest department stores, and he received seeds of all the *Rhododendron* species we collected on Taiwan. When the plants collected as *R. lasiostylum* (under expedition number 136) flowered in his garden, he realised that it differed sufficiently from existing species in section *Brachycalyx* of subgenus *Tsutsusi* to distinguish it as something new. DNA analysis confirmed Yuji's suspicions. His formal description of this new species was published in the *Edinburgh Journal of Botany*, the scientific publication of the Royal Botanic Garden, Edinburgh, as *R. chilanshanense*. The specific name

The first few flowers on *Rhododendron chilanshanense* in cultivation in Japan
(photograph courtesy Yuji Kurashige)

recognises the locality where the plant was collected—sadly, it doesn't recognise one of the collectors (*R. flanaganii* has a nice ring to it). Unfortunately, this plant has not proved easy to grow in the English climate; it is not represented at Kew or Wakehurst Place, and I have one poor, ailing little plant in the nursery at Windsor Great Park. This isn't the case for Yuji, who is now curator of the Niigata Prefectural Botanical Garden. In his new garden, *R. chilanshanense* flowers every spring and is thriving in his comprehensive and ever expanding azalea collection.

I have dwelt on the success of the plants from our trips in the gardens at Kew and Wakehurst Place, but this is only part of the story. Kew has always been a clearinghouse for plants, a central hub in an exchange network that extends to gardens around the world. Yuji Kurashige was not the only recipient of seed; many other gardens and individuals have also benefited. There is a truism in horticulture, often repeated, that the best way to keep a plant is to give it away. This seemingly contradictory statement recognises the fact that the more widely grown a plant is, the less likely it is to be lost to cultivation. At first it was relatively easy to distribute plants to other collections, and the South Korean material was made available to a wide range of organisations. I was thrilled to discover our collection of *Betula davurica* from South Korea growing in the arboretum of my own alma mater, the Royal Botanic Garden, Edinburgh; and I recall admiring a thriving clump of the suckering *Aralia bipinnata*, from Taiwan, at Westonbirt Arboretum, where curator Hugh Angus also proudly took me to see saplings of *B. costata* from South Korea. Perhaps the greatest pleasure, in this regard, was that which Tony and I experienced in the same place but on separate occasions. The place in question was the marvellous David C. Lam Asian Garden at the University of British Columbia's Botanical Garden in Vancouver. Here, in a favoured site on a promontory projecting out into the Strait of Georgia, where tall Douglas firs, western red cedars and western hemlocks provide shelter and shade, Peter Wharton has developed a wonderful garden, literally carved out of the wild. His technique is unorthodox but effective. He earmarks areas for development and plants a vanguard of exotic trees amongst the brush. Keeping a close eye on their development, he waits until they have achieved a reasonable size before beginning the task of clearing the ground vegetation, selecting and thinning the canopy trees and creating paths and beds. In this way, his middlestorey trees are already well established by the time the main development and planting takes place.

Tony visited Peter early in the summer of 2000 during time off from an American Association of Botanic Gardens and Arboreta conference. In the course of a walk around the Asian Garden, Peter gestured Tony to come across to have a look at an area awaiting development—'You might be interested in the trees' was Peter's understated remark. As Tony pushed his way through the undergrowth he came upon glades of Taiwanese maples raised from seed sent from Kew in 1993 following the previous autumn's trip. *Acer caudatifolium* was followed by *A. rubescens* and *A. oliverianum* subsp. *formosanum*—all were doing wonderfully well. I had the same experience the following spring, when Peter, along with Doug Justice, maple specialist and associate director of the UBC Botanical Garden, took me on the same route. Peter has been conspicuously successful with our Taiwanese material, probably because his climate is just that bit more congenial to these plants, especially in the spring, when the British weather can be especially capricious. Most recently I had a surprise when coming across a sapling of our collection of *Pinus taiwanensis* in the wonderful private garden of Rosemary and Maurice Foster at White Farm House, near Sevenoaks in Kent. Almost idly Maurice pointed to a beanpole of plant. 'That's your Taiwan black pine', he said. Sure enough, emerging from between its companions, was a tall, spindly pine, seemingly forgetting to develop a branch structure in its haste to climb into space.

Increasingly, however, the exchange of plants has become more regulated. When we journeyed to Taiwan in 1992, the first Earth Summit, the popular name for the United Nations Conference on the Environment and Development (UNCED), had just been held in Rio de Janeiro. Amongst the many important principles established at this groundbreaking conference, two—in particular—were to affect the field activities of Tony and me and all other responsible collectors. The first principle was that the ownership of the genetic resources of any plant lies with the country from which it originated, and this ownership exists in perpetuity. This means that should one country or group of countries exploit the potential of any plant, a proportion of the benefits, financial or otherwise, generated by that action should be returned to the country in which the plant was collected. It is sobering to reflect on this: the greatest diversity of plants is in the Third World, and yet the countries that gain the most revenue from exploiting these plants are First World countries. International pharmaceutical companies and agrochemical companies have systematically screened plants from the tropical areas of the earth to reveal useful compounds. Sadly, little or none of the huge revenues generated from the products derived from these plants have benefited local people. For the first time, Rio recognised this iniquitous situation and challenged the West to rectify it. Kew was quick to sign up to the letter and spirit of this challenge and rapidly put in place a series of legally-binding agreements which regulated the transfer of plant material to third parties. In this way, it was hoped that any exploitation of Kew-acquired plants would see a fair and equitable return of benefits to the original donor country. Thus all subsequent plants released from our trips were underpinned by a Material Transfer Agreement.

The second principle established at Rio is Prior Informed Consent. By this mechanism, collectors of wild plants are obliged to secure all necessary permissions to gather plants from the relevant authorities before they depart from their home country and to sign any memorandum of understanding required by the host country. Historically, many collectors have not secured proper permission, and their activities have been completely unregulated; as a result, overcollecting of wild plants has been all too common (certain groups, notably orchids and cacti, have been plagued by this problem). After our trip to South Korea (which, in any case, was conducted under the aegis of the Forestry Research Institute in Seoul), we were obliged to adopt a very proactive approach to the Convention on Biological Diversity, the treaty that emerged from the Rio Summit. In practise, this was little more than we had been doing and was far from onerous. We enjoyed knowing that, as ambassadors for Kew, we were setting an example of good practise and, in working collaboratively, were benefiting not just ourselves but our hosts. One of the more pleasant aspects of our time in the East was the friendships that we forged with our field companions, friendships that in many cases endure to this day. In the cases of Peter Gorovoy and Fuh-Jiunn Pan, we were delighted to be able to welcome them to Kew and support them during their time in England—small recompense for their unstinting efforts on our behalf.

An element of our expeditionary work that has not been mentioned hitherto formed the final part of the discussion that Tony and I engaged in following our afternoon at Kew, as we relaxed over a pint of beer in the nearby Orange Tree pub. Though Tony had participated in a seed collecting trip to Chile in 1985, when we left Kew for South Korea in September 1989 we were very much rookies. Not just in terms of fieldwork but as travellers and, perhaps most importantly, in our own intellectual development. We were starting families and building homes for our wives and children. That we shared an affinity was clear: both proud Lancastrians with a passion for plants and the wild places. In hindsight, it seemed that our careers were destined to converge. During our time together in the field, we developed as individuals, drawing not just from the cultures we experienced and the people we met, but from each other. We experienced the highs and lows that demanding fieldwork always brings. We endured ill health, fatigue and disappointment, but most of all we experienced elation, excitement and the satisfaction that comes with achieving hard-won objectives. Throughout this roller coaster of emotions in the mountains and valleys of eastern Asia, Tony Kirkham and Mark Flanagan grew up and left a legacy that we are satisfied we can be judged by.

Bean, W. J. 1980. *Trees and Shrubs Hardy in the British Isles*. 8th ed., vols. 1–4, 1970–1980, and Supplement by D. E. Clarke, 1988. London, John Murray.

Blunt, W. S. 1978. *In for a Penny: A Prospect of Kew Gardens, Their Flora, Fauna and Falballas*. London, Hamish Hamilton.

Briggs, R. W. 1993. *Chinese Wilson: A Life of Ernest H. Wilson*. London, HMSO.

Brown, G., and T. Kirkham. 2004. *The Pruning of Trees, Shrubs and Conifers*. 2nd ed. Portland, Ore., Timber Press.

Chamberlain, D. F. 1982. A Revision of *Rhododendron*: 2. Subgenus *Hymenanthes*. *Notes from the Royal Botanic Garden, Edinburgh* 39 (2):209–486.

Chamberlain, D. F., and S. J. Rae. 1990. A Revision of *Rhododendron*: 4. Subgenus *Tsutsusi*. *Edinburgh Journal of Botany* 47 (2).

Compton, J. A., A. Culham and S. L. Jury. 1998. Reclassification of *Actaea* to Include *Cimicifuga* and *Souliea* (Ranunculaceae): Phylogeny Inferred from Morphology, nr DNA ITS and cpDNA truL-F Sequence Variation. *Taxon* 47: 543–634.

Cox, E. H. M. 1945. *Plant Hunting in China: A History of Botanical Exploration in China and the Tibetan Marches*. London, Collins.

Cullen, J. 1980. A Revision of *Rhododendron*: 1. Subgenus *Rhododendron*, Sections *Rhododendron* and *Pogonanthum*. *Notes from the Royal Botanic Garden, Edinburgh* 39 (1): 1–207.

Desmond, R. 1998. *Kew: The History of the Royal Botanic Gardens*. London, Havill Press and Royal Botanic Gardens, Kew.

Evans, A. 1974. *The Peat Garden and Its Plants*. London, Dent.

Flanagan, M. 1988. The Damage Caused by the Hurricane Force Winds to the Trees at the Royal Botanic Gardens, Kew. *Arboricultural Journal* 12 (2): 181–188.

———. 1989. Recovery from the 1988 Storm at Wakehurst Place. *Kew Magazine* 6 (3): 134–139.

———. 1993. Wakehurst Place: A Walk Through the Temperate Woodlands of the World. In Hunt, D. R., ed. *Betula: Proceedings of the IDS Betula Symposium*. 89–93.

———. 1995a. Plants in Peril, 22: *Fagus hayatae*. *Curtis's Botanical Magazine* 12 (1): 42–45.

———. 1995b. Ussuri Adventure. *The Garden* 120 (7): 412–415.

———. 1997. *Rhododendron camtschaticum* on Sakhalin Island. *Rhododendrons with Camellias and Magnolias* 48: 27–30.

Flanagan, M., and A. S. Kirkham. 1995. Tree Planting at the Royal Botanic Gardens, Kew and Wakehurst Place. RHS *The New Plantsman 2 (3)*: 142–151.

Flanagan, M., and T. Kirkham. 1994. Brought from a Far Land: Recent Tree Planting at the Royal Botanic Gardens, Kew and Wakehurst Place. RHS *The New Plantsman* 1 (3) 131–137.

———. Taiwan's Foggy Forest. *Kew* (Autumn issue) 8–11.

Flanagan, M., and M. Pitman. 1988. Lost Treasures, New Hopes. *Hortus* 8: 94–98.

Gardiner, J. 2000. *Magnolias: A Gardener's Guide*. Portland, Ore., Timber Press.

Galle, F. C. 1997. *Hollies: The Genus Ilex*. Portland, Ore., Timber Press.

Green, P. S., and J. B. E. Simmons. 1978. *Report of a Visit to the Peoples' Republic of China*. Kew, Surrey, Royal Botanic Gardens, Kew.

Hadfield, M., R. Harling and L. Highton. 1980. *British Gardeners*. London, A. Zwemmer.

Hayata, B. 1906. On *Taiwania*, a New Genus of Coniferae from the Island of Formosa. *Journal of Linnaean Society* 37: 330–331.

———. 1911–1921. *Icones of the Plants of Formosa and Materials for a Flora of the Island, Based on a Study of the Collections of the Botanical Survey of the Government of Formosa*. 10 vols. Taihoku, Bureau of Productive Industry, Government of Formosa.

Henry, A. 1898. A List of Plants of Formosa, with Some Preliminary Remarks on the Geography of the Island. *Transactions of the Asiatic Society of Japan*. 24.

Hillier, J., and A. Coombes, eds. 2002. *The Hillier Manual of Trees and Shrubs*. Devon, England, David and Charles.

Johnson, H. 1979. *The Principles of Gardening*. London, Mitchell Beazley.

———. 1981. The Origins of Plants. Part 1. *Telegraph Sunday Magazine* 242.

Kirkham, T., and M. Flanagan. 1999. Closing the Temperate Loop. *The Dendrologist* 13 (2) 1–4.

Kron, K. A. 1993. A Revision of *Rhododendron*: 5. Section *Pentanthera*. *Edinburgh Journal of Botany* 50: 249–364.

Krüssmann, G. 1984–1986. *The Manual of Cultivated Broad-leaved Trees and Shrubs*. 3 vols. Portland, Ore., Timber Press.

———. 1985. *The Manual of Cultivated Conifers*. Portland, Ore., Timber Press.

Kurashige, Y. 1999. *Rhododendron chilanshanense* (Ericaceae), a New Species from Taiwan. *Edinburgh Jorunal of Botany* 56 (1): 75–78.

Lamb, H. H. 1964. *The English Climate*. London, English Universities Press.

Lee, S. C. 1962. Taiwan Red and Yellow Cypress and Their Conservation. *Taiwania* 8:1–15.

Lee, Y. N. 1996. *Flora of Korea*. Seoul, Kyo-Hak Publishing Company Ltd.

Li, H. L. 1963. *The Woody Flora of Taiwan*. Narberth, Pa., Livingston Publishing Company.

McAllister, H. A. 1986. *The Rowan and Its Relatives (Sorbus spp.)*. Neston, University of Liverpool.

Mitchell, A. 1974. *A Field Guide to the Trees of Britain and Northern Europe*. London, Collins.

Mitchell, A. F., V. E. Schilling and J. E. J. White. 1994. *Champion Trees of the British Isles*. Edinburgh, Forestry Commission.

Philipson, M. N., and W. R. Philipson. 1975. A Revision of *Rhododendron* Section *Lapponicum*. *Notes from the Royal Botanic Garden, Edinburgh* 34: 1–72.

———. 1986. A Revision of *Rhododendron*: 3. Subgenera *Azaleastrum, Mumeazalea, Candidastrum* and *Therorhodion*. *Notes from the Royal Botanic Garden, Edinburgh* 44:1–23.

Pim, S. 1966. *The Wood and the Trees. A Biography of Augustine Henry*. London, Macdonald.

Rehder, A. 1920. The American and Asiatic Species of Sassafras. *Journal of the Arnold Arboretum* I (4): 242–245.

Reid, E. M., and M. E. J. Chandler. 1933. *The London Clay Flora*. London, British Museum.

RHS Plantfinder 2002–2003. London, Dorling Kindersley.

Rushforth, K. D. 1987. *Conifers*. London, Christopher Helm.

Sargent, C. S., ed. 1912. *Plantae Wilsoniae: An Enumeration of the Woody Plants Collected in Western China for the Arnold Arboretum of Harvard University during the Years 1907, 1908 and 1910 by E. H. Wilson*. Cambridge, Mass., The University Press.

Schilling, A. D., and M. Flanagan. 1990. Wakehurst Looks to the Future. *The Garden* 115 (6): 288–293.

Severinghaus, S., and C. E. De Vol. 1974. Notes on the Distribution of Taiwan Beech. *Taiwania* 19 (2): 235–237.

Simmons, J. B. E. 1981. The History and Development of the Arboretum at the Royal Botanic Gardens, Kew. *Arboricultural Journal* 5 (3): 173–188.

———. 1986. A 7000 Foot Mountain with a Five Step Snake. *The Garden* 111 (12): 567–572.

Spongberg, S. A. 1990. *A Reunion of Trees. The Discovery of Exotic Plants and Their Introduction into North American and European Landscapes*. Cambridge, Mass., Harvard University Press.

Takhtajan, A. L. 1986. *Floristic Regions of the World*. Berkeley, California, University of California.

Taylor, N. P. 1987. A Revision of the Genus *Skimmia* (Rutaceae). *Kew Magazine* 4 (4): 168–194.

van Gelderen, D. M., P. C. de Jong, H. J. Oterdoom and J. R. P. van Hoey Smith. 1994. *Maples of the World*. Portland, Ore., Timber Press.

Wilson, E. H. 1927. *Plant Hunting*, vol. 2. Boston, Stratford.

———. 1929. *China, Mother of Gardens*. Boston, Stratford.

INDEX